Security and Policy Driven Computing

Security and Policy Driven Computing

Lei Liu
Oracle Corporation
Menlo Park, California, USA

CRC Press
Taylor & Francis Group
Boca Raton London New York

CRC Press is an imprint of the
Taylor & Francis Group, an **informa** business

CRC Press
Taylor & Francis Group
6000 Broken Sound Parkway NW, Suite 300
Boca Raton, FL 33487-2742

Printed in the United States of America on acid-free paper
10 9 8 7 6 5 4 3 2 1

International Standard Book Number: 978-1-4398-2579-2 (Hardback)

Visit the Taylor & Francis Web site at
http://www.taylorandfrancis.com

and the CRC Press Web site at
http://www.crcpress.com

Contents

Preface

Unified Universe: From Real Computing to Imaginary Computing

Scientists and engineers have been studying the organization, properties, structures, and flows of computing universe. This book analyzes intuitions, induces their relations, and deduces common practices.

A. Generalized Computing Representation

$$e^{-x} = O(1) \qquad where\ x \to +\infty,\ x \in R \tag{1}$$

Using a real variable and real valued function e^{-x} to represent our universe, we need to measure the physical computation continuously to be bounded to the intrinsic unity of the computing universe $O(1)$. Specifically, it is a future directive and not invertible $x \to +\infty$. Good examples of these types of real quantities are time t, Euclidean geometric parameters (x, y, z), spherical geometric parameters (r, θ), and Riemann metrics (vector fields X, Y on M). Without high dimensional relations, this real computing representation has implications for the cause of the structures of the computing universe, which is the result of continuous measurement such as motions and data flows. The measuring can be the process of structure construction, transformation of time or displacement, and deformation of shapes. The computing universe becomes the result of dynamic trajectories and rays of divergency. The asymptotic structure continuously expands and approaches the unity. Hence, to understand our computing universe, we need to observe and probe system and computational objects with continuity. This representation is a macroscopic computing representation.

$$e^{ix} = O(1) \qquad where\ x \in R \tag{2}$$

This equation is a real variable and complex valued function. This generalization creates a mixture of the real computing and an imaginary computing, which is not measurable. However, the mixed representation shows that we do not need continuous activities. We need to measure only one variable without repetition to obtain unity of the universe. No transformation, such as data flows, is required. There is no progression of construction involved with a one-dimensional representation. Traveling back and forth through the mixture can be possible. This equation is a regular computing representation. If we substitute $x \in R$ with a sector $x \in C(|phx| < \frac{1}{2}\pi)$, it explains the harmonic divergency existing in the universe, including sun rays and atomic computing.

$$e^z = 1 + z + O(z^2) \qquad where\ z \to 0,\ z \in C \tag{3}$$

A even more generalized representation is a complex variable and complex valued function. z represents space-time curvature. This equation is a purely imaginary computing representation. This equation shows the relations between the universe and space-time. Space-time and the computing universe can be independent. Moreover, space-time can be interactive and have a causal effect. The computing universe can have one copy of itself and one copy of space-time. Space-time can be self-referenced so that time and space can interact with each other. The interactions between space-time can be independent of the original copy of space-time. We can also see that space-time can be unique to the computing universe. This equation not only gives a microscopic computing representation but also illustrates relativistic views of computing representation. Considering the universe and space-time, this equation gives an initial unified view of our computing universe and space-time.

B. Computing Representation by Security and Policy

Security forms protection structures or surfaces to systems and data flows such as firewall and encryption methods. Computing can be further generalized with a space-time function. It depends on time and the contour.

$$Q(z) = \int_0^\infty k(t, z) f(t) dt \tag{4}$$

where t represents time. z represents a contour. $k(t, z)$ represents a policy or a security method that has a four-dimensional structure. $f(t)$ is a local hardware or software functionality. $Q(z)$ is a three-dimensional structure such as stopped data flows, denied service requests, and encrypted packets, and so on.

Hence, to create computational governance, security and policy are required. The policy represents a complex valued function such as a quantum policy.

$$I(z) = \int_0^\infty k(z, p(t)) f(t) dt \tag{5}$$

where $p(t)$ is the potential to release or schedule a data flow. $k(z, p(t))$ represents a four-dimensional policy or security method. $f(t)$ is a local hardware or software functionality. $I(z)$ is a data flow.

Similarly, interactions between policy and activities can construct information flows.

$$I(x) = \int_0^\infty g(x,t)f(t)dt \tag{6}$$

where $g(x,t)$ is an interactive policy. $f(t)$ is a local hardware or software functionality. $I(z)$ is a three-dimensional data flow.

Hence, policy can be defined without contour structures. The policy is location specific such as load balancing rules or routing rules. The policy can be formed dynamically during interactions with data flows. Furthermore, this equation indicates time-based policies for atomic computing without four-dimensional structures. In this way, information flows become shadows of system activities and policies to achieve autonomic unity of the computing universe.

C. Layout of the Book

This book discusses these topics from security and policy driven computing to storage management. For high dimensional data distribution, we study multiple variables and derivation of index structures. The numeric methods are applied to the proposed search method. In the computing universe, we focus on discovering relations, logic, and knowledge for policy management. To manage performance, we discuss contention management for transactional structures, buffer tuning, and test environments. To obtain geometric information, we study truncated functions with paralleled techniques for search optimization. The proposed method can reduce the conditions of domain overlapped transformation. For quantum policies, we study structures, recovery, message conflicts, and test coverage. Finally, we exploit methods of quantum protection mechanism for intrusion prevention.

D. Motivation to Readers

Where and how do we keep the original copy of the computing universe? How does space-time look like across the multiverse? Without measurables, how can we travel to history? If we travel to history, how can we travel back to where we are now? If we go back to the original space-time, can we still stay in the same universe and backup and restore the changes of space-time? These questions are left to all curious readers.

Chapter 1

A Parallel Search Optimization Using an Adaptive State-Action Index Structure

1.1 Introduction

In problem solving, search formulation involves many combinatorial optimizations of search approximation, including action-control optimizations. All aspects of the search-task environment represent various classes of applications, such as routing, scheduling, speech recognition, scene analysis, and intrusion-detection pattern matching.

Given a directional graph G with distinguished starting state S_{start} and a set of goal states $\overrightarrow{S}_{goal}$, search means following the edges to visit vertices and locating the set of state-action sequences with least cost or maximized reward to go from S_{start} to any element of $\overrightarrow{S}_{goal}$. In addition, search can discover the structure or subset of the computational presentation of the given graphs. The set of information to search is not explicitly stored, but candidate solutions may be generated as the search process expands.

The rest of the chapter is organized as follows. Section 1.2 illustrates the significance of complexity problems and convergence issues and proposes search optimizations. Section 1.3 formulates the search problem and its associated properties. Section 1.4 briefly reviews the proposed solutions from the search literature. Section 1.5 briefly summarizes the contributions. Section 1.6 proposes a set of dynamic search strategies, including algorithmic operations and data structures for stochastic systems. Section 1.7 presents performance evaluation and convergence analysis of the proposed algorithms and data structures. Section 1.8 introduces experimental studies and simulation results from the proposed search-utility framework. Finally, Section 1.9 lists conclusions.

1.2 Significance of Research

The most influential search optimization is the informed algorithmic operations. Informed searches use problem-specific knowledge to exploit heuristic information [1]. The informed method continues to explore along the direction with local optimum. The most commonly used informed search strategies are variants of A^* search [2], best-first search [3], and its variant of greedy best-first search. Specifically, researchers discussed the A^* algorithms on the optimality proof. With high-level assumptions on system modeling, heuristic search has the lowest level of complexity on modeling efforts. However, heuristic search provides solution quality with a risk of local optimum. The search method may be prohibitive because of algorithmic space complexity and intensive computation to provide approximated solutions. In addition, cost functions or utilities may be hard to formulate with closed forms. This results in the limited usage in dynamic search spaces.

One of the main threads of search optimization is local search. Local search provides an optimal solution with or without gradient information [4]. Variants of hill-climbing algorithms were proposed for nonlinear-programming numeric methods, such as gradient descent with finite differences and tabu search [5]. Simulated annealing is one of the active optimization research areas. Local search recently provided good results for large constraint satisfaction problems [6]. Furthermore, genetic algorithms [7] have evolved for the search optimization. In general, local search strategies share a common issue: which computation procedures may be trapped into local optimum instead of global optimum points? Local search methods also share the common space and computation complexity with traditional AI search techniques. Moreover, learning-based methods may require supervised training for search optimization. Furthermore, search function approximation may result in issues of error convergence. This is one of the major constraints of online search methods.

In another thread of study on state space search for problem solving, uninformed search strategies are the central topic. Conventional uninformed search strategies execute computation on the basis of variants of problem definition to generate successor states for a goal test. Some of the well-known algorithms are breath-first search [8], method of dynamic programming [9], uniform-cost search [10], depth-first search, depth-limited search, and iterative deepening search. Dynamic programming formulated optimization guarantees search optimality. However, state enumeration is restricted due to large-state transitions or high-dimensional feature extraction during search computation.

Hence, this chapter suggests optimization of learning-based search with reduced time and space complexity, especially for memory bound problems and error convergence problems. It proposes search optimality with constrained resources such as central processing unit (CPU) and main memory.

1.3 Problem Formulation

Search is a stochastic process generating random state changes with dynamic optimization in which the goal is to find an optimal action for each state visited during state transitions. Intuitively, an adaptive search is a state-action control optimization problem. Hence, search actions and associated state changes form a stochastic decision process resulting in search-state transitions, which is usually probabilistic. Search is a problem of dynamic computation optimization.

Search is a memoryless process. Specifically, each state transition probability is dependent only on the current state but not on the previous states. In addition, state transition time is not a unity time step. Hence, it is a semi-Markov decision problem (SMDP). However, in real-world systems, state transition probabilities and reward discount factors are unknown or hard to compute. Without transition probability matrices (TPM), transition reward matrices (TRM), and transition time matrices (TTM) as the foundation of a theoretical model, adaptive search is hard to formulate as a traditional Markov decision problem (MDP), which can be solved by decision problem (DP) algorithms.

In addition, search objective functions may have high-dimensional random decision variables in large state spaces. The search may have difficulty obtaining the probability mass or distribution function of these parameters. Furthermore, given a distribution function, optimization may not be solved in closed forms. With distribution of system-inbound random decision variables, estimated transition probability and reward matrices could generate TPMs and TRMs via simulators. However, the solution does not scale up to large-state and solution spaces. For large-state spaces, state aggregation is required to approximate models with a manageable number of states.

Traditional search is explicitly computed in the space of state action along the edges to the vertices. Approximation, such as explorations or revolutionary methods, would climb policy spaces for state generation and evaluation to obtain policy improvements. In general, by direct searching, entire policy spaces are formulated and evaluated with scalar quantities. Intuitively, a fixed policy is held with practices many times, which could result in biased local optimum points. Search against large-state spaces or high-dimensional task environment as an explicit search approximation problem is also hard to resolve.

With reinforcement learning (RL) optimization, search costs and rewards can be assigned or computed as environmental feedback treated as state values learned by interactions. Therefore, with RL methods, optimal policies can be reached without explicit search over a possible sequence of entire states and actions. Hence, search is a dynamic problem that can be resolved with large and even infinite spaces.

Consequently, the dynamic search problem is formulated as a RL- and DP-based SMDP problem.

A MDP for a single agent can be illustrated by a quadruple (S, A, R, T) consisting of

- A finite set of states S, $s \in S$
- A finite set of actions A, $a \in A$

- A reward function c, $S \times A \times S \rightarrow \Re$
- A state transition function, $T : S \times A \rightarrow PD(S)$ that maps the agent's current state and action into a set of probability distributions over the entire state space.

1.3.1 Task environment formulation

Environment Properties

- The search process has a discrete set of percepts and actions.
- Search environment is deterministic since the next state is completely dependent on the current state and action, which will be taken further.
- Search optimization is a discrete task environment with a set of state transitions and environmental feedback signals.

1.3.2 Goal formulation

Goal Properties

- State: A goal state specified by s_{goal}. However, the goal state might be unknown or hard to formulate within a dynamic or partial observable task environment.
- Performance: (1) Unknown objective functions. (2) The lowest cost function or the highest reward function. (3) Expected rewards within every unit time calculated over an infinitely long trajectory of the SMDP process. (4) An average reward or cost function.

1.3.3 Problem formulation

Problem Properties

- States: A set of system properties $\overrightarrow{S}$ reachable from an initial state that is specified as $s_i = In(s_i)$. For a finite state space, the total count of states, $count[S] = M$.
- Initial state: $In(s_{start})$. Search starts from the location with $s_1 = In(s_{goal})$.
- Goal state: May or may not be formulated with simple presentation.
- Actions: Actions are commonly formulated as a successor function to generate states with actions. There is a set of action-state pairs. Both

state-action and value-action mapping are defined in Section 1.4.

$$AS_i = \{ < Go(s_i, a_i), In(s_i, a_i) > \\ , \dots, \\ < Go(s_{goal}, a_{goal}), In(s_{goal}, a_{goal}) > \} \tag{1.1}$$

- Goal test(): It may be hard to formulate the goal evaluation equation, but it may approximate the optimal policy.
- $Go(s_i, a_i)$: Represents the action expending function from state s_i with action a_i.
- Policy: It is a control mechanism. For n state decision process, it is formulated as n tuple, π_i specifies the action to be selected in the state associated with that element.
- Path: In state space, a set of states S is connected by a set of actions A.
- $N = |S|$ denotes the number of elements in the state decision states.
- A: A finite set of action state spaces. A_i is an element of action vector associated with state s_i
- Decision value function: Search decision value function is stored in a finite set of vector $\overrightarrow{Q}$.
- Search cost: A cost function assigns numeric cost to each path as a performance measure specified in Section 1.4 as the negative forms of scalar values computed by a reward function.

1.4 Review of Literature

For search-action control optimization, MDP yields optimal solutions on a control optimization problem as additional nonlinear-programming methods in stochastic dynamic programming, such as value and policy iterations. However, for a complex system, it is hard to construct the theoretical model specifically required for MDP formulation.

As a random variable, the expected immediate reward of state transition with action a from state s_i to state s_j can be conceptually defined as

$$\overline{r}(s_i, a) = E[r(s_i, a)] = \sum_{s_i, s_j \in S} p(s_i, a, s_j) r(s_i, a, s_j) \tag{1.2}$$

- $p(s_i, a, s_j)$ is the long run transition probability from state s_i to state s_j when MDP is running with action a selected in state s_i.

- $r(s_i, a, s_j)$ is the immediate reward earned from state s_i to state s_j.
- $\overline{r}(s_i, a)$ denotes the mean of the rewards at state s_i with action a.

If a deterministic stationary policy $\overrightarrow{\pi}$ is followed, $\pi(s_i)$ is the action that will be selected in state s_i. Intuitively, the average reward associated with policy $\overrightarrow{\pi}$ is derived as

$$\overline{r}(\pi(s_i)) = E[r(\pi(s_i))] = \sum_{s_i \in S} p(s_i)\overline{r}(s_i, \pi(s_i)) \tag{1.3}$$

- $\overrightarrow{\pi}$ is an n tuple associated with n states.
- $p(s_i)$ is the infinitely long run transition probability of state i when MDP is running with the policy $\overrightarrow{\pi}$.
- S denotes a set of decision states in the sample space.
- Under policy $\pi(s_i)$, $\overline{r}(s_i, \pi(s_i))$ denotes the expected immediate reward earned in the state s_i when action $\pi(s_i)$ is selected in state i.

With the above equation, optimal policy can be evaluated by maximizing the rewards. Therefore, the above performance objective function provides a conceptual model for control optimization. However, it suggests the policy enumeration to compute the transition probability matrices and transition reward matrices to evaluate the objective performance metrics resulted from each policy. It derives the optimal action value and associated policy. This limits the solution to small state spaces due to the exponential computation for $m \times n$ (n states and m actions) introduced by the above conceptual model. To optimize controls, DP algorithms [11] were evolved to solve the MDP problems. DP algorithms were proposed as a linear system of equations [12] to resolve MDP problems. By solving Bellman equations, the value components of the value function vector can be utilized to locate the optimal actions or policies. There are various forms of Bellman equations [12] to resolve MDP problems. The Bellman equation for a given policy in the average reward context requires k iterations of evaluation on linear equations pertaining to each policy selected in the iteration to derive the optimal policies. Value iteration is another form of Bellman equations that does not require solving any equation. It is the foundation of RL algorithms.

From Bellman optimality equation for average reward

$$V^*(s_i) = \max_{a \in A(s_i), s_i, s_j \in S} \left[\overline{r}(s_i, a) - \rho^* + \sum_{s_j=1}^{N} p(s_i, a, s_j) V^*(s_j) \right] \tag{1.4}$$

where

- $A(s_i)$ denotes a finite set of actions taken in state s_i by following policy $\overrightarrow{\pi}$.

- $V^*(s_i)$ denotes the element of a value function vector $\overrightarrow{V}$ associated with the optimal policy for state s_i.
- $\overline{r}(s_i, a, s_j)$ denotes the expected immediate reward in state s_i as action a is taken.
- ρ^* denotes the average reward associated with the optimal policy.

To resolve the value-bound problem, relative value interaction was proposed. For the *kth* interaction

$$V_{k+1}(s_i) = \max_{a \in A(s_i), s_i, s_j \in S} \left[\overline{r}(s_i, a) - \rho^* + \sum_{s_j=1}^{N} p(s_i, a, s_j) V_k(s_j) \right] - V^*_{k+1}(s_i) \tag{1.5}$$

In the setting of nonunity transition times, relative value interaction was proposed. For *kth* interaction

$$V_{k+1}(s_i) = \max_{a \in A(s_i), s_i \in S} \left[\overline{r}(s_i, a) - \rho^* t(s_i, a, s_j) + \sum_{s_j=1}^{N} p(s_i, a, s_j) V_k(s_j) \right] - V^*_{k+1}(s_i) \tag{1.6}$$

where $t(s_i, a, s_j)$ denotes the transition time from state s_i to state s_j followed by policy $\overrightarrow{\pi}$ where action a has taken place. This equation indicates that the maximum value V^* selection may run away from regular value iterations with deterministic optimal path locations. The above interactive conceptual model requires intensive computation. In addition, it requires a theoretical model.

From RL literature, a provable convergent approach has been developed for learning optimal policies in continuous state and action spaces under average rewards [13]. This technique has been applied to research with nontrivial configurations [14]. However, there is no existing discussion on RL and optimization within search state and action space. This chapter proposes self-organization of an index structure for state-action value mapping for a search function numeric method approximation.

1.5 Contribution

The purpose of this chapter is to provide an adaptive search apparatus and a method for problem solving and reasoning within next generation SMDP systems and associative task environment. To serve large continuous system spaces with reduced space complexity, a self-organized index data structure partitions data sets to provide exact state-action and reward/cost factor mapping. Exact function mapping eliminates error convergence. Thread-safe algorithms are proposed for system parallelization and pipelined processors for time complexity reduction. Specifically, RL search approximation and learning factor index mapping are proposed to simplify search decision organization and prediction. In addition, a set of RL interactive algorithmic operations and augmented index operations are suggested.

1.6 Methodology

With the formulated SMDP and DP problem, the following characteristics are critical in this chapter.

- Memoryless: Each state transition probability is independent of previous states but not of the current state. Hence, it is a memoryless process.
- Dynamic: Since search optimization is formulated as a stochastic DP problem, it has dynamic search properties.
- Adaptive: To handle large state space and unknown objective functions, the DP problem is transformed into the RL-based adaptive learning problem. Adaptiveness implies that search is conducted interactively with converged resources.
- Parallelization: With data parallelization, time complexity is further optimized by algorithmic parallelism with core-based systems and pipelined processors.

Dynamic programming algorithms require computation of a theoretical model of a system on transition probabilities, on transition rewards, and on transition time. These quantities are unknown or hard to evaluate. Specifically, to obtain transition probabilities, multiple integrals with the probability distribution functions of many random variables are involved in the calculation on a complex stochastic system.

Both DP and RL algorithms have a dependency on $\Sigma_{x \leq t} p_x(x)$, the distributions of the random variables that govern the system behavior for a time interval t. For continuous random variables, $\int_{-\infty}^{x} f(x)dt$ is applied. However, RL does not need the above theoretical model quantity evaluation or estimations but needs to simulate the system using the distributions of the governing random variables. For adaptive search, one needs the distribution of random decision variables.

Value function and state mapping can be directly done by table lookup. However, the result is a memory contention problem due to large state transitions. Hence, value state mapping was generalized by function approximation to reduce time and space complexity in literature. But function approximation introduces error convergence problems to achieve the approximated state value mapping. To resolve the time and space complexity of value mapping without approximation error convergence issue, this chapter proposes value state mapping using storage-based index structure for exact mapping function. This is a logarithmic space reduction data structure and algorithmic operation to map the state and solution space.

However, reinforcement learning techniques provide near-optimal solutions without evaluation of the above quantities. As in DP techniques, one element of the value function vector is associated with each state variable. The RL search algorithm associates each element of the value mapping vector with a given state-action pair (i, a) as $Q(i, a)$ for search cost or reward evaluation to derive optimal policies.

Value iteration algorithms do not compute the system of linear equations. However, value iteration for MDP poses difficulties for Bellman optimality equation computation with an unknown value of the average reward (ρ^*). For SMDP in the average reward context, learning is transformed into approximation solution space. However, regular DP value iteration becomes unbounded for average reward MDP. Hence, relative value iteration keeps the operation bound. Since the discounting factor is hard to measure in real-world systems, average reward tends to be more popular in measuring performance.

- Discrete environmental signal: After each action, the learning agent receives immediate feedback from the above task environment. The reinforcement immediate reward signals $r \in \Re$ are listed below.

$$r = \begin{cases} a & \text{A penalty resulted from a wrong action} \\ b & \text{A reward is granted as a target is learned} \\ c & \text{The goal state is reached} \\ -1 & \text{Cost of any action during learning} \\ 0.0 & \text{Otherwise for all nonterminal states} \end{cases}$$

The move to the target is less than the absolute value of moving to the wrong direction since keeping the agent in a valid task environment is more important than getting to the target ($|a| > c > b$). Intuitively, the agent needs to learn to achieve the goal without rewards. In other words, the absolute value of the penalty should be significantly larger than the reward from the excepted move. The agent is required to stay in the task environment to move to the goal state. However, the sooner the action is rewarded, the sooner the agent will learn. The cost of moving is measured by a negative unit reward from the task environment. It is larger than the reward from getting to the correct positions so that the steps in the path are considered in search evaluation to achieve the minimized path ($0 < b < c < 1$).

- Traditionally, value action function computation is done by in-memory table lookup. This is limited to small-state and solution spaces. With large-state and solution spaces or high-dimensional state space, table-based lookup is prohibitive due to limited computational resources because of space complexity, such as memory constraints. In addition to table-based exact function computation, value action function approximation is another numeric method to fit the possible state and value mapping. However, function approximation introduces the error convergence problem in information theory. With an unknown dynamic task environment and partial observable decision variables, the error propagation will be hard to predict. Hence, it is hard to obtain formal proof of convergence with approximation methods. This is the root cause of the convergence problems to resolve in the proposed method.

- To resolve convergence issues within a dynamic and partially observable task environment, exact function mapping is considered. However, exact function mapping results in significant memory contentions. This can be demonstrated by a puzzle [15] state transition and action value function mapping. $8 - puzzle$ problem is selected as an experimental study for the proposed method. Section 1.8 has detailed discussions on $8 - puzzle$ problems solving.

$$\begin{aligned} total\ memory &= 4 * 4 + 362{,}880 * 9 * 4 \\ &\quad + 362{,}880 * 4 * 8 \approx 30\ MB \end{aligned} \tag{1.7}$$

Apparently, with $k - puzzle$, space complexity will grow with $O(k^2)$. To eliminate the space complexity resulting from memory bound operations for large-state and solution spaces or high-dimensional state spaces, this chapter proposes a index data structure (Figure 1.1) to construct the RL value and state function. With such index data structure, only the root of any arbitrary state space stays in memory. All other states are dynamically saved and loaded from secondary storage devices as learning proceeds. This index structure transforms memory-intensive computation into unbounded storage input/output (I/O) issues. Hence, the relaxed version of value state function mapping is to resolve the algorithmic time complexity from native I/O. Therefore, a common logarithmic cost reduction model is taken to reduce the data lookup time and steps. To amortize the cost of I/O, page-based lookup ($8\ kB$–$256\ MB$) and persistence is proposed for different initial and target states.

- Page-based index structure partitions the state-action value function with initial and goal states. This derives parallelized data sets, which are ready for straight system parallel processing and pipelined processor computation. In addition, application threads can execute the algorithmic operations without running into data hazards. This leads to reduction of time complexity, which is another core benefit of the proposed method. According to Amdahl's law [16], the speedup can be obtained from a specific feature.

$$speedup = \frac{execution\ time_{without\ enhancement}}{execution\ time_{with\ enhancement}} \tag{1.8}$$

Hence, the execution time with parabolization of pages of function mapping will be

$$speedup_{overall} = \frac{1}{(1 - fraction_{new}) + \frac{fraction_{new}}{speedup_{new}}} \tag{1.9}$$

- Another common memory strategy is to defer memory management to the kernel virtual memory (VM) module of the underlining operating system. It is not utilized in the proposed method for the following reasons. First, VM or shared memory has a common lock mechanism to handle data hazards. Locks are major contentions for data parallelization. With data parallelization, system parallelism and application thread parallelization are not effective. Hence, VM or shared memory may not leverage parallelism to improve time complexity without significant optimization of scheduling policies, which is not the focus of this chapter. Second, VM is normally implemented with fixed policies such as LRU or MRU. It does page-based swapping to resolve resource starvation. However, it lacks intelligent management. It is not efficient for high-volume computation against large data sets since it could cause recursive dependency of page loading. Third, it limits the memory usage within a single host environment. Even though distributed shared memory could be used to enforce resource sharing across different hosts, there are limitations of resources joining the search-task environment.

The proposed 8 kB–256 MB based index structure is illustrated in Figure 1.1.

For large-state spaces or high-dimensional solution spaces, value-mapping vectors are not stored explicitly. Instead, function approximation is used to solve the high-dimensionality problem during RL value iterations. If the time spent in a transition is not unity, the average reward per unit time over an infinite time horizon is defined as

$$\rho = \lim_{k \to \infty} \frac{E\left[\sum_{i=k}^{k} r(x_i, \pi(x_i), x_{i+1})\right]}{k} \tag{1.10}$$

From Bellman optimality, the equation for average reward becomes

$$V^*(s_i) = \max_{a \in A(s_i), s_i, s_j \in S} \sum_{s_j=1}^{N} p(s_i, a, s_j)[r(s_i, a, s_j) + V^*(s_j)] \tag{1.11}$$

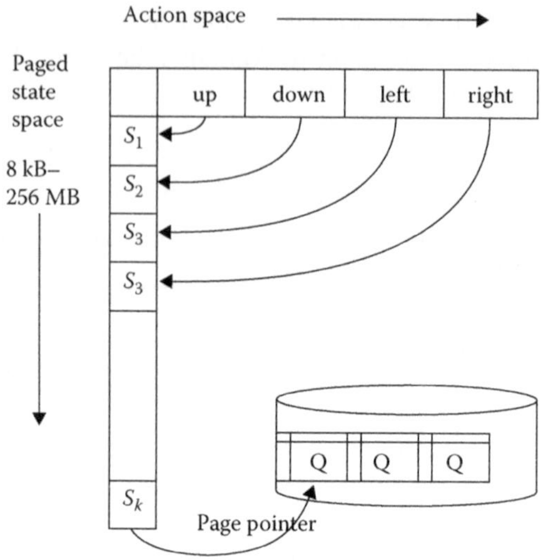

FIGURE 1.1: A paged index structure of state-action value mapping.

where

- $V^*(s_i)$ denotes the element of value function vector $\vec{V}$ associated with optimal policy for state s_i.
- $p(s_i, a, s_j)$ denotes the transition probability from state s_i to state s_j under action a.
- $\overline{r}(s_i, a, s_j)$ is the mean of long-term rewards from state i to state j.

From the Robbins-Monro algorithm [17], value and state-action mapping vectors in the Bellman equation are defined without the dependency of transition probability:

$$Q(i, a) \leftarrow (1 - \alpha)Q(i, a) + \alpha[\gamma(i, a, j) + \max_{b \in A(j)} Q(j, b)] \quad (1.12)$$

To resolve the divergent iteration problem of traditional Bellman optimality equations and associated DP algorithms, a relative value function proposition can be utilized.

$$Q(i, a) \leftarrow (1 - \alpha)Q(i, a) + \alpha[\gamma(i, a, j) + \max_{b \in A(j)} Q(j, b) - Q(i^*, a^*)] \quad (1.13)$$

where a state-action pair (i^*, a^*) is selected arbitrarily.

Since the discounting factor is usually unknown in the real-world problems, taking transition time without unity into consideration, the Bellman equation has difficulties in being applied to value iterations with an unknown average reward of the optimal policy ρ^* without uniformization of SMDP. However, by estimation of $\widehat{\rho}$, the above equation is given as

$$Q(s_i, a) = (1 - \alpha)Q(s_i, a) + \alpha[\gamma(s_i, a, s_j) - \widehat{\rho}t(s_i, a, s_j) + \max_{b \in A(s_j)} Q(s_j, b) - Q(s_i^*, a^*)] \quad (1.14)$$

With indexed data partition and parallelization, the proposed parallelized search algorithm (Figure 1.2) is to initialize and load a page-sized state-action data set. It is the subspace of the entire state and solution space. This is the algorithmic design to resolve memory bound issues with index pointers of each initial state data set. It is based on the upper bound of interactions to resolve state-action value function mapping by page basis. For each initial state, an action will be randomly selected to avoid local greedy optimality. In addition, simulation plays the major role in the search exploration. On the basis of Q factors of learning during search computation, it is updated incrementally instead of by traditional batch data training. The final optimal action policy is computed with the maximum action value.

Initialization (Figure 1.3) of state space and action value mapping is done with 0 as its starting point. However, as it is specified in the feedback of the task environment, rewards and costs are assigned by predefined discrete real values. The simulation routine is set as a large number, which ensures the sufficiently long run to avoid local optimum.

Randomization (Figure 1.4) is very critical for ensuring that the action selector is not trapped into local optimality. In addition, a long run of simulation is important to the algorithm design and implementation.

Simulation (Figure 1.5) updates the state-action value pairs and associated iteration parameters.

Parallel-SEARCH(s, a, limit)

> **Description**: Parallel search with a value and state-action mapping index
> **INPUT**: state space, action space and maximum iteration jumps
> **OUTPUT**: solution to the problem
> $S_{sub}, A_{sub} \leftarrow$ **SUB-SPACE**(S,A)
> **INIT-FACTORS**($S_{sub}, A_{sub}, limit$)
> **for each** k **in** k_max **do**
>   **LOCATE-ACTION**(S, A, Q)
> $r_{s_i,a,s_j}, t_{s_i,a,s_j} \leftarrow$ **PROBE**(s_i, a, s_j)
>   **SIMULATE − ACTION**($r_{s_i,a,s_j}, t_{s_i,a,s_j}$)
>   **UPDATE − ACTION**($Q(s_i, a), A$)
>   **LOCATE − POLICY**($Q(s_i, a)$)
> return $\max Q(l, b)$

FIGURE 1.2: Parallel search algorithm with value and state-action mapping index.

INIT-FACTORS(s, a, limit)

Description: Initialize a value and state-action mapping,
Visiting Factors for state space S
INPUT: state space, action space and maximum iteration jumps
INIT-FACTORS(S, A, limit)
count $\leftarrow$ max($length[S], length[A]$)
for each s_i **in** count **do**
  $Q(s_i, a_i) \leftarrow 0$
  $Visit(s_i, a_i) \leftarrow 0$
$k \leftarrow 0$
$\alpha \leftarrow 0.1$
$total\_reward \leftarrow 0$
$total\_time \leftarrow 0$
$\rho \leftarrow 0$
$\phi \leftarrow 0$
$k_{max} \leftarrow limit$

FIGURE 1.3: Initialization of all parameters.

LOCATE − ACTION(s, a, Q)

Description: locate an action with the maximum Q factor value starting from
state s_i, randomly select action a
Input: state space, action space and Q factors
Output: action a which generate maximum Q factor
$s_i \leftarrow$ **RANDOMIZE**(S)
$a_i \leftarrow$ **RANDOMIZE**(A)
for each a_i **in** Q **do**
  if $Q(s_i, a_i) == \max(Q(i, A))$
    $\phi \leftarrow 0$
    return a_i
$\phi \leftarrow 1$
return NIL

FIGURE 1.4: Randomized algorithm to locate action with maximum state-action value mapping.

SIMULATE − ACTION$(r_{s_i,a,s_j}, t_{s_i,a,s_j})$

Description: Simulate action a
Input: immediate reward from action a,transition time from state s_i to
state s_j
$Visit(s_i, a) \leftarrow Visit(s_i, a) + 1$
$k \leftarrow k + 1$
$\alpha \leftarrow A/V(s_i, a)$

FIGURE 1.5: Action simulation algorithm.

UPDATE – ACTION$(Q(s_i, a), A)$

Description: Update the state-action value mapping
Input: State-Action Value Mapping
Output: updated State-Action Value Mapping
$Q(s_i, a) \leftarrow (1-\alpha)Q(s_i, a) + \alpha[r_{s_i,a,s_j} - \rho t(s_i, a, s_j)$
$\quad + \max(Q(s_j, A) - Q(s*, a*)]$
return $Q(s_j, a)$

FIGURE 1.6: Update state-action value mapping algorithm.

LOCATE – POLICY$(Q(s_i, a))$

Description: Locate a policy with the optimal State-Action Value Mapping
Input: state space
$IF(\phi == 0)$
THEN
$total\_reward \leftarrow total\_reward + r(s_i, a, s_j)$
$total\_time \leftarrow total\_time + t(s_i, a, s_j)$
$\rho \leftarrow [total\_reward/total\_time]$

FIGURE 1.7: Locate policy algorithm.

INIT – INDEX()

Description: Initialize a state-action value mapping index
node ← **LOCATE – NODE**()
tree ← **CONSTRUCT – TREE**()
$root[tree] \leftarrow node$
$leaf[tree] \leftarrow FALSE$
$PAGE - OUT(root)$

FIGURE 1.8: Initialize index structure.

Q factor is an incremental learning algorithm (Figure 1.6). It updates the learning result based on the environmental feedback. The distinguished state is selected right after the first update of s_1.

The optimal policy is based on the maximum Q factors of each state-action pair so that the policy becomes deterministic as a goal state is reached or the maximum iteration is exceeded (Figure 1.7).

The life cycle management of the proposed index structure is illustrated in Figures 1.8, 1.9, and 1.10. The initialization (Figure 1.8) of indices always keeps the root node in the main memory. Nodes are loaded on demand. For amortization, data activities are completed through page-in and page-out routines. Node insertion and lookup routines depend on the key, which is the vectors of state-action values.

INSERT$(tree, key)$

Description: Insert a new state-action value pair into the index tree
$root[tree] \leftarrow node$
$degree \leftarrow degree[tree]$
$leaf[tree] \leftarrow FALSE$
IF$(keyCount[root] == 2 * degree - 1)$
  $newNode \leftarrow$ **LOCATE − NODE**()
  $root[tree] \leftarrow newNode$
  $isRoot[newNode] \leftarrow FALSE$
  ADD − NODE$(1, newNode)$
  SPLIT$(degree, newRoot, 1, key)$
  INSERT − NOT − FULL$(degree, newRoot, key)$
INSERT − NOT − FULL$(degree, root, key)$

FIGURE 1.9: Insert a node into index structure.

LOOK − UP$(node, key)$

Description: Search a state-action value pair from the index tree
$index \leftarrow 1$
$count \leftarrow keyCount[node]$
while$(index <= count\&\&key > key[node])$
  $index + +$
if$(index <= count\&\&key == key[node])$
  $keyIndex[node] \leftarrow index$
  return node
if$hasChild[node]$
  $child \leftarrow child[index, node]$
  PAGE − IN$(child)$
  SEARCH$(child, key)$
return NIL

FIGURE 1.10: Locate a node from index structure.

1.7 Evaluation

The fundamental property of the value function used throughout the entire study of adaptive learning for search optimization is tuning. This can produce accurate estimation. Moreover, this estimation is represented as a table with a set of tuples, which are states or state-action pairs.

$$Q(s, a) = Q(s_t, a_t) + \alpha_t \delta_t \tag{1.15}$$

$$\delta_t = r(s_t, \pi(s_t), s_{t+k}) - \rho_t + \max_a(Q(s_{t+1}, a) - Q(s_t, a_t)) \tag{1.16}$$

$$\rho_{t+1} = \rho_t + \beta_t(\gamma(s_t, a_t, s_{t+1}) - \rho_t) \tag{1.17}$$

where ρ_t, β_t are positive step parameters set to $\frac{1}{t}$. The discount rate is $\gamma \in [0, 1)$. The above iterative learning converges to the optimal state-action value with a discount. However, there is no convergence proof in the average reward cases. In addition, the above equations are not suitable for large or continuous action and state spaces.

Let $\tilde{Q}(s, a, p)$ approximate to $Q^*(s, a)$ on the basis of a linear combination of basis functions with a parameter vector p:

$$\tilde{Q}(s, a, p) = \sum_{1<=i<M} p^i \phi^i(s, a) \tag{1.18}$$

where a column vector with a fixed number of real valued components $p = (p^1, p^2, \ldots, p^M)^T$ and

$$\phi(s, a) = (\phi^1(s, a), \phi^2(s, a), \ldots, \phi^M(s, a))^T \tag{1.19}$$

Hence, $\tilde{Q}(s, a, p)$ is a smooth differentiable function of p for all $s \in S$. The above Bellman equation error can be estimated by the mean-squared error over a distribution P of inputs.

$$MSE(\vec{p_t}) = \sum_{s \in S} P(s)[Q^*(s, a) - \tilde{Q}(s, a, p)]^2 \tag{1.20}$$

$$p_{t+1} = p_t + \alpha[Q^*(s, a) - \tilde{Q}(s, a, p)]\nabla_{\vec{p_t}} \tilde{Q}(s_t, a_t, p_t) \tag{1.21}$$

where α is a positive step-size parameter, and $\nabla_{\vec{p}_t} Q(p)$, for any function Q denotes the vector of partial derivatives.

$$\nabla_{\vec{p}_t} Q(p) = \left(\frac{\partial Q(\vec{p_t})}{\partial p_t(1)}, \frac{\partial Q(\vec{p_t})}{\partial p_t(2)}, \ldots, \frac{\partial Q(\vec{p_t})}{\partial p_t(t)} \right)^T \tag{1.22}$$

where $\phi(s_t, a_t)$ is a vector of all basis functions.

Since

$$\nabla_{\vec{p_t}} \tilde{Q}(s_t, a_t, p_t) = \phi^i(s, a) \tag{1.23}$$

Above equation is updated as

$$p_{t+1} = p_t + \alpha[Q^*(s, a) - \tilde{Q}(s, a, p)]\phi^i(s, a) \tag{1.24}$$

Hence, the average reward estimate is updated as follows:

$$\rho_{t+1} = (1 - \alpha)\rho_t + \alpha_t(r(s_t, a_t, s_{t+1}) - \rho_t) \tag{1.25}$$

As noted earlier, this choice results in the sample average method, which is guaranteed to converge to the true action values by central-limit theorem. A well-known result in stochastic approximation theory gives us the conditions about learning rate ($\Sigma_{1 \leq k < \infty} \alpha_t = \infty$ and $\Sigma_{1 \leq k < \infty} \alpha_t^2 < \infty$) required to assure convergence with probability 1.

In addition, exact state-action value function mapping acts like linear function exact fitting. Hence, the error convergence problem is resolved with exact mapping.

As discussed earlier, real-life systems and real-time measurement have a large state and action space resulting in latency and errors to reach a convergent state. Hence, adaptive search depends on the nature of the exact state-action value function to generalize from a limited subset of current state space over a much larger subset of state and action space. The proposed method applies index data structure mapping techniques to look up a state-action value function to construct numeric value exact mapping of the entire search function.

1.8 Experimental Study

The $k-puzzle$ [15] is formulated with numerous variants. A sliding puzzle consists of a grid of numbered squares with one square missing as a space in the grid. A numeric label on the squares swaps with the space at any given time. If the grid is 3×3, the puzzle is known as the $8-puzzle$ or $9-puzzle$. However, if the grid is 4×4, the puzzle is named as the $15 - puzzle$ or $16 - puzzle$. The puzzle solution is to rearrange the numbers to achieve the specified goal state.

There are several reasons to select $8 - puzzle$ problem to evaluate the proposed search methods in this chapter.

- The $k-puzzle$ is a classical problem for modeling and evaluating search algorithms. For larger states of the $k - puzzle$, locating a solution is easy, but the problem of finding the optimal solution is $NP - hard$.

- The $8-puzzle$ has been adopted to study new search algorithms, neural network, and path finding. It's usually one of the first instruments that computer researchers use to test a new search algorithm. Hence, the proposed methods for optimal or approximated optimal decisions for solutions can be validated by the classic AI $8 - puzzle$ problem.

- The $8 - puzzle$ has been utilized by AI researchers as a toy problem. It is not a real-life problem but a simplification of the problem definition and constraints. Hence, an exact description of the problem is possible, and factors that affect the problem are deterministic. Therefore, with problem abstraction, it is a problem that can be solved efficiently with AI search algorithms.

- There are combinational $P_9^9 = 362880$ states existing in $8 - puzzle$ grid. It has about 30 MB of memory requirement for state-action value function mapping. It is a sufficiently large state space with space complexity to evaluate the proposed search methods.

1.8.1 Test selection

The candidate solutions could be lists of moves from a specific hypothetical initial state matrix and a hypothetical goal state matrix shown below.

A random initial state of the 3×3 matrix is

$$\begin{bmatrix} 2 & 8 & 3 \\ 1 & 6 & 4 \\ 7 & & 5 \end{bmatrix}$$

The goal state of the 3×3 matrix is

$$\begin{bmatrix} 1 & 2 & 3 \\ 8 & & 4 \\ 7 & 6 & 5 \end{bmatrix}$$

1.8.2 Test description

The test starts with an initial state, a set of candidate actions, and criteria for identifying the goal state. It is often guided by heuristics but is not guaranteed to make the optimal choices. Starting from an initial state, the search process selects actions to transform that state into new states until a goal state is generated. For example, consider a search program to solve the $8-puzzle$. A child solves the puzzle by sliding the numbered tiles (without lifting them) to reach a configuration in which the tiles are all in an ordered set. When the $8-puzzle$ is formulated as a search problem, the initial state is a starting position. Each action is a possible move of space to swap with any labeled tile. The possible actions are up, down, left, and right. The proposed search methods suggest candidate moves by computing learning rewards, to favor those moves that make progress toward the solution. For some search problems, what is of interest is the solution path. However, for other search problems, only the final state is important.

The agent arranges the tiles so that all the tiles are in the correct positions. The agent does this by moving tiles. The agent can move a tile up, down, left, or right, so long as the following terminal goal state is met.

- Task environment: The $8-puzzle$ consists of a 3×3 grid with eight consecutively numbered tiles arranged on it. Any tile adjacent to the space can be moved on it. One agent learns a solution path to move labeled tiles to reach a targeted state. There is no other tile blocking the agent in the direction of the movement. The agent does not try to move outside of the boundaries or edges.
- State representation: A state is an ordered set of numbers $i \in [0, 8]$ to capture the position of each labeled tile in the grid.

- State space: If the space in the grid is considered as number 0, there are nine states to be assigned to nine slots. Hence, there are combinational $P_9^9 = 362880$ states existing in the puzzle grid. It is a classic combinational search optimization problem.
- Initial state: Randomization shuffles a set of numbers $i \in [0, 8]$. A possible initial state could be $\{\{5, 4, 0\}, \{6, 1, 8\}, \{7, 3, 2\}\}$.
- Goal state: A single identity of a goal state in the puzzle grid could be $\{\{1, 2, 3\}, \{4, 5, 6\}, \{7, 8, 0\}\}$ in a conventional $8 - puzzle$ problem.

- Action representation: There are four actions that deterministically result in corresponding state transitions at each state. These do not include the actions that take the agent off the puzzle grid.
  - At each state, the agent may take a set of actions as {*up, down, right, left*}.
  - The agent selects from all four actions with equal probability in all states (random policy with equal probability). As proposed in the learning algorithmic operation, the action probability is $1/|length[\overrightarrow{A(i)}]|$, where $length[\overrightarrow{A(i)}]$ is the total number of actions from state i. However, this property is used only to define the problem specification. It is not required by algorithm computation since the probability calculation is removed from operations. Some actions leave the agent off the grid but result in no state change.
- Goal definition: The learning agent tries to discover the optimal path to the goal and to maximize the reward it receives.
- Utility representation: The single output of the evaluation represents the rewards of the given input state.
- Discrete environmental signal: After each move, the learning agent receives from the above task environment one of the following reinforcement immediate reward signals $r \in \Re$.

$$r = \begin{cases} -10 & \text{If agent moves out of the grid} \\ 0.1 & \text{If a tile is moved on the correct position} \\ 0.4 & \text{If the goal state is reached} \\ -1 & \text{The cost of moving to any direction} \\ 0.0 & \text{Otherwise for all nonterminal states} \end{cases}$$

The move to the correct position is less than the absolute value of moving out of the grid since keeping the agent in the grid is more important than getting to the target. Intuitively, the agent needs to learn to achieve the goal without rewards. The agent is required to stay in the grid to move to the goal state. However, the sooner the action is rewarded, the sooner the agent will learn. The cost of moving is measured by a negative unit reward from the task environment. It is larger than the reward from getting to the correct position so that the steps in the path are considered in the search evaluation.

1.8.3 Test sample analysis

A random initial state s_1 from 362880 state spaces:
3×3 matrix

$$\begin{bmatrix} 2 & 8 & 3 \\ 1 & 6 & 4 \\ 7 & & 5 \end{bmatrix}$$

Select an action of $A(s_1) = down$ from $\overrightarrow{A} = \{up, down, left, right\}$ with a probability of $1/|A| = 0.25$. With simulation of the action $A(s_1) = down$, the state remains as s_1 with $r = -11$ due to the wrong action of taking the agent out of the grid with additional moving costs. This action value mapping increases the number of visited state-action pairs by $V(1) = V(1)+1$. This state transition also increases the number of interactions by 1. Hence, the $\alpha = 0.1/V = 0.1$. Hence, the Q factor is updated as follows. Since all $Q(s_1, A(s_1))$ pairs are initialized as -10, Equation 1.11 is evaluated as

$$\begin{aligned} Q(s_1, down) &= (1 - 0.1) * Q(s_1, down) + 0.1 * [(-11) \\ &+ \max Q(s_1, A) - 0] = -11.2 \end{aligned} \tag{1.26}$$

Since the iteration is less than the maximum iteration, select an action $A(s_1) = up$ with current state s_1. The state is updated to s_2 with a reward of $+0.1$ and a moving cost of -1 due to the expected action to move number 6 to the target position as s_2. Hence, $r = -0.9$ is the total reward of computation.
3×3 matrix

$$\begin{bmatrix} 2 & 8 & 3 \\ 1 & & 4 \\ 7 & 6 & 5 \end{bmatrix}$$

This action value mapping increases the number of visited state-action pairs by $V(2) = V(2) + 1$. This state transition also increases the number of interactions by 1. Hence, the $\alpha = 0.1/V = 0.1$. Hence, the Q factor is updated as

$$\begin{aligned} Q(s_1, up) &= (1 - 0.1) * Q(s_1, up) + 0.1 * [(-0.9) \\ &+ \max Q(s_2, A) + 10] = -9.09 \end{aligned} \tag{1.27}$$

Hence, the state s_1 with action $A(s_1) = up$ is selected as a significant state as $Q(s*, a*) = -10.09$ for further Q factor computation.

Now, the current state is set to s_2 to select an action of $A(s_2) = up$ from $\overrightarrow{A} = \{up, down, left, right\}$ with a probability of $1/|A| = 0.25$. With the simulation of action $A(s_2) = up$, the state is changed to s_3 with $r = -1$ due to the action taken by the agent.

3 × 3 matrix

$$\begin{bmatrix} 2 & & 3 \\ 1 & 8 & 4 \\ 7 & 6 & 5 \end{bmatrix}$$

This action value mapping increases the number of visited state-action pairs by $V(3) = V(3) + 1$. This state transition also increases the number of interactions by 1. Hence, the $\alpha = 0.1/V = 0.1$. Hence, the Q factor is updated as

$$\begin{aligned} Q(s_2, up) &= (1 - 0.1) * Q(s_2, up) + 0.1 * [(-1) \\ &\quad + \max Q(s_3, A) + 9.09] = -9.191 \end{aligned} \tag{1.28}$$

Now, the current state is set to s_3 to continue to select an action of $A(s_3) = left$ from $\overrightarrow{A} = \{up, down, left, right\}$ with a probability of $1/|A| = 0.25$. With the simulation of action $A(s_3) = left$, the state is changed to s_4 with $r = -1$ due to the action taken by the agent. This action value mapping increases the number of visited state-action pairs by $V(4) = V(4) + 1$.

3 × 3 matrix

$$\begin{bmatrix} & 2 & 3 \\ 1 & 8 & 4 \\ 7 & 6 & 5 \end{bmatrix}$$

This state transition also increases the number of interactions by 1. Hence, the $\alpha = 0.1/V = 0.1$. Hence, the Q factor is updated as

$$\begin{aligned} Q(s_3, left) &= (1 - 0.1) * Q(s_3, left) + 0.1 * [(-1) \\ &\quad + \max Q(s_4, A) + 9.09] = -9.191 \end{aligned} \tag{1.29}$$

Now, set the current state to s_4 to continue to select an action of $A(s_4) = down$ from $\overrightarrow{A} = \{up, down, left, right\}$ with a probability of $1/|A| = 0.25$. With the simulation of action $A(s_1) = down$, the state is changed to s_5 with $r = -0.9$ due to the action taken by the agent to move number 1 to the expected position.

3 × 3 matrix

$$\begin{bmatrix} 1 & 2 & 3 \\ & 8 & 4 \\ 7 & 6 & 5 \end{bmatrix}$$

This action value mapping increases the number of visited state-action pairs by $V(5) = V(5) + 1$. This state transition also increases the number of interactions by 1. Hence, the $\alpha = 0.1/V = 0.1$. Hence, the Q factor is updated as

$$\begin{aligned} Q(s_4, down) = {} & (1 - 0.1) * Q(s_4, down) + 0.1 * [(-0.9) \\ & + \max Q(s_5, A) + 9.09] = -9.181 \end{aligned} \tag{1.30}$$

Now, set the current state to s_5 to continue to select an action of $A(s_5) = right$ from $\overrightarrow{A} = \{up, down, left, right\}$ with a probability of $1/|A| = 0.25$. With the simulation of action $A(s_5) = right$, the state is changed to s_6 with $r = -0.5$ due to the action taken by agent to move number 8 to the expected position. In addition, this is the goal state. Hence, this action value mapping increases the number of visited state-action pairs by $V(6) = V(6) + 1$.

3×3 matrix

$$\begin{bmatrix} 1 & 2 & 3 \\ 8 & & 4 \\ 7 & 6 & 5 \end{bmatrix}$$

This state transition also increases the number of interactions by 1. Hence, the $\alpha = 0.1/V = 0.1$. Hence, the Q factor is updated as

$$\begin{aligned} Q(s_5, right) = {} & (1 - 0.1) * Q(s_5, right) + 0.1 * [(-0.5) \\ & + \max Q(s_6, A) + 9.09] = -9.141 \end{aligned} \tag{1.31}$$

To summarize the above search computation, the optimal action policy for the above station transition to reach the final goal state will be illustrated as

3×3 matrix

$$\begin{bmatrix} \downarrow & \leftarrow & \\ \rightarrow & \uparrow & \\ & \uparrow & \end{bmatrix}$$

To avoid the greedy local optimum, iterations should continue until the search reaches the maximum interaction number, then set the current state back to s_1 to continue to select an action from $\overrightarrow{A} = \{up, down, left, right\}$ with a probability of $1/|A| = 0.25$. Since $V(1) = V(2) = 1$, we need to randomly select an action $A(s_1, left)$ to ensure 0.25. With the simulation of action $A(s_1) = left$, the state is changed to s_7 with $r = -1$ due to the action taken by the agent. This action value mapping increases the number of visited state-action pairs by $V(7) = V(7) + 1$.

3×3 matrix

$$\begin{bmatrix} 2 & 8 & 3 \\ 1 & 6 & 4 \\ & 7 & 5 \end{bmatrix}$$

This state transition also increases the number of interactions by 1. Hence, the $\alpha = 0.1/V(7) = 0.1$. Hence, the Q factor is updated as

$$Q(s_1, left) = (1 - 0.1) * Q(s_1, left) + 0.1 * [(-1) + \max Q(s_7, A) + 9.09] = -9.191 \tag{1.32}$$

The search will continue until the goal state is reached or the maximum number of iterations is exceeded. However, as the above halt condition is satisfied, the original state is set back to s_1. To continue to select an action from $\overrightarrow{A} = \{up, down, left, right\}$ with a probability of $1/|A| = 0.25$. Since $V(1) = V(2) = V(7) = 1$, we need randomly select an action $A(s_1, right)$ to ensure 0.25.

With the simulation of action $A(s_1) = right$, the state is changed to s_8 with $r = -1$ due to the action taken by the agent. This action value mapping increases the number of visited state-action pairs by $V(8) = V(8) + 1$.

3 × 3 matrix

$$\begin{bmatrix} 2 & 8 & 3 \\ 1 & 6 & 4 \\ & 7 & 5 \end{bmatrix}$$

This state transition also increases the number of interactions by 1. Hence, the $\alpha = 0.1/V(7) = 0.1$. Hence, the Q factor is updated as

$$Q(s_1, right) = (1 - 0.1) * Q(s_1, right) + 0.1 * [(-1) + \max Q(s_8, A) + 9.09] = -9.191 \tag{1.33}$$

The search will continue until the goal state is reached or the maximum iteration number is exceeded. However, as the above halt condition is satisfied, the original state is set back to s_1. This will further explore state transitions. To continue to select an action from $\overrightarrow{A} = \{up, down, left, right\}$ with a probability of $1/|A| = 0.25$. Since $V(1) = V(2) = V(7) = V(8) = 1$, we randomly select an action $A(s_1, up)$ to ensure 0.25.

With the simulation of action $A(s_1) = up$, the state is changed to s_2 again with $r = -0.9$ due to the action taken by the agent. This action value mapping increases the number of visited state-action pairs by $V(2) = V(2) + 1$. This state transition also increases the number of interactions by 1. Hence, the $\alpha = 0.1/V(2) = 0.05$. Hence, the Q factor is updated as

$$Q(s_1, up) = (1 - 0.05) * Q(s_1, up) + 0.05 * [(-0.9) + \max Q(s_2, A) + 9.09] = -8.6855 \tag{1.34}$$

As you can see, $Q(s_1, up)$ is improved from -9.09 to -8.6855 during the learning process. It will converge to its optimal value as the $maxQ(s_2, A)$ grows. However, other actions from $Q(s_1, A)$ continue to select an action from $\overrightarrow{A} = \{up, down, left, right\}$ with a probability of $1/|A| = 0.25$. We randomly select an action $A(s_1, right)$ to ensure 0.25.

With the simulation of action $A(s_1) = right$, the state is changed to s_8 again with $r = -1$ due to the action taken by the agent. This action value mapping increases the number of visited state-action pairs by $V(8) = V(8)+1$. This state transition also increases the number of interactions by 1. Hence, the $\alpha = 0.1/V(8) = 0.05$. Hence, the Q factor is updated as

$$
\begin{aligned}
Q(s_1, right) = {} & (1 - 0.05) * Q(s_1, right) + 0.05 * [(-1) \\
& + \max Q(s_8, A) + 9.09] = -8.82695
\end{aligned}
\tag{1.35}
$$

Apparently, $Q(s_1, up)$ is the optimal state action for the specified initial and goal state. Consequently, state s_2 is the optimal subsequent state from state s_1. Finally, it is concluded that state transitions $\{s_1, s_2, s_3, s_4, s_5, s_6\}$ is the optimal path to the goal state. The experimental evaluation of the proposed search optimization is achieved with the following figure (Figure 1.11). It is a simplified version of search goal discovery without the paged index structure.

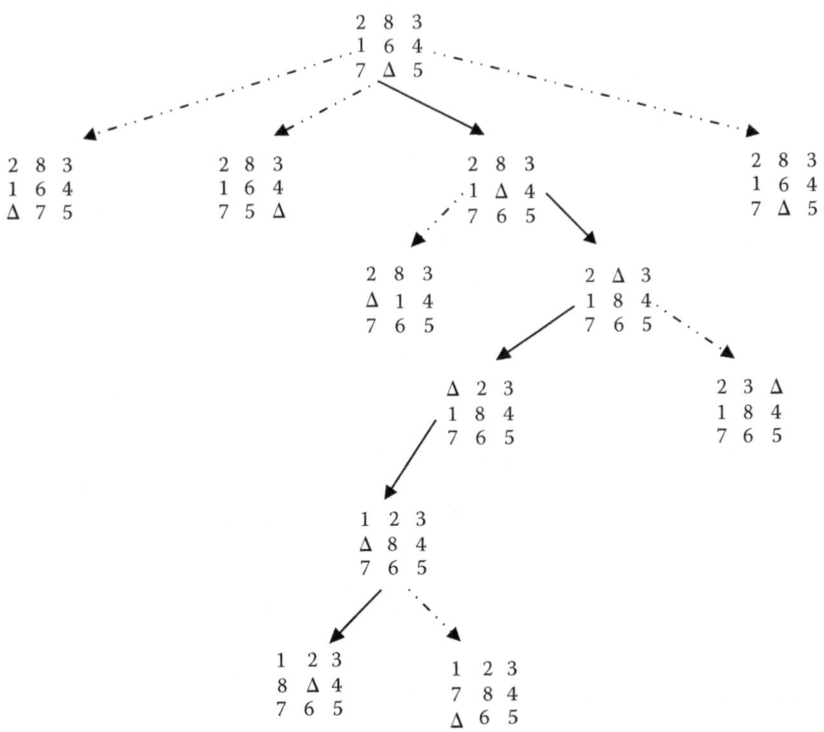

FIGURE 1.11: A search simulation scenario.

1.9 Discussion

General findings from this chapter are itemized below:

- The above search computation illustrates that the proposed Q learning-based search algorithm rooted from RL optimization methods exploits the solution space with incremental calculation of the immediate and future rewards from any given state. This ensures optimality, which is inherited from conventional DP methods. Specifically, the index-based exact Q function eliminates the error convergence resulting from numeric approximation methods. In addition, the transformation of traditional in-memory computation to I/O lazy loading guarantees the logarithmic cost reduction of disk read/write with converged space complexity.

- Only the root of initial state is originally kept in main memory. However, the current state and subset of state-action mapping with associated Q values are loaded into memory as search computation proceeds.

- To avoid the local optimum, the proposed search method randomizes the action selection for any given state to explore within a large solution space. Specifically, state enumeration does not terminate until the threshold of search iterations is exceeded.

- Simulation plays a critical role in the proposed search optimization. To obtain the entire solution space, the proposed search method is optimized by simulation. As shown, simulation does not enumerate the state space for Q function mapping but for search optimization to obtain the optimal action policy and the expected state transition costs. This is different from traditional simulation experiments.

- Stochastic exploration tends to result in a breadth-first search (BFS) tree if the maximum iteration is sufficiently large and simulation does a possible long run. This indicates the optimality of the proposed search methods. However, performance degradation within a limited episode is reduced by randomization instead of expansion of BFS nodes. In addition, for any known goal state, a monotonically converged Q value indicates the approximation to the goal state. Intuitively, unless the goal state is unknown, the simulation is normally halted at the goal states.

- For unknown goal state search, optimality is obtained by a possible long run of the entire state space. However, this generates an index-based BFS tree that is located on the secondary storage to reduce space complexity. A Q function does index I/O-based lazy loading.

- Within a routine of local path discovery, the proposed search method shows the depth-first search (DFS) similar logic to expand the single path of state transition. The upper bound of iterations could be the maximum threshold of iterations or terminated at a local goal state if the goal state is known. However, to avoid trapping into the local optimum, randomization is required to conduct further state via simulation as BFS type of enumeration to ensure global optimality.

- The Q factor provides an indication of optimal path search as heuristics-based search does. This could reduce search time complexity. However, to avoid trapping into the local optimum, randomization is required to conduction further state via simulation as BFS type of enumeration to ensure global optimality.
- A genetic algorithm could be applied to the proposed search optimization. However, a genetic algorithm is an evolutional approximation to the traditional memory bound problem for large-state spaces and solution spaces. The proposed search optimization is an incremental learning search. In addition, it does online learning that is different from genetic algorithms. Traditional genetic algorithms depend on clearly defined objective functions with supervised training. This is prohibitive in dynamic search optimization problems.
- Unlike conventional local search methods such as tabu search, gradient descent, hill climbing, and simulated annealing techniques, the proposed search optimization enhances conventional DP techniques for optimality. With Q function exact mapping, the proposed search optimization resolves the error convergence problem resulting from traditional function approximation problem.
- Data parallelization is critical for system parallelism and pipelined processors. Time complexity is reduced by the speedup derived from parallelized search computation and simulations. In addition, each randomized initial state is searched with indexed value function mapping without the risk of data hazard.
- The proposed index data structure is a simple lookup pointer structure to locate the target states on the secondary storage devices. At any time, only a single root node, which owns the pointers to the disk-based states, loads an initial state to begin the search. Afterward, the pointers of search-state transition for action space A logically construct the search tree with state simulation.

1.9.1 Conclusion

This derives the conclusion that the proposed dynamic search with adaptive index structure provides a parallelized formal framework with data parallelization to reduce time complexity and resolve the memory bound and convergence problems existing in AI search community.

References

[1] Bagchi, A. and Mathanti, A. Search algorithms under different kinds of heuristics-A competitive study. *Journal of ACM,* 30(1):1–21, 1983.

[2] Hart et al. A formal basis for the heuristic determination of minimum cost paths. *IEEE Transactions on Systems Science and Cybernetics,* 4(2):100–107, 1968.

[3] Pearl, J. *Heuristics: Intelligent Search Strategies for Computer Problem Solving.* Addison-Wesley, Reading, MA, 1983.

[4] Brent, R. P. *Algorithms for Minimization Without Derivatives.* Prentice-Hall, Upper Saddle River, NJ, 1973.

[5] Glover, F. Tabu search: 1. *ORSA Journal on Computing,* 1(3):190–206, 1989.

[6] Minton et al. Minimizing conflicts: A heuristic-repair method for constraint satisfaction and scheduling problems. *Artificial Intelligence,* 58(1-3):161–205, 1992.

[7] Goldberg, D. E. *Genetic Algorithms in Search, Optimization and Machine Learning.* Kluwer Academic Publishers, Boston, MA, 1989.

[8] Moore, E. F. The shortest path through a maze. *In Proceedings of an International Symposium on the Theory of Switching, Part II.* 285–292, 1959.

[9] Bellman, R. E. and S. E. Dreyfus. *Applied Dynamic Programming.* Princeton University Press, Princeton, NJ, 1962.

[10] Dijkstra, E. W. A note on two problems in connexion with graphs. *Numerishe Mathematik,* 1:269–271, 1959.

[11] Howard, R. *Dynamic Programming and Markov Process.* MIT Press, Cambridge, MA, 1960.

[12] Bellman, R. E. *Dynamic Programming.* Princeton University Press, Princeton, NJ, 1957.

[13] Konda,V. R. and J. N. Tsitsiklis. Actor-critic algorithms. SIAM. *Journal on Control and Optimization,* 42(4):1143–1166, 2003.

[14] Vengerov et al. A fuzzy reinforcement learning approach to power control in wireless transmitters. *IEEE Transactions on Systems, Man, and Cybernetics, Part B,* 35(4):159, 2005.

[15] Ratner, D. and M. K. Warmuth. Finding a shortest solution for the extension of the 15-PUZZLE is intractable. *Proceedings of the 5th National Conference on the Artificial Intelligence*, 1986.

[16] Amdahl, G. M. et al. Architecture of the IBM System 360. *IBM Journal of Research and Development,* 8(2):87–101, 1964.

[17] Robbinsi, H. and S. Monro. A stochastic approximation method. *Annals of Mathematical Statistics,* 22(3):400–407, 1951.

Chapter 2

A Method of Policy Discovery for Storage and Data Management

2.1 Introduction

2.1.1 Background

Policy usually copes with storage environments with partial observability and uncertainty. In addition, these environments evolve over time space. So the policy deals with large complex policy objects and relations. Also, it requires taking actions in the limited time domain. During input/output (I/O) operations, policy management is a major step towards connecting, storing, and filing among storage pools. Real-life policy management networks acquire, evaluate, and execute 10^6 discrete storage events and processes. The environment is overwhelmed by irrelevant information and actions. It manages 10^9 physical objects with imperfect information.

Due to uncertainty and observability, situations and activities may be described incompletely or incorrectly with hidden variables. In representing the storage objects and relationships, the ambiguity of a policy language leads to hidden states. In addition, a structure of goals may need reformulation. For critical events, activities are monitored during and after execution. Hence, a common practice is to specify and execute policies with least domain-dependent human interactions. With a continuum of operational and business objectives, new birth of applications and hyper-exponential growth of arrival density impose contingencies in the storage environment. In general, storage policy space exhibits a stochastic and dynamic state space without fixed goals.

To represent the above policy environment with an atomic sentence of n variables in first order logic, $O(d^n)$ is exponential in n given d, which are the computation steps required to infer each predicate in the worst case. If the n variables are partitioned into at most c variables in a domain, $O(d^c \times n/c)$ is linear in n. Hence, a policy library can take advantage of hierarchical decomposition to reduce the exponential explosion problem into a linear one. Specifically, constructing a plan with n actions and maximal b actions at each state results in state transitions with a branch factor of b at most. $O(b^n)$ is exponential in n without decomposition. A policy hierarchy with a regular $B+$ tree structure has branch factor b for each level of decomposition. The

$B+$ node space is $O((n-1)/(b-1))$, which is linear in n.

$$1 + b + b^2 + \cdots + b^{\log_b n} = (n-1)/(b-1) \tag{2.1}$$

In Equation 2.1, the activity space is bounded to $O(d^{(n-1)/(b-1)})$ if each node has up to d decomposition.

In addition to traditional discrete methods, differentiable variables can be approximated as polynomial functions with smooth continuity. From power series, a real or complex function $p(x)$ is infinitely differentiable in a neighborhood of a real or complex number a.

$$p(x) = \sum_{n=0}^{\infty} \frac{p^{(n)}(a)}{n!}(x-a)^n \tag{2.2}$$

where $n!$ is the factorial of n and $p^{(n)}(a)$ denotes the nth derivative of f evaluated at the point a.

Hence, a linear approximation could be

$$p(x, y) \approx p(a, b) + p_x(a, b)(x-a) + f_y(a, b)(y-b) \tag{2.3}$$

For completeness, this chapter combines partial ordering with the $B+$ tree structure to derive a decidable inference. However, classic hierarchy decomposes physical state space with full observability. Hence, hierarchy is augmented with an AND-OR graph for conditional probabilities. Hierarchy does action decomposition, whereas knowledge effects on chance nodes represent uncertainty of optimal performance or behavior of storage activities.

Unlike attribute relations of a single object, both policy consistency and conflicts can be consistent relationships between attributes of different objects. In addition, no policy trajectory can exist at critical values. Policy conflicts may also arise as inconsistent effects negate each other. An effect may interfere with a precondition of another activity. A precondition of an action may be mutually exclusive with a precondition of another. Conflicts may occur in higher-order relations other than the binary ones. Higher-order constraints such as performance (time, IOops, etc.), resource (watermark), and preference (cost, priority) impose policy conflicts in real-life storage environments. The physics of policy impose an ontological commitment in a storage environment.

2.1.2 Review of literature

From the literature, a classic search-based method [1] is a possible option for solving conflicts. However, pure search methods cannot formulate states with internal structures. Instead, search routines use arbitrary data structures to represent objects and relations. Search methods rely on domain-specific definitions of successor states and heuristics for fixed goals without contingencies of the storage environment. Hence, classic search methods are not optimal for stochastic and dynamic policy space without a fixed goal.

Intuition of constrained-based conflicts leads to conflict formulation as a (constraint satisfaction problem) CSP [2, 3]. CSP can propose a general structure of problem formulation to derive domain independent heuristics to goals. CSP can develop a general principle for policy variable selection and value assignment in addition to problem decomposition by connected-independent problems. To resolve preference satisfiability, a preference is encoded with a cost scheme. The assigned values can be used to evaluate objective functions. However, the proposal infers upon a set of policy attributes of a single storage object. Hence, high-dimensional relationships between storage objects cannot be effectively represented by attributed-based inference. In addition, CSP can be formulated with a fixed goal description and it cannot reason about uncertainty. Hence, CSP has a limitation for policy discovery in storage space.

Due to hyper-exponential growth with contingencies in storage policy space, situation calculus [4] provides one of the formal tools for conflict analysis. Logic inference [5] in policy space reduces a infinite belief domain into a finite one. In addition, hidden policy variables can be inferred and hidden storage states can be reasoned with partial observability or without policy sensors. However, the systematic theorem proving in situation calculus has been shown to be an inefficient reasoning method in literature. CSP has been studied with propositional logic for sentence satisfiability.

To represent policy resulting from higher dimensional relationships among storage activities and objects, a planning-based method [6] can infer the hidden factors in an exponential policy and conflict space. With unbounded uncertainty, continuous planning methods evaluate policy during and after execution of storage activities. Specifically, the methods may reformulate goals of storage activities. But a single hierarchical planner does not reason the probability of policy optimality. In addition, existing planning methods compute with indeterminacy. They do not evaluate the cost of solutions. Utility methods were proposed as a model-based tool for decision making.

Another potential method is a model-based policy representation where utility can be applied to derive optimality. Specifically, dynamic decision networks [7] can be used for policy decision making. A policy causal model represents storage objects and relationships where probabilities and utilities can be assigned for satisfiability. However, the causal model is defined upon domain-specific knowledge. In addition, for a finite set of variables with a fixed domain, Bayes networks [8] are encoded as random variables, which are attribute-based systems. To express object relationships, the object relational model was proposed. This is still an active research area.

In machine learning space, making discovery using inductive logic programming [9] is studied. The method uses logic programming as a uniform representation for sample description, background knowledge, and hypotheses. With the encoding of prior knowledge and ground facts in logical databases, an inductive logic programming (ILP) system was reported to derive a hypothesized logic program that entails examples with 80% from database and 20% from ILP instead of linear regression.

For noisy processing, Kalman filters [10], hidden markov models (HMMs), and dynamic Bayes nets represent transition models and sensor models with partial observability. There are exact and approximate algorithms to update the posterior probability distribution over internal state representation. Storage policies would be providing accurate, continuously updated information about the states of storage objects and applications given only a sequence of observations about its random variables, each of which includes some error. The Kalman filter exploits the dynamics of the storage targets with its time evolution. It removes the effects of the noise and gets a good estimate of the location of the targets by filtering, prediction, and interpolation or smoothing. However, the Kalman filter estimates states of a linear dynamic system from a series of noisy measurements.

In a simulated environment, it is possible to use enforcement-learning algorithms such as Q-learning [11] to learn with millions of trials in hours. On real-life systems, it might take years to run these trials. In addition, real crashes of systems and activities may not be like the simulated ones. Furthermore, it may require domain knowledge about the storage activities and its physical environment to perform and learn quicker. Therefore, in this paper, we augment traditional planning methods for policy discovery.

The rest of the chapter is organized as follows. Section 2.2 gives the problem presentation for policy discovery in a storage environment. Section 2.3 introduces policy discovery with uncertainty. It analyzes their completeness and consistency. Section 2.4 presents performance analysis of the proposed method with cost of the solution. Finally, we draw some conclusions in Section 2.5.

2.2 Problem Analysis

Hierarchical categories of storage policy are not a simple set of structural relations. The inconsistency and consistency of relationship between policy and storage effects is a representational and inferential problem for policies, which may be relations between objects rather than attributes of a single object. Backup window and service response time of an application, data, resource (bandwidth), and forcing functions represent the relations among objects. Integration is a resource attraction and repelling force. Data could result in locks, dependencies, and so on.

The following sections give a more general and flexible representation for this complex domain.

2.2.1 State representation

(1) *Discrete States:* State representations of environment are internal states structured for belief updates corresponding to physical variables. Policy space in a storage environment can be represented with a logical structure. With general-purpose state descriptions, there are four state-structure representations. They are full physical state, logical state, knowledge state, and information state. They represent possibilities for policy hidden states and variables. A state represents the process of continuous nonchange. To model the rate of changes, an instantaneous state representation is introduced.

Full-Joint expression: a complete set enumeration with all possible state variables.

$$P(x_1, x_2, \ldots, x_n) \tag{2.4}$$

In Equation 2.4, for a n variable policy specification, there is a set of $O(3^n)$ physical states with its epistemological commitment. With partial or ambiguous information, it will be an exponential distribution of possible current states. Even algebraic inequity, bound propagation, and fuzzy membership can be reduction techniques for discrete variables such as the status of activities. Function approximation and linear programming can reduce continuous variables such as watermark and IOops. It is not possible to encode a complete description of policy states with full-join description due to ignorance and laziness. Hence, the full physical states are not adequate for conflict analysis.

Conditioning expression: Given perfect or incorrect sensor evidences, conditioning the subset of a policy model focuses on the set of observed derivation of all possible policy states.

$$\begin{aligned} P(x_i|x_{i-1}, \ldots, x_1) = &P(x_i|parents(x_i), children(x_i), \\ &parent - children(x_i)) \end{aligned} \tag{2.5}$$

In Equation 2.5, for a n variable policy specification, there is a set of 2^n physical states. From k-consistency, parents, children, and children's parents are sufficient to represent states. Indifference is also denoted in the above policy state expression. Hence, with an open world assumption, logical states include hidden variables, evidence variables, and states in logical reduction.

Knowledge state expression: A planner updates existing knowledge base with current evidence.

$$Tell(x_i) \wedge Tell(x_j) \wedge Tell(x_k) \tag{2.6}$$

In Equation 2.6, for a n variable policy specification, there is a set of 2^n physical states. The significance of the knowledge state is to have a close world assumption. With such a knowledge proposition, a policy state may negate the truth of hidden variables.

(2) *Continuous States:* In addition to representation of physical states, dynamic states are specified with governance rules. Instantaneous state representation of a storage activity is illustrated in the following section. Response time is defused as

$$r'' + \gamma r' + \alpha r + \beta r^3 = A \cos \omega t \tag{2.7}$$

where system resources, specifically central processing unit (CPU) capacity, are modeled as a hard spring force that grows to its limits as r increases. Data arrival rate is modeled as a periodic force function. System utilization and network capacity such as congestion and bandwidth contribute as dump factors. Resources are attraction and repelling forces of constraints.

Entropy duffing is modeled as

$$x'' + \gamma x' + \alpha x + \beta x^3 = A \cos \omega t \tag{2.8}$$

where system resources, specifically CPU capacity is modeled as a hard spring force. The data arrival rate is modeled as a periodic force function. Throughput is the dump factor.

Service time has a closed policy trajectory as

$$s'' + \epsilon(1 - s^2)x' + \alpha s + \beta s^3 = 0 \tag{2.9}$$

where system resources, specifically CPU capacity is modeled as a hard spring force. The dump factor is $L2$ cache, memory, and so on.

(3) *Information States:* In cases of current state unknown, information regarding the state is obtained from sensors during the execution of a plan. Some tasks can be solved without requiring states to be sensed. To do so, the policy discovery problem should be expressed in terms of information space. The three sources of policy information space are initial conditions, sensor observations during execution, and action executed.

(4) *Configuration States:* The complexity of policy space can be hard and uncertain in storage environment. Instead of constructing policy sets explicitly, it is practical to probe the configuration of policy space. Hence, policy discovery may generate a configuration and test to see if it is consistent by applying related transformation and computation and then checking for relations in policy space.

2.2.2 Relation representation

Both causal and conflict mapping represent orders of relations among objects and along the paths. Specifically, mutex and constraints can be used. Topological connectivity and associated causal knowledge represent spatial relations.

2.2.3 Policy representation

Storage and data management involve continuous random variables such as response time, throughput, and service time. To transform infinity into a finite problem, a standard family of probability density functions is specified with a finite number of parameters. With the linear Gaussian distribution, the child in Equation 2.5 has a Gaussian distribution whose mean μ varies linearly with the value of the parent and whose standard deviation δ is fixed.

$$\pi_\theta(x_i|x_{i-1}, ..., x_1) = N(\mu_\theta, \delta^2)(x_i) \tag{2.10}$$

where μ_θ is the linear approximation of causes of a policy activity.

A policy can be represented as discrete relations. At each state s_i, a policy can be represented as the activity a_i achieving better performance of $Q_\theta(s_i, a_i)$. For discrete activities $\overrightarrow{a}$ at each discrete state s_i, the policy $\pi(s_i)$ becomes discontinuous. Hence, policy can be represented as a probability for the discrete relations. It transfers a discrete policy function into a differential function of θ.

$$\pi_\theta(s, a_j) = \frac{e^{\widehat{Q}_\theta(a,s)}}{\sum_{a'} e^{\widehat{Q}_\theta(a',s)}} \tag{2.11}$$

In Equation 2.11, tuning linear parameters $\{\theta_0, \theta_1, \ldots, \theta_6\}$ improves policy without approximating an optimal function Q^*.

2.2.4 Activity representation

For a discrete fluent, a policy activity is described by effects of a possible execution or a logical operation. Storage ontology can be represented by initial situation, by possibility axiom, and by effect axiom.

$$\begin{aligned} Preconditions &\Rightarrow Poss(a, s) \\ Poss(a, s) &\Rightarrow F_i(o, Result(a, s)) \\ Poss(a, s) &\Rightarrow F_i(Result(a, s)) \\ &\Leftrightarrow PosEffect(a, F_i) \\ \vee[F_i(s) &\wedge \neg NegEffect(a, F_i)] \\ &PosEffect(A_i, F_i) \\ &NegEffect(A_j, F_j) \end{aligned} \tag{2.12}$$

Preconditions specify the logical expression that should be evaluated for action execution. $Poss(a, s)$ extends the activity description from a single activity to a sequence of time steps t. At each time step t_i, $F_i(o, Result(a, s))$ denotes the derivation resulting from taking a policy activity a involved with a set of storage objects o. To represent the indifference of a storage effect, at time t_i, $F_i(Result(a, s))$ is projected by $PosEffect(A_i, F_i)$, which is a policy activity making F_i true, and $NegEffect(A_j, F_j)$, which is a policy activity negating F_i. With close world assumption, knowledge activity can be represented with true value of F_i.

This derives the delta rule of policy activities and state relations at each time step, $Result(a, s_i)$ is represented by $Result(a, s_i)$ with changes F_i.

For continuous activities and fluents, event-based ontology represents the relations with an atemporal axiom.

$$\begin{aligned} T(f, t_2) \Rightarrow \exists e, t Happens(e, t) \wedge Initiates(e, f, t) \\ \wedge (t < t_2) \wedge \neg Interrupted(f, t, t_2) \\ Interrupted(f, t, t_2) \Rightarrow \exists e, t_1 Happens(e, t_1) \\ \wedge Terminates(e, f, t_1) \wedge (t < t_1) \wedge (t_1 < t_2) \end{aligned} \tag{2.13}$$

In responding to a discrete event e occurring at t_2, a fluent f represents the temporal substance (between t and t_2) of policy and storage relations and is denoted as $T(f, t_2)$. As it is interrupted at t_1, the storage process is terminated. Event Calculus [12–14] was introduced as a logic programming formalism for reasoning about events and fluents. Hence, within the condition body, activity, and fluent relations may include combinations of predicate propositions and time relationships.

2.2.5 Activity space

Hence, given activities, the relational deduction of change effects is reduced to a finite domain $O(AF)$, where F represents changes resulting from activities A. For storage facts that are not changed, complexity is reduced to $O(Et)$, where E is effects of each action and t is a sequence of time steps. There are $O(INTS)$ event spaces where $INTS$ are interrupts of events causing fluents. In addition, policy algorithms can infer preferred storage effects by a sequence of activities with hidden states and variables.

However, there is no completeness to enumerate all preconditions of a given activity a due to ignorance and laziness.

2.2.6 Upper ontology of policies

In information science, an upper ontology [15] is a method to create an ontology denoting general concepts across all domains. Upper ontology of policy represents a general framework of concepts on storage governance. Topology of the upper ontology is specified with general policy relations at the top and more specific policy relations below them. A proposed upper ontology of policy categories and subclass relationships are represented by the following taxonomy hierarchy.

$$\begin{aligned}
GeneralPolicy &\subset Policy \\
BasisPolicy &\subset Policy \\
SpecificPolicy &\subset Policy \\
GeneralEvents &\subset Policy \\
PolicySets &\subset GeneralPolicy \\
RepresentationalObjects &\subset GeneralPolicy \\
PolicySentences &\subset RepresentationalObjects \\
Measurements &\subset RepresentationalObjects \\
Times &\subset Measurements \\
Frequencies &\subset Measurements \\
Probabilities &\subset Measurements \\
Interval &\subset GeneralEvents \\
Places &\subset GeneralEvents \\
Objects &\subset GeneralEvents \\
Processes &\subset GeneralEvents \\
Categories &\subset PolicySets \\
Local &\subset Places \\
Distributed &\subset Places \\
Domains &\subset Objects \\
StorageObjects &\subset Domains \\
StorageApplications &\subset Domains \\
StructureBasedPolicy &\subset Processes \\
ConstraintBasedPolicy &\subset Processes \\
DefaultPolicy &\subset StructureBasedPolicy \\
LocalPolicy &\subset StructureBasedPolicy \\
DistributedPolicy &\subset StructureBasedPolicy \\
TimeBasedPolicy &\subset ConstraintBasedPolicy \\
ResourceBasedPolicy &\subset ConstraintBasedPolicy
\end{aligned} \tag{2.14}$$

As shown in Equation 2.14, a policy domain is partitioned by basis policy trajectories, by specific solutions, and by general solutions. With linear independency, a general policy is composed of a set of basis policies and specific policies. General policies do not contain physical policy objects but do contain presentational sentences. General policies also include measurements. General policy events are composed of spatial relations, temporal relations, times, concrete objects, and policy fluents. The objects are further classified by domains of storage objects and applications.

(1) *Structure-based Policies:* Due to the structure of problem decomposition, policy discovery at a node level always has consistent relations, which means that there are consistent values for each variable by itself in policy space. However, inconsistent relations may exist between adjacent nodes and propagate to a third neighboring node. Hence, there are structure-based conflict relations at both local nodes and along the paths in a decomposed policy graph.

Default policy: Semantics of objects, categories of objects, and relations can be used for property reasoning. Inheritance inference follows subset and super-set relations until it finds a category that has the property. Conflict values may occur when multiple inheritance exists. Normally, the default value should be overridden by the more specific value. Default reasoning under exceptions also relies on precedence and preference operations for conflict computation.

Local policy: Local policy relations may result from a pair of policy activities.

Distributed policy: With decomposition of policy activities, independent subpolicies are connected. Policy relations may exist between any pair of variables among two or more peer nodes. Furthermore, policy relations may occur across different subpolicies.

(2) *Constraint-based Policies:*

- Time: A complex state and event are denoted as a pair of storage activities to be executed concurrently or separately or in interleaving steps.

$$\begin{aligned}
&\exists a, i(a \in \mathit{Activity})\\
&\wedge T(\mathit{Backup}(a) \circ \mathit{Replication}(a), i))\\
&\exists a, i(a \in \mathit{Activity})\\
&\wedge T(\mathit{OneOf}(\mathit{Backup}(a), \mathit{Replication}(a)), i))\\
&\exists a, i(a \in \mathit{Activity})\\
&\wedge T(\mathit{Either}(\mathit{Backup}(a), \mathit{Replication}(a)), i))
\end{aligned} \tag{2.15}$$

- Resource: Numeric values are assigned to a specific resource such as CPU(75), Watermark(90), Power consumption and energy level(25), and Temperature(75).

- Preference: Preference structure U can be modeled with k attributes

$$U(x_1, \ldots, x_k) = \sum_i V_i(x_i)$$
$$= max_A \sum_i U(Result_i(A))P(Result_i(A)|Do(A), E) \quad (2.16)$$

where $Result_i(A)$ represents the differentiable outcome instead of a single state transition. $V_i(x_i)$ is the value of information at state i. $P(Result_i(A)|Do(A), E)$ is the probability of taking action A with evidence variables E.

2.2.7 Semantics of policies

This section studies policy relations more generally rather than procedure mechanisms.

- Binary relations: The semantics of inconsistent policy relations can be represented as functions. $Conflict(R, Backup(a))$ or $Conflict\ (Watermark(90), Reduction(a))$ or $Conflict(Mount(a), Reduction(a))$, and so on.

- High order relations: Implicit state representation is critical for policy analysis. However, in a continuous-temporal domain, the state transition function $T(s, a)$ yields another causal model other than the next state s' in discrete cases. The relation is formalized as a set of differentiable relations which is denoted as a N tuple Q.

$$Q(\lambda, R, S, \mu, \rho) = T(s, a) \quad (2.17)$$

where λ is the arrival rate. R represents response time. S denotes service time. Throughput is μ and utilization is specified as ρ.

$$E[R] = 1/[\mu \times (1 - \rho)] \quad (2.18)$$

where μ is throughput and ρ is channel utilization for a specific storage application. The velocity of change increases the probability of conflicts.

- Noisy logical relations: Uncertain relationships.

- Identity uncertainty: Object is another source of conflicts.

2.3 Method of Policy Discovery

Storage policy discovery can operate directly on a probabilistic representation of the policy by a performance critic. Dynamic Bayes net models represent states, observations, and activities to be taken and the past activities. The past activities are included for plan reconstruction as conflict relations are deduced. Absolute independency and relation independency are computed by conditional probability.

In addition, linear independency is evaluated by Wronskian. Coupling elimination and reduction can be applied with leaving the policy solution intact. Consistent policy activities, inconsistent effects, and nonelementary policy trajectories can be solved analytically.

2.3.1 Continuous policies

To solve problems that involve dynamic states, a policy can be represented by trajectories with one or more variables. Hence, continuous policy relations can be represented by Taylor series. But the relations involved with discontinuity can be represented in infinite Fourier series. For nonperiodic relations, Fourier transformation represents the policies. In cases of discrete policy relations, discrete Fourier transformation (DFT) deals with discrete samples of storage activities and effects.

However, Fourier and Laplace have a dependency on the time variable. This dependency can be eliminated by decomposing a general policy trajectory with basis trajectories and particular trajectories. A general policy contains all trajectories, which are a spectrum of policies. Hence, a general system behavior or global flow of policy sets can be linearized with local flows about critical values such as watermark, throughput, and response time.

Real-life nonlinearity is rarely solvable analytically. Storage simulation methods can provide quantitative results. Using auxiliary variable y, the higher-order policy relations $p(x)$ can be reduced into a first order differential equation $p(x, y)$ with a single integration constant. With conservational law, the constant becomes the total energy. If we take it as the end result and study it by a (x, y) plane, the energy parameter gives a family of policy curves or surfaces representing possible activities resulting from the consequence of policy decisions.

Instead of obtaining policy decisions, the qualitative and topological nature of nonlinear policy solutions can be partitioned by the following geometric approach. The unique policy relation exists in some open intervals containing t_0. The types of equilibrium points are categorized by policy characteristics. The stability of policy trajectories is further studied in the following paragraphs.

If we substitute $x' = y$ in Equation 2.9, service time has a outward flow about $(0, 0)$. The linearized version is

$$\begin{aligned} X' &= Y \\ Y' &= -X + \epsilon Y \end{aligned} \tag{2.19}$$

Due to the theorem of Levinson and Smith, service time does admit a closed trajectory. It is a periodic function with a single limit cycle for every positive value of ϵ. It is a self-managed computing mode. If storage activities start on the cycle, service time enters steady states. However, for all other local states, policy governance requires winding into the cycle asymptotically. If $\epsilon > 0$, a limit cycle exists. However, the cycle distorts considerably as ϵ becomes large and even discrete. If $\epsilon < 0$, the origin becomes a inward flow. If $\epsilon \to 0$, the inward flow changes to central. Hence, $\epsilon = 0$ is bifurcation value of ϵ. The case of large ϵ is especially important.

Potential activities occur as oscillation exceeds the threshold during firing of policy rules. The rules fire repetitively as oscillation exceeds the threshold. The magnitude of the action potential remains unchanged but the firing frequency increases.

In Equation 2.7, the nonlinearity string force causes the response curve to bend to one side as frequency grows. The dump factor results in a further phase shift. In addition, a continuous increasing of arrival frequency creates a jumping phenomenon. Hence, continuous changes in arrival rate to a storage system may lead to a discrete response time. Specifically, the middle branch will never repeat. Hence, governing rules walk away from the middle range.

Dump behavior occurs due to continuous variation of one or more policy parameters such as arrival rate for load balancing or routing in the network settings. For two or more policy parameters, the trajectory is a surface above the policy plane. These quantities compose the policy parameters or plane of a storage system.

The effects of the periodic forcing function are the results of oscillations. But the periodic degradation and motion becomes chaotic as it increases. Storage systems may look random but are actually deterministic systems. Policies are predictable if you have enough information governed by physical laws. However, they are very difficult to predict accurately for a long-term range. The difficulty of prediction means an aperiodic deterministic behavior that is very sensitive to its initial conditions. Infinitesimal perturbations of initial conditions for a chaotic state lead to large variations of the orbit in the phase space. The sensitivity and associated chaotic states are governed under discrete policies.

2.3.2 Discrete policies

A policy can also be represented by a probability instead of an optimal solution. Each storage activity derives effects to system behaviors. Due to the sequential characteristics of storage activities, a discrete policy function can be approximated by samples generated from the probability distribution of policy relations.

Policy is discovered as performance improves and then terminates. Intuitively, policy is represented by a set of Q functions associated with storage parameters. Policy discovery is finding values of the parameters that result in good performance of applications and storage activities such as backup and de-duplication. The best performed discovery may still be far away from its true optimal point. Conflicts become a continuous function of parameters with discrete storage activities. Since the value may vary, the discovery process might not find conflicts.

The gradient of the expected value of policy relation in Equation 2.11 is computed in Equation 2.20.

$$\nabla_\theta \rho(\theta) \approx \frac{1}{N} \sum_{i=1}^{N} \frac{(\nabla_\theta \pi_\theta(s, a_i)) R_j(s)}{\pi_\theta(s, a_i)} \tag{2.20}$$

The changes of policy values depend on the gradient of the action selection probability of each generated sample. For each discrete state s, $R_i(s)$ is the total reward received from state s toward the ith sample. The rewards could be assigned as discrete numeric categories such as $(-1, 0, 1)$ or as continuous value intervals.

To eliminate measurement errors, N sequences of random numbers are generated in advance as the index of an activity selected at state s_i. Each sequence can be used to run a trial of the policy space. Policy search is carried out by evaluating each candidate policy using the same set of random sequences to determine the activity outcomes.

N required for the values of every policy depends on the complexity of the policy space but not the complexity of domain. Hence, the randomness and stability of chaotic behaviors can be approximated by fixing the randomness in advance. In addition, to ensure bounded uncertainty, 10 look-ahead search with θ is based on observed performance.

2.3.3 Simulator

To repeat the outcomes of each action, the automatic cartridge system simulator (ACSSimis) is developed to observe the effects of various storage activities. ACSSim simulates a wide variety of sun automated tape library hardware. Both the control path using the hardware layer interface (HLI) and small computer system interface (SCSI)-based media changer protocols and the data path using multiple virtual storage (MVS)-based 3480/3490/3590 command set protocols are described in the hardware reference manuals for each of the types of 3xxx tape drives (GA32-0127 for 3490 or its equivalents for 3480 and 3590). Control path simulation is achieved using the internet-domain socket interface to ACSSim for HSC and VTCS and using the SCSI pseudo driver for automated cartridge system library software (ACSLS). Data path simulation for tape drives is achieved using the virtual tape drives defined to a z/OS (a.k.a. OS/390, MVS) system that is executing as a virtual machine operating systems (VM) guest.

ACS Simulator (ACSSim) has been integrated with VTAPE using REXEC client and server facilities where the simulator is executing, and where LSTC1VM is executing, respectively. VTAPE modifies the VMs CP component to allow virtual tape drives, (using minidisks to store data in a tape image format) to be defined to an MVS guest (i.e., OS/390, z/OS). The tape drives can be, brought online to the MVS system just as real tape drives are. A variety of drive types can be defined to your MVS environment.

N sequence of random numbers are generated. Policy search is carried out by evaluating each candidate policy by the same set of random sequences. It determines the action outcomes from repeatable effects.

2.3.4 Assign values to relations

To reduce unexpected relations, an initial variable is selected on the basis of the most constraints enforced on other unassigned variables. In addition, the ordering of variables is chosen from the most constrained variable with least possible values. Values are selected with the least constraints to their neighbor nodes. The propagation of properties and relations inherit top-down behavior with less explicit representation and computation. Properties can be inferred from relations. A specific value overwrites its parent nodes. However, the natural reasoning process exhibits nonmonotonicity. Hence, precedence and preference are mathematical operations to ensure expected effects. Conventions and standard specifications can constrain storage activities ruling out violations. In addition, they provide feedback to policy discovery elements to evaluate against standards.

2.3.5 Conflict relations

Policy conflicts may exist during discovery. Conflict conditions between two storage activities are

- Inconsistent effects: An effect of a storage activity negates another.
- Interference: An effect of a storage activity negates the precondition of another activity.
- Competing needs: A pair of preconditions of two storage activities are in conflict with each other.

Conflicts may exist between two literals of storage states.

- Negated literals: State representation contains complementary pairs.
- Inconsistent support: Two activities lead to two literals that are mutually exclusive.

2.3.6 Compute uncertainty

Bounded uncertainty is a key characteristic of policy discovery problem. In addition to state transitions, uncertainty results from a partial observable environment or stochastic effects of actions. Consistency exists with temporal characteristics. The conditional relation is computed below.

Conditional representation encodes each value of continuous random variables as the tuple Q. Probability density functions (PDF) are considered with the finite set of parameters. To model relations with response time r, given discrete backup activities, the probability distribution over response time $P(r|s, backup)$ is represented as a linear model due to an empirical interval boundary in the domain of service time $s \in [0, 15]$.

$$P(r|s, backup) = \frac{1}{\delta_t\sqrt{2\pi}} EXP\left[-\frac{1}{2}\left(\frac{r-\mu}{\delta_t}\right)^2\right] \tag{2.21}$$

where $\mu = (a_t s + b_t)$ and a, b are linear factors of approximation.

To include all other possible causes, a leak node is added to cover miscellaneous causes. Specifically, an implicit representation $\neg backup$ can be applied to compute the distribution over response time.

$$P(r|s, \neg backup) = \frac{1}{\delta_f\sqrt{2\pi}} EXP\left[-\frac{1}{2}\left(\frac{r-\mu}{\delta_f}\right)^2\right] \tag{2.22}$$

where $\mu = (a_f s + b_f)$.

In addition, the interval of backup activity $T(r, t)$ results in fluents of response time r and is computed as the prior probability of backup activities within $T(r, DAY)$

$$P(backup) = \frac{Hours(T(backup, t))}{Hours(DAY)} \tag{2.23}$$

where $T(backup, t)$ is a backup interval starting at time t.

Due to decomposition of storage activities, the service time s_i spent in each phase is independent and could be exponentially distributed. Then the overall service time s is exponentially distributed for discrete and memoryless Poisson arrival rate λ.

$$P(s \geq T_0) = \int_s^{\infty} \lambda e^{-\lambda s} ds \tag{2.24}$$

where λ is an average rate of storage service requests.

Hence, the relation of conflicts $Conflict(r, a)$ denotes possible degradation of response time r due to a specific storage activity at time t, such as $Happened(backup, t)$.

$$P(conflicts|r) = \frac{1}{1 + EXP[-2 \times \frac{-r+\mu}{\delta}]} \tag{2.25}$$

In Equation 2.25, linear combination can be applied to compute conflicts with multiple parent values. However, enumeration may be exhaustive as the number of parameters grow or the narrow range of domain is broken.

2.3.7 Hierarchy of policy relational model

To generalize the method of policy discovery, a relational probability model (PRM) is applied to translate PRM representation into an equivalent Bayesian network with a finite structure. Complexity of network construction grows with the size and density of interconnections. However, an equilibrium of stationary distribution exists during a long run in each state. Hence approximation of policy computation is evaluated by the possibility of state transitions.

$$P(x_i|x_h, x_e) = \alpha P(x_i|parents(X_i)) \times \prod_{Y_i \in Children(X_i)} P(y_i|parents(Y_j)) \tag{2.26}$$

where x_h are hidden variables and x_e are evidence variables. α is a normalized factor.

2.3.8 Granularity of relations

For real time policies and fine controlled storage applications, a planner may not be able to measure and control activities accurately. In addition, the storage environment itself may be uncertain. It may not be feasible to compute a specific probabilistic value. However, the uncertainty can be treated as finite conditional planning in such an environment. Hence, a series of guarded command controls and a termination condition can achieve a complete prevention method at a fine level for real time policies.

2.3.9 Relevance of information

Both consistent and inconsistent relations may be discovered upon relevant observations rather than all applicable storage activities. In logical senses, relevant activities are to achieve one of conjuncts of the goals. For differentiable quantities, watermark W and response time R are dominant relations with storage activities that provide qualitative relevance for the preference structure of conflict information. With parameters service time S, arrival rate λ, throughput μ, and utilization ρ, structure can be approximated with the following linearity. It computes the relevance and consistency of observations. With noise, the approximated storage relation is represented by

$$P(Q|s, backup) = \frac{1}{\sqrt{(2\pi)^n|\Sigma_Q|}} e^{-\frac{1}{2}((Q-\mu)^T \Sigma_Q^{-1} (Q-\mu))} \tag{2.27}$$

where Σ is the covariance matrix of the distribution. μ is the mean vector.

Irrelevant information is a noise aspect of learning. The value of information is a good clue to irrelevance. However, early pruning may pass the optimality.

2.3.10 Parameter estimation

Due to Murphy's Law on sensor failure, noisy information or imperfection in measurement, policy discovery is required to estimate parameters and activities chosen by storage applications. Noise can be modeled as a second action of storage activities. The noise is modeled with a Gaussian distribution. The optimal parameter estimation based on observation e is obtained by selecting policy action u to minimize

$$\int_a^b Cost(u,\theta)p(e|\theta)d\theta \tag{2.28}$$

where the prior probability density $p(\theta)$ is given as uniform over an interval $[a,b]$. The $p(e|\theta)$ is

$$p(y|\theta) = \frac{1}{\sqrt{2\pi\delta^2}}e^{-\frac{(y-\theta)^2}{2\delta^2}} \tag{2.29}$$

2.3.11 Biological model

Emergent behavior of a biological model suggests feasible joint plans of storage activities. With the Boid model, storage activities can be separated with hieratical partitions. Operational windows for each activity steer away from each other as they become too close. Peaks of each storage activity keep cohesion around the mean values of the activity's probabilistic distribution. In addition, each activity aligns toward global feasibility and optimality.

If two activities such as reduction and replication are separated against storage volumes within a same operational window, the reduction activity, with throughput μ_d, responds to a customer arrival rate λ_d upon dismount events. λ_d is available in unlimited quantity. The replication activity is executed with α throughput μ_p and an unlimited arrival rate λ_p. If a linear approximation is applied to model rate equations of these activities, Equation 2.30 is derived.

$$\begin{aligned} \mu_d' &= \alpha\mu_d \\ \mu_p' &= -\beta\mu_p \end{aligned} \tag{2.30}$$

where $\mu_d(t)$ and $\mu_p(t)$ can be approximated by continuous variables. α and β are positive real numbers representing the net rate of changes.

However, activities may not be perfectly separated in practice. Hence, the two parallel activities are satisfying the same resource constraints. The above model is obtained as

$$\begin{aligned} \mu_d' &= (\alpha - \gamma\mu_p)\mu_d \\ \mu_p' &= -(\beta - \delta\mu(d))\mu_p \\ \frac{d\mu_d}{d\mu_p} &= -\frac{(\alpha - \gamma\mu_p)\mu_d}{(\beta - \delta\mu_d)\mu_p} \end{aligned} \tag{2.31}$$

The system in Equation 2.31 becomes representable with two-dimensional μ_d,μ_p phase plane. It has no explicit dependency on independent variable t.

2.3.12 Policy decomposition

For policy relations, policy sets can be transformed into a finite set of consistent activities with policy decomposition. Conflicts within a single partition can be solved by discrete methods. The value of each partition can be computed in the above learning sections. Subactivities are inserted as actions of a global activity. Mutex relations along the path and even among different zone partitions of policy library may exist. Arbitrary interleaving steps, a fair share, queuing, or other scheduling of conflict sets can speed up the policy discovery without total orders. Hence, a complete policy discovery must follow interleaving of activities from different subactivities within a single sequence. In addition, interleaving of activities may be effective for policy exploration. Serialized storage activities are conflict free.

2.4 Performance Evaluation

Policy discovery may be intractable in the worst case. It is a nondeterministic polynomial (NP)-hard problem. The level of hardness from PSAPCE-COMPLETE to EXPTIME. depends on precise problem conditions. For example, not all operations of storage activities are known in advance.

However, as storage state parameters and activity operators grow monotonically, unexpected relations will decrease monotonically. For activity-based conflicts, inconsistent effects, activity interference, and competing needs will result in conflicts at any level if mutexes exist. In addition, the possibility of conflicts will decrease as all applicable activities are increased. Hence, methods of conflict prevention will reach stability due to the decreasing of conflicts. In this section, we consider performance analysis of the structures in case of detecting policy relations.

2.5 Conclusions

This chapter proposes a policy discovery method. In literature, Fuzzy logic, logic reasoning, contention tree, and query tree were studied in policy systems. However, this is still an active research area for policy design and refinement. This work imposes a critical resource and time constraint on policies used in these systems.

2.5.1 Closure

In this chapter, we applied augmentation to existing planning methods. We defined policy representation in both continuous and discrete domains, which consider reduction of problem space by compression and compactness. We also studied completeness, consistency, and stability of policy discovery with storage activities.

References

[1] Selman, B. Compute-intensive methods in artificial intelligence. *Annals of Mathematics and Artificial Intelligence*, 28:35–38, 2000.

[2] Miguel, I. Dynamic flexible constraint satisfaction and its application to ai planning. *PhD Thesis*, University of Edinburgh, 2001.

[3] Apt, K. *Principles of Constraint Programming.* Cambridge University Press, Cambridge, 2003.

[4] Reiter, R. *Knowledge in Action: Logical Foundations for Specifying and Implementing Dynamical Systems.* The MIT Press, Cambridge, 2001.

[5] Kowalski, R. The logical way to be artificially intelligent. *Computational Logic in Multi-Agent Systems (CLIMA VI Post-Proceedings), LNAI 3900*, 1–22, 2006.

[6] Nguyen, X., S. Kambhampati, and R. S. Nigenda. Planning graph as the basis for deriving heuristics for plan synthesis by state space and csp search. *Artificial Intelligence*, 135:73–123, 2002.

[7] Chen, Y., W. Xu, T. Rikakis, H. Sundaram, and S.-M. Liu. A dynamic decision network framework for online media adaptation in stroke rehabilitation. *ACM Transactions on Multimedia Computing, Communications, and Applications*, 5(4):35–38, 2008.

[8] Ben-Gal, I. Bayesian networks. In *Encyclopedia of Statistics in Quality and Reliability*, Ruggeri, F., R. Kenett, F. Faltin. (Eds.). John Wiley & Sons, Chichester, England. 2007.

[9] Bartlett, M., I. Bate, and D. Kazakov. Challenges in relational learning for real time systems applications. *18th International Conference on Inductive Logic Programming, ILP 2008*, 2008.

[10] Julier, S.J. and J. K. Uhlmann. A new extension of the kalman filter to nonlinear systems. In *International Symposium Of Aerospace/Defense Sensing, Simulations and Controls, 3*, 2008.

[11] Strehl, A. L., S. Li, E. Wiewiora, J. Langford, and M. Littman. Pac model-free reinforcement learning. In *Proceedings of the 23rd International Conference on Machine Learning*, 2006.

[12] Kowalsky, R. A logic-based calculus of events. *New Generation Computing*, 4:67–95, 1986.

[13] Kowalsky, R. Database updates in event calculus. *Journal of Logic Programming*, 12:121–146, 2001.

[14] Farrell, A. D. H., M. J. Sergot, M. Sall, and C. Bartolini. Using the event calculus for tracking the normative state of contracts. *International Journal of Cooperative Information Systems*, 14(2–3):99–129. Oct. 2005.

[15] Mascardi, V., V. Cord, and P. Rosso. A comparison of upper ontologies. *Technical Report DISI-TR-06-21*, 2006.

Chapter 3

Knowledge-Based Policy Discovery for Storage and Data Management

3.1 Introduction

3.1.1 Background

Data archiving is a common data management application that refers to the long-term data copying algorithms to targeted secondary or tertiary storage. As a medium is recorded in secondary or tertiary storage, it is physically removed and disconnected as off-line storage. Archiving operations will mount and dismount removable mass storage media such as tape libraries and optical jukeboxes into a storage device according to system demands. Upon the occurrence of mount and dismount events, archiving rules specify backup streams to copy data or files to secondary storage by executing read and write routines. In general, archiving is primarily a data management operation in large data center automation.

Hence, archiving rules are specified for rarely accessed information or long-preserved data. When authorized data hosts or applications request information from the tertiary storage, the semantic of archiving rules will first retrieve a catalog database to determine the locality of tapes or disks containing the information. Next, archiving rules instruct a robotic arm to fetch the medium and place it in a drive. Upon completion of archiving algorithmic procedures, the robotic arm returns the medium to its location in the tape library.

In well-modularized object-oriented practices, policy concerns exist with the modularization of rule management, security, logging, audit, and backup stream. The scattered complementary code blocks are tangled with core rule inference routines. The tangled code includes other concerns such as sensor data processing and dispatching, state classification, rule classification, session management, page management, and fact management. Hence, the archive policy is a crosscutting concern. Due to the distributed nature of policy decision points, policy enforcement, and data collection points, it is uncertain that quality of service (QoS) of archiving operations can be enforced by means of programming techniques.

There is no way to customize the reaction of the system with respect to context information and backup requests with time properties. Further, changing any rule functionalities or programming interfaces often results in changing of many other modules and visa versa.

Policy exploration is one of the evolution issues in policy specification and refinement. Some policy concerns are functionalities or features denoted by the production of concrete syntax trees with source language grammars. The abstract syntax trees are built of records with type definitions based on the abstract syntax names given by the grammar. A context free notation of a Backus normal form (BNF) rule formalizes a list of concerns in Equation 3.1.

$$\begin{aligned} &< concerns >::=< concern >:< concerns > \\ &< concern >::=< class > \mid < constructor > \\ &\mid < method > \mid < variable > \mid < exception > \\ &\mid < advice > \end{aligned} \tag{3.1}$$

Crosscutting concerns span a list of modules and apply to a list of join points in a system. This chapter is limited to exposed join points for reusable policy-aspect discovery. As depicted in Equation 3.2, a concern is a lexical structure. Specifically, a concern could be a class or structure that shares the hidden states among a set of procedures. It is also a method, which is a procedure acting on a state. In addition, a concern may be a variable. In first order logic, crosscutting concerns are represented by a relation predicate of the above program entities.

$$\begin{aligned} \forall x, y Concern(x) \vee Concern(y) \vee (Scatter(x, y) \\ \wedge Tangle(x, y)) \Rightarrow Crosscut(x, y) \end{aligned} \tag{3.2}$$

As asserted in Equation 3.2, the semantics of two program entities x and y are encoded by the concerns of storage functionalities. The program entities are scattered or tangled with each other.

The above knowledge of policy aspect is represented upon definite knowledge in terms of programming calculus. But real life program analysis may not have precise measurement. Uniform join points exhibit syntactic properties to optimize learning accuracy and precision on policy discovery. Tangled or scattered code space without uniformity requires semantic analysis even for trivial policy aspects such as logging, error handling, and monitoring. Intuitively, policy discovery has a degree of information uncertainty about a finite but stochastic code space. The probabilistic nature of falling into an imprecise range suggests a logical approach that deals with imprecise concepts in a partially observable environment.

3.1.2 Review of literature

Both functional policy and nonfunctional policy are discussed in the literature. Business rules are the focus of study on functional concerns, whereas nonfunctional policy aspects are limited to security properties. Specifically, access control, availability, integrity, monitoring, and recovery rules are discussed.

Traditional program-aspect identification [1] relies on the observation that scattered or crosscutting functionalities are discovered with high fan-in values. This method is the guideline to apply aspect solutions to the same functionality. However, the functions may be required in many places throughout a system.

The main threads of common mining techniques [2, 3] are fan-in analysis [4, 5], identifier analysis [6], and dynamic analysis [7, 8]. Fan-in metric was used for evaluating the number of locations from control passed into a module or method. This method discovers well-known crosscutting concerns. In addition, the method identifies seeds that are largely scattered throughout systems that involve a lot of invocations of the same method. It is not effective for a small code base. Identifier analysis relies on some assumptions to identify aspect seeds by grouping program entities with similar names. It locates seeds with low fan-in values with common identifers. However, it requires manual analysis. Dynamic analysis is used to identify aspects with formal concept analysis to locate features in a procedural lexical structure. It locates seeds without high fan-in values and common identifiers. But it depends on execution paths. Another thread studies crosscutting mining with a randomization algorithm [9]. In addition, natural language processing techniques are proposed for discovery [10].

In the state-of-the-art rule discovery, the concerns of rules [11–14] are exploited in the setting of web service composition and several middleware web services. Specifically, aspectization toward business rule processes is proposed in [15]. Researchers found that join points exist in both business process execution language (BPEL) and engine internal implementation. Advices are BPEL activities and XPath is the pointcut language to specify weaving rules. In addition to functional rule aspects, security rule concerns [16–18] were exploited to express the requirements for messaging and service interoperatability between parties without tangling and scattering. Researchers discovered that aspect-based web service adaptability weaves policies and web service handlers with modularization. Similarly, an aspect-oriented application model [19] was proposed to solve access control concerns with primary models and aspects.

The closest arts are availability policies [20] and monitoring and recovery concerns [21] with aspectized rules. In regard to availability, researchers found that aspects can be formalized as a timed automat and that the weaving rules are automata product. For monitoring and recovery concerns, researchers discovered that a set of super-visioning rules can be enabled to support time constructs for both monitoring and recovery advices. Researchers [22] found a framework for rule-based autonomic management with control aspects, access aspects, and rule aspects. However, it is an aspect-oriented weaving solution rather than rule specific methods.

However, there are no study-related policy concerns on classes of storage and data management applications and their wellness other than conventional security policy concerns. In addition, rule conflict detection and resolution are absent in most studies on aspectized policy concerns. A primary conflict resolution is suggested by a static priority setting [22].

This chapter proposes a logical reasoning formalism for the suggested problem. It proposes a policy discovery utility to specify, match, evaluate, and execute policy aspects to enforce storage policies. An information-theoretic model is applied with lay separation of data, information, and knowledge. Specifically, a set of policy facts, rule management, and data management concerns have been studied.

The rest of this chapter is organized as follows. Section 3.2 gives the problem presentation for policy aspects in a storage environment. Section 3.3 introduces conflict discovery with uncertainty. It analyzes their completeness and consistency. Section 3.4 presents performance analysis of the proposed method with cost of the solution. Finally, we draw some conclusions in Section 3.5.

3.2 Problem Analysis

A real-life policy management network acquires, evaluates, and executes stochastic continuous storage events and pervasive objects crossing a parallel community. Policy is a crosscutting concern spanning multiple modules and applying to multiple join points in storage and data management systems. Identification of policy concerns within storage settings is to discover, collect, and understand all source code related to storage policy concepts. Policy concern location needs to define an aspect detect function to compute and classify policy methods.

3.2.1 Syntax

A program construct p is defined by a set of instructions $\{I_1, \ldots, I_n\}$ Ing of the form in Equation 3.3, where l_1, l_2, l_3 are program labels.

$$\begin{aligned} < I > &::= < command > \mid < test > \\ < command > &::= l_1 : c \Rightarrow l_2 \\ < test > &::= l_1 : t \Rightarrow l_2 ; l_3 \end{aligned} \tag{3.3}$$

Type c is a command, such as a variable assignment, whereas t represents a boolean expression. Hence, if command c is executed, the current program will move from l_1 to l_2. When test t is evaluated as true, the current program becomes l_2 otherwise, it moves to l_3. Hence, the property of a crosscutting concern is conjunctivity.

3.2.2 Semantics

Policy discovery consists of finite many program constructs with exponential growth of dependency graphs. Execution paths of archiving routines and rule execution of policy management may be nondeterministic due to changes of underlying infrastructure and operational requirements. The formalism of an aspect location originates from automata theory and is motivated by a Petri net [23]. Conventional Petri nets graphically depict structures of distributed systems as directed bipartite graphs $G = (V, E)$ with annotations. This chapter models a crosscutting concern with a Petri net of a tuple (P, T, C, R, H, M_0, W) where:

- P is the set of program constructs $\{p_1, p_2, ..., p_n\}$, in which p_i represents each concern.
- T is the set of transitions $\{\tau_1, \tau_2, ..., \tau_n\}$.
- S and T are disjoint so that no object can be both a place and a transition.
- C, R, H are, respectively, the set of calling, returning, and hidden invocation mapping the set of transitions T to the bag of P. The set of arcs is known as flow relation representing a transition function.
- M_0 defines the initial marking of the net.
- W is a set of arc weights denoting how many tokens are consumed by a transition.

A method of the graph in Figure 3.1 can be utilized to represent the policy relations. A concern of a program construct is represented by a circle, with tokens represented by black dots. The tokens are enumerated as the number of data management requests in the program routine shaped as a circle. Transactions of states are represented by rectangular bars, while input and output arcs are represented by an arrow line whose arrow head points to the flow control. Inhibitor arcs are represented by a line with a bubble at its end. The flat rectangles are immediate transitions such as asynchronous calls, while the rectangles with a nonzero width represent timed transitions with synchronous calls of blocking or waiting contexts.

As illustrated above, p_0 has a join point with p_2 whereas p_1 crosscuts with p_3. p_2 has a hidden invocation routine with p_4 while p_3 has join points with p_4.

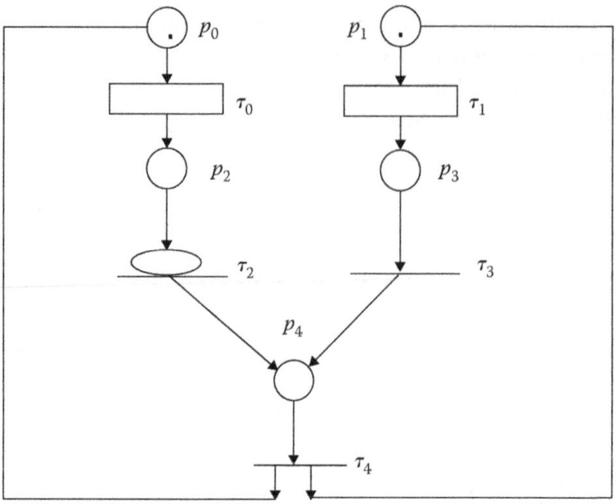

FIGURE 3.1: A graph representation of policy relations.

With the specified execution path, p_0 and p_1 receive their return values. The Petri net abstraction approximates the execution trace of crosscutting concerns. Hence, the crosscutting concern problem is a combinational problem of conjunctivity (reachability) and disjunctivity (modularity).

The semantics of data management services are given by a set of rules.

$$\frac{l_1 : c \Rightarrow l_2 \in Ps_1 \Rightarrow s_2}{(l_1, s_1) \Rightarrow (l_2, s_2)}$$
$$\frac{l_1 : t \Rightarrow l_2; l_3 \in Ps_1 \Rightarrow s_2}{(l_1, s_1) \Rightarrow (l_2, s_1)}$$
$$\frac{l_1 : t \Rightarrow l_2; l_3 \in Ps_1 \Rightarrow s_2}{(l_1, s_1) \Rightarrow (l_3, s_1)} \tag{3.4}$$

To model invariant

$$I(p_1, \ldots, p_i, \ldots, p_n) = I_{p_1}(p_1), \ldots, \cup I_{p_i}(p_i), \ldots, \cup I_{p_n}(p_n) \tag{3.5}$$

Expressiveness of a few axioms generalizes policy discovery rules. Each rule is specified with precise and clear functions, predicates, and constants. The semantics of the language define the truth of each sentence with respect to each possible aspect world. Modularity evolves as a problem of concern classification problem.

3.3 Method of Discovery

3.3.1 Upper ontology

A Petri net formalizes policy aspect discovery with a mathematical model and virtual representation of a concern crosscutting graph. The readability, liveness, and inherently k-boundedness properties ensure the soundness and completeness of policy aspect discovery. The relaxed version of problem formulation is to resolve crosscutting by a structure of a name space as shown in Figure 3.2.

Given that the branch factor is bounded to constant B for a naming space tree representing a finite many of source files N, the height of naming space is bounded to $\log BN$. To measure the concern rule base, the discrete information is specified as the following figure in bits, where $P(n)$ is the probability that a random program construct equals n.

$$H(N) = \Sigma_{i=1}^{N} - P(n) \times \log_B P(n) \tag{3.6}$$

Hence, the expected information gain is higher when selecting naming from the top down to the leaf nodes, which represent concrete program constructs. For a given input symbol, the proper question is to partition from naming spaces to specific type information.

3.3.2 Perception specification

Policy discovery receives a percept with two variables for program construct y and the location of construct in type x. The time step t is included for truth management of concern knowledge base. Hence, a precept can be represented by a percept predicate.

$$Percept(x, y, t) \tag{3.7}$$

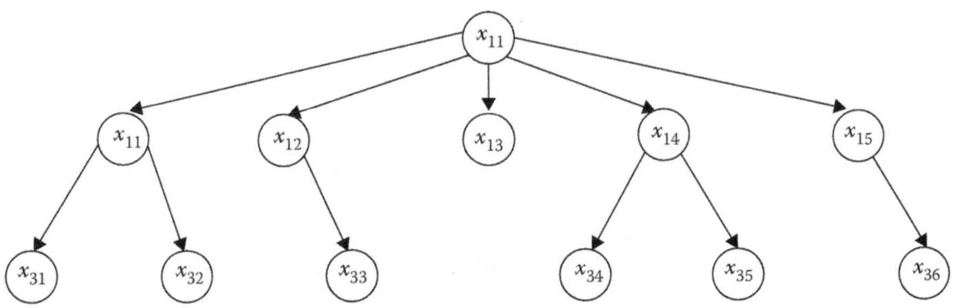

FIGURE 3.2: Upper ontology of policy aspects.

3.3.3 Action specification

To describe actions and reason about the effects of the actions, the following axioms, in Equation 3.8, map a possible policy discovery action **a** and possible effects **Result** of executing the action **a** without redundant copies of action description at each time step **t**.

$$
\begin{aligned}
At(PolicyDiscovery, x, s) \wedge Crosscut(x, y) \\
\Rightarrow Poss(Go(x, y), s) \\
Poss(Go(x, y), s)) \Rightarrow \\
At(PolicyDiscovery, y, Result(Go(x, y), s)) \\
Aspect(cc) \wedge At(PolicyDiscovery, x, s) \\
\Rightarrow Poss(Discover(cc), s) \\
Poss(Discover(cc), s) \Rightarrow \\
Exploitation(cc, Result(Discover(cc), s)) \\
Exploitation(cc, s) \Rightarrow Poss(Stop(cc), s) \\
Poss(Stop(cc), s) \Rightarrow \\
\neg Exploitation(cc, Result(Stop(cc), s))
\end{aligned} \tag{3.8}
$$

The above axioms state that a policy discovery action traverses to a program construct y if a crosscutting occurs at program construct x and y. Policy-aspect discovery identifies a crosscutting concern as it exists at program x. If there are other potential crosscutting concerns, the discovery will continue to exploit the process. The consequent exploitation repeats the $Go(x, y)$. Otherwise, it will stop at x, where the policy aspect cc is discovered. Since there are no additional constraints for discovery to proceed upon source files, all actions will succeed without other conditions.

To model things unchanged, axioms are specified in Equation 3.9. The possibility axioms show that **PolicyDiscovery** stays at a situation as it does not **Go** further along the connected module files whereas exploitation continues until it stops discovery.

$$
\begin{aligned}
Poss(a, s) \Rightarrow (At(PolicyDiscovery, x, s), a \\
\Longleftrightarrow Go(x, y) \vee (At(PolicyDiscovery, y, s) \\
\wedge a \neq Go(y, z))) \\
Poss(a, s) \Rightarrow (Exploitation(cc, Result(a, s)) \\
\Longleftrightarrow Discover(cc) \\
\vee(Exploitation(cc; s) \wedge a \neq Stop(cc)))
\end{aligned} \tag{3.9}
$$

A set of unique name assumptions is specified for inequality of constant names in Equation 3.10.

$$
\begin{aligned}
Go(x_1, \ldots, x_m) &\neq Discover(x_1, \ldots, x_n) \\
Go(x_1, \ldots, x_m) &\neq Stop(x_1, \ldots, x_n) \\
Discover(x_1, \ldots, x_m) &\neq Stop(x_1, \ldots, x_n) \\
Go(x_1, \ldots, x_m) &= Go(y_1, \ldots, y_n) \\
&\Longleftrightarrow x_1 = y_1 \wedge \ldots \wedge x_m = y_m \\
Discover(x_1, \ldots, x_m) &= Discover(y_1, \ldots, y_n) \\
&\Longleftrightarrow x_1 = y_1 \wedge \ldots \wedge x_m = y_m \\
Stop(x_1, \ldots, x_m) &= Stop(y_1, \ldots, y_n) \\
&\Longleftrightarrow x_1 = y_1 \wedge \ldots \wedge x_m = y_m
\end{aligned}
\tag{3.10}
$$

3.3.4 Environment specification

(1) *Encode General Concern*: The uniqueness of name space specifies the ontology of the policy-aspect knowledge base. It is encoded as the general concern rules in Equation 3.11.

$$
\begin{aligned}
\forall x Leaf(x) \wedge Source(x) &\Longleftrightarrow Type(x) \\
\forall y, x : Leaf(y) \wedge Connected(y, x) &\Longleftrightarrow Parent(y, x) \\
\forall x, y, j Type(x) \wedge Parent(y, x) &\Rightarrow \neg Parent(j, x) \\
\forall y, x \neg Parent(y, x) &\Longleftrightarrow Root(x)
\end{aligned}
\tag{3.11}
$$

The root node does not have any parent nodes. The leaf nodes have no child nodes but share a same parent node. They are located in the same module. However, intermediate nodes are located in different modules. Adding axioms to constrain the naming space tree, there is no child node sharing the same parent node. The four predicates are **Leaf, Root, Parent, Type**, and they form facts. As the naming predicate Parent illustrates, the expressiveness of FOL eliminates the **Child** predicate and its associated axiom. The knowledge of modularization is encoded in Equation 3.12 with a module predicate.

$$
\begin{aligned}
\forall x, y Root(x) \neq Root(y) &\Rightarrow \neg Module(x, y) \\
\forall x, y Root(X) \wedge Root(Y) &\Rightarrow \neg Module(X, Y) \\
\forall x, y \exists j, k \neg Root(x) \wedge Height(x) &> 3 \\
&\wedge Parent(x, j)
\end{aligned}
$$

$$
\begin{aligned}
\wedge(\neg Root(y) \wedge Parent(y,k) \wedge Height(x) = Height(y) \\
\wedge Name(x) \neq Name(y)) \Rightarrow Module(x,y) \\
\forall x, y, z Type(x) \wedge Type(y) \wedge Parent(z,x,y) \\
\Rightarrow Module(x,y)
\end{aligned} \tag{3.12}
$$

As specified, any leaf and source files are type nodes. A connected node has a parent and child bidirectional relationship. The leaf does not have children. The root does not have parent.

Crosscutting concerns are formally deduced by the rule specified in Equation 3.13.

$$
\begin{aligned}
\forall x, y, j, k Concern(x,j) \wedge Concern(y,k) \\
\wedge(Module(j) \neq Module(k)) \\
\Rightarrow Crosscut(Concern(x,j), (Concern(y,k))
\end{aligned} \tag{3.13}
$$

As defined, node **x** and node **y** belong to different modules if they own different roots. Two all **Root** ground facts are not modules; only **Type** source files are module files. Specifically, two **Type** source files are different modules if they have the same parent nodes. Empirically, naming definition starts with an organizational structure such as "org.ABC," "com.ABC," or "net.ABC." In addition, the third-level element in naming space would be product or module names. By heuristics, module inference may initiate from level of 3. Hence, two nodes may be classified into the same module if they have different naming but share a same parent node among the same sibling level.

Considering crosscutting of concerns as events overlapping execution of program constructs, a fluent of program execution traces can be reasoned over intervals of time. **Crosscuts(e,f,t)** denotes the occurrence of concern execution event **e**, which results in the true value of crosscutting effect **f** at time **t**. **Executes(e,t)** means concern execution trace **e** is taken place at time **t**. **Terminates(e,f,t)** means that **f** is toggled on at time **t** for executing the event **e**. Formally, the axiom is derived as

$$
\begin{aligned}
T(f, t2) \iff \exists e_1, t Executes(e_1, t) \\
\wedge(t < t_2) \wedge Crosscuts(f, t, t_2) \\
Crosscuts(f, t, t_2) \iff \exists e_2, t_1 Executes(e2; t1) \wedge \\
Terminates(e_2, f, t_1) \wedge (t < t_1) \wedge (t_1 < t_2)
\end{aligned} \tag{3.14}
$$

(2) *Encode Data Management:* Data management specific concerns are encoded with ground terms shown in Equation 3.15.

$$\begin{aligned} &Module(SENSOR), Module(BROKER),\\ &Module(INFORMATION), Module(KNOWLEDGE),\\ &Concern(CLASS), Concern(CONSTRUCTOR),\\ &Concern(METHOD), Concern(VARIABLE),\\ &Concern(EXCEPTION), Concern(ADVICE) \end{aligned} \tag{3.15}$$

3.3.5 Knowledge base

Any atomic sentence about concerns and crosscutting represents a fact of policy discovery. It initially contains the physics of concerns spaces. The policy mining sensor adds assertions during the preprocessing of input program symbols. The larger the environment, the larger the initial knowledge base needs to be. The clause proliferation problem and partial information require that the expressiveness of logical representation is defined as first order logic rather than traditional propositional logic. A complete and correct knowledge is built upon the ontology of concern space and expressiveness of the calculus discussed above to encode concern and crosscutting knowledge to track concern discovery.

3.3.6 Policy aspect inference algorithm

With the exponential growth of data management, storage source files increase during evolution of specification and operational requirements. The number of source files becomes infinity. One of the major efficient inference algorithms in literature is backward chaining [24], which provides goal-based incomplete aspect discovery with a depth-first search method. But policy aspect discovery requires precision and accuracy according to information theory. Another major inference algorithm is forward chaining [25].

- Policy aspect discovery with forward chaining is data-driven inference with an unknown goal but input program symbols.
- From dynamic programming, forward chaining for policy-aspect reasoning is sound and complete to derive all crosscutting concerns.
- Given problem formulation, a policy-aspect inference rule has more premise clauses than body on average so that the identified programs can lead to many more reasoning questions.
- Relevant policy-aspect facts are known, and the purpose of policy inference is to identify where those storage crosscutting concerns lead.

Hence, a forward chaining algorithm is selected because policy-aspect discovery is usually started without precise and specific queries. A forward chaining algorithm unifies all premises of all rules with a subset of relevant facts. Significant time complexity results from partial pattern matching and redundant rule matching during rule inference.

Among well-known published forward chaining inference algorithms, the ReteII algorithm [26] was proposed to optimize the proposed knowledge-based policy-aspect inference. It is selected to optimize partial matching and redundant computation of unification. Hence, Rete networks make substitutions only for required inferencing. For policy-aspect discovery, the algorithm is a data-driven reasoning to derive aspects without a specific query but incoming program symbols. Policy-aspect sensor inputs its percepts to its knowledge base. It suggests an incremental forward-chaining algorithm in which facts are updated and added to KB for new inference.

The Rete algorithm is formulated with numerous variants. It processes a set of rules in a knowledge base by constructing a data-flow network where a node represents a concept or rule literal. The root node is where all objects enter the network. Variable bindings flow through the network and are filtered out when they fail to match a concept or rule literal. In the case of variable sharing across multiple nodes archive(x,y,z), pool(x), file(y) and volume(z) in a rule, a bindings from each node are filtered through an equality node. In addition, binding for an nary rule literal such as archive(x,y,z) needs to wait for binding for other variables to be established. AlphaNodes are used to evaluate literal conditions. When a rule has multiple literal conditions for a single node, they are evaluated as a chain. Hence, at any given point, the state of a Rete network captures all the partial matches of the rules without recomputation. BetaNodes are used to compare two objects by their fields. The left input for a BetaNode is a Tuple, whereas the right input is a single ObjectTypeNode. TerminalNodes represents a single rule with a full match.

3.4 Performance Evaluation

It is easy to see that the proposed policy-aspect reasoning method. It is sound since every inference is essentially an application of Modus Ponens. In addition, it is complete since every entailed atomic sentence will be derived. For large and high-dimensional discovery, irrelevant consequences should be avoided.

3.4.1 Soundness

From an initial ground-fact existing aspect knowledge base, since $f_1, f_2, \ldots, f_n$ holds then a substitution θ supports $Subst(\theta, p_1) \wedge Subst(\theta, p_2) \wedge \ldots \wedge$

$Subst(\theta, p_n)$. If $p_1 \wedge p_2 \wedge \ldots \wedge p_n \Rightarrow q$ holds with universal qualifiers, aspect inference holds with substitution θ.

$$\frac{\begin{array}{r} f_1, f_2, \cdots f_n \\ Subst(\theta, p_1) \wedge Subst(\theta, p_2) \wedge \ldots \wedge Subst(\theta, p_n) \\ p_1 \wedge p_2 \wedge \ldots \wedge p_n \Rightarrow q \\ f_1, f_2, \ldots, f_n, (p_1 \wedge p_2 \wedge \ldots \wedge p_n \Rightarrow q) \end{array}}{Subst(\theta, q)} \tag{3.16}$$

3.4.2 Completeness

A complete inference method derives all entailed sentences. First order inference of crosscutting concern is complete given that the space of possible concerns is infinite. Since there are no function symbols in definite clauses, the proposed aspect discovery method is complete to derive all entailed facts. With specified data management knowledge, there are j predicates and the maximum arity of any predicate is about k. In addition, the number of constant symbols is n.

Hence, the distinct ground facts required for a complete inference to reach a fixed point is bounded to O(facts) below. For the formalized aspect problem, where $j = 20$, $k = 5$, and $n = 20$, the worst case iterations are required.

$$O(facts) = j \times \bigcup_{i=k} P_n^1 = 20 \times \bigcup_{i=5} P_{20}^1 = 20^6 \tag{3.17}$$

However, the proposed method shares the common issues of propositional and first order logic inference. It is semidecidable when no answer exists in the knowledge base. But crosscutting concerns are common in well object-oriented (OO) design and implementation. In addition, the rule space is small with optimized knowledge formulation. This concludes the completeness analysis of the proposed aspect inference method.

3.4.3 Time complexity

The completeness analysis illustrates the bounded time complexity of aspect inference. However, indexing and hashing optimize matching and evaluation of aspect inference by a constant factor of O(1). Since the above aspect axioms are proposed with multiclauses, a multiattribute indexing strategy is required. However, policy aspect discovery is not a query-driven inference; the query-based indexing is not optimal for the proposed policy aspect discovery method. Hence, constrained conjunction ordering is proposed in the above aspect axioms. The most constrained heuristics are applied to reduce the matching complexity. In addition, an average of E of these updates results in complexity of O(E) updates and O(F) matching in cases of the changes involved. However, with proper indexing and hashing, working memory updates become complexity of O(1). Intuitively, O(1) is not a straight gain factor in policy aspect discovery. But the proposed method is a K bound inference method with the number of ground facts.

3.4.4 Space complexity

Action axioms specify changes due to a set of three actions {*Go*, *Discover*, *Stop*} during crosscutting discovery. Each action is associated with each effect of the discovery action. Hence, O(A) is needed to reason about the action effects. However, to represent that those things stay the same, additional axioms are required. As specified in the successor state axiom, the next state is completely specified from the current state. Consequently, O(AE) is required to model the unchanged aspect. Since effects E is smaller than F as illustrated in formulation, O(AE) is the bounded estimation of aspect axiom space complexity. The average size of aspect axioms is O(AE = F).

However, in real-life policy aspect discovery, the size of rules and the arity of predicates are bounded to a constant. Hence the complexity is transformed into data complexity. Complexity of inference is a function of the number of ground facts. It has been proved that data complexity in forward chaining is polynomial.

3.4.5 Experiment

The selected storage and data management source files present a large fact and state problem to evaluate the proposed policy-aspect inference methods in this paper.

- Rete inference solving is a classical rule-based system problem.
- Large facts may lead to intensive matching, firing, and execution complexity to evaluate performance speedup.
- This large-state problem may simulate a real-life rule inference problem with random workload. A simplification of the problem could be batch workload by reducing number of threads for fact insertions but increasing number of facts per thread. Hence, an exact description of the problem is possible, and factors that affect the problem are deterministic. Therefore, with problem abstraction, it is a problem that can be solved efficiently with rule-based performance optimization.
- There are processor and memory requirements for state, event, and situation value function mapping. The policy discovery is a sufficiently large-state space with space complexity to evaluate proposed optimization methods. It can demonstrate the parallelism and reduction performance with core systems.

(1) *Testbed Setup:* A dual core SPARC IV (50 × 2.4 GHZ, 64 GB RAM) servers with the Solaris™ operating system are considered to setup a test environment for this paper. The servers are hosting rule-based system software programs. Inference software packages were developed and deployed on a Sun(TM) Enterprise M5000 server. In addition, JDK6 Update 6 was installed on the system. During test cycles, execution time was collected from test scripts and central processing unit (CPU) utilization was sampled by a Solaris built-in utility tool: cpustat with a 3-second interval. In addition, CPU and memory contention are analyzed by java development kit (JDK) agentlib and a heap tool to produce reproducible experiment test results. Discussion and test results on parallelism are presented in following sections.

The policy aspect inference rules are associated with state transitions for each fact. The objective of the test is to evaluate the throughput and service time of the proposed aspect inference methods and identify system bottlenecks during aspect inference with finite large fact and rule management by running test cases locally on the M5000.

(2) *Discussion:* As it is proposed in axioms, a set of implementations have discovered the result of following aspect space.

Name	**Multitude**
Root	4
Source files	1.475×10^3
Naming directory	2.06×10^2
Ground facts	1.681×10^3
Modules	1.18×10^2
Concerns	1.0466×10^4
Crosscutting concerns	6.471×10^3

(3) *Memory Management:* Memory and SWAP allocation: For the Solaris operating system, a swap file is backing for pages used for the software process heap and stack. Swap space is reserved each time a heap segment is created. The root cause of an adequate SWAP configuration results from the working principle of the software due to heap size optimization. For policy to handle more than 10 million facts and 40 million rule executions, it requires about 2 GB heap, 2874 MB software process image, 1591 MB resident set size, and 750 MB new generation size. A software heap segment utilizes the SWAP area. The amount of swap space reserved is the entire size of the segment being created. Empirically, swap size is 0.5–1.5 times of physical memory. A large rule-based system that requires an amount of memory, swap can be potentially less than total physical memory. However, swap configuration is workload dependent in terms of random workload and batch workload. In our case, swap is reserved as 50 GB, which is allocated for the

software process. It seems reasonable for policy since it is a memory bound workload for large fact-rule management.

$$k \approx b + \sqrt{b \times E[L]} = 5 + \sqrt{2 \times 5 \times 0.02} \approx 5 \text{ GB} \tag{3.18}$$

For the software process, control information b is the number garbage collection (GC) times average GC size.

The software heap and GC profiling result is listed below for a use case running 1000 threads with each thread inserting 1000 facts.

```
[GC 589824K->65536K(2260992K),0.0486280s]
[GC 655360K->69632K(2260992K),0.0474786s]
[GC 659456K->69632K(2260992K),0.0428354s]
[GC 659456K->69632K(2260992K),0.0396579s]
[GC 659456K->69632K(2260992K),0.0384900s]
[GC 659456K->69632K(2287360K),0.0402092s]
[GC 712128K->95961K(2260416K),1.0221868s]
[GC 738457K->120537K(2282944K),0.0114766s]
[GC 753817K->120473K(2282496K),0.0139290s]
[GC 753753K->122777K(2284928K),0.0165853s]
[GC 759577K->124761K(2284032K),0.0090867s]
[GC 761561K->126745K(2286464K),0.0118910s]
[GC 766809K->128729K(2285760K),0.0122748s]
[GC 768793K->130713K(2287744K),0.0113439s]
[GC 773465K->132697K(2287168K),0.0097565s]
[GC 775449K->134681K(2288832K),0.0097477s]
[GC 779673K->136833K(2288320K),0.0151087s]
[GC 781825K->138817K(2289728K),0.0116511s]
[GC 785665K->140801K(2289280K),0.0098111s]
[GC 787649K->142785K(2290432K),0.0092022s]
[GC 791105K->144769K(2290048K),0.0151499s]
[GC 793089K->146753K(2291008K),0.0090408s]
[GC 796353K->150785K(2290048K),0.0245672s]
```

The example shows health rule assertions and inference cycle without FullGC but 1-second new generation garbage collection (NGC) that occurred at about 18 seconds of intervals.

To eliminate NGC, we reduce the NG area to make an earlier NGC running at about two seconds.

```
[GC 393203K->65664K(4390912K),0.2800647s]
[GC 458880K->65664K(4390912K),0.0212565s]
[GC 458880K->68575K(4390912K),0.0473655s]
[GC 461791K->68767K(4390912K),0.0359721s]
```

```
[GC 461983K->68831K(4390912K),0.0352179s]
[GC 462047K->68895K(4386048K),0.0351329s]
[GC 457247K->89994K(4388096K),0.0332675s]
[GC 478346K->117898K(4388096K),0.0237485s]
[GC 505482K->109322K(4375040K),0.0043056s]
[GC 496906K->120970K(4386624K),0.0074727s]
[GC 505290K->122890K(4386304K),0.0087036s]
[GC 507210K->126986K(4385920K),0.0123612s]
[GC 511242K->122698K(4377856K),0.0126731s]
[GC 506954K->124298K(4386112K),0.0086229s]
[GC 508042K->124106K(4375296K),0.0053168s]
[GC 507850K->134218K(4384576K),0.0111051s]
[GC 516042K->134154K(4385216K),0.0057666s]
[GC 515978K->129610K(4384960K),0.0064375s]
[GC 511434K->135562K(4385216K),0.0084429s]
[GC 517386K->139530K(4385920K),0.0122201s]
[GC 522698K->139338K(4385856K),0.0082830s]
[GC 522506K->141194K(4386944K),0.0080610s]
[GC 526026K->145034K(4386496K),0.0090619s]
[GC 529866K->140490K(4386432K),0.0078386s]
[GC 525258K->148618K(4382464K),0.0114459s]
[GC 533386K->150834K(4386560K),0.0281213s]
[GC 535346K->150642K(4386560K),0.0060170s]
[GC 535154K->152498K(4387520K),0.0056894s]
[GC 538482K->154354K(4387072K),0.0085414s]
[GC 540338K->137458K(4382400K),0.0081301s]
[GC 519154K->142514K(4363008K),0.0061246s]
[GC 524210K->160754K(4382656K),0.0059271s]
[GC 538738K->164722K(4377728K),0.0108237s]
[GC 542706K->162610K(4382784K),0.0080006s]
[GC 538930K->145522K(4353536K),0.0050109s]
[GC 521842K->165618K(4381376K),0.0144086s]
[GC 539442K->171695K(4373568K),0.0159445s]
[GC 545519K->169583K(4380928K),0.0108134s]
[GC 542120K->175471K(4372288K),0.0136062s]
```

As shown, GC is no longer holding 1 second with frequent NGC. It shows we have optimized GC with a proper NG size.

Software tuning: The selected software tunnables are listed below on M5000.

$$java - server - d64 - XX : +PrintGC$$
$$-XX : +PrintGCTimeStamps$$
$$-XX : +AggressiveHeap$$

$$\begin{aligned} -XX: LargePageSizeInBytes268435456 \\ -XX: +UseParallelGC \\ -XX: ParallelGCThreads = 32 \\ -Xmsm4096m - Xmx4096m - Xmn480m \end{aligned} \tag{3.19}$$

3.5 Conclusions

Things learned from this chapter and proposed future topics are enumerated in this section.

This paper proposed knowledge-based policy aspect inference axioms and its proof for moderate to large spaces. A relaxed naming presentation and inference are proposed to resolve the complexity of the dependency graph for storage and data management systems. In addition, this paper identifies a performance critical path of policy-aspect construction and inference, which are composed of fact assertions, rule matching, and rule executions.

For storage fact management, the complexity of insertion operations is critical for optimization. It suggests precreating the first fact for each thread if possible. However, for any random workload without join points for assertions, it is recommended to use the proposed session-based fact management method to reduce space complexity with the factor of k. In addition to preassertion for batch workload, a page-based fact management brings space reduction with the factor of k. Facts update is O(1) with optimization. Hence, throughput of working memory update is no longer a performance issue. For fact retraction, the elapsed time has negative linear independency with the number of facts and the threads to lookup facts. The above proposed working memory management techniques will reduce the contention. Therefore, working memory retraction is recommended with finite state management machine at terminal states. Fact lookup gets benefits from optimization. Dynamic fact update and lookup are suggested.

In regard to aspect rule management, this work proposes to eliminate and decouple rule execution logics with expensive external calls. In addition, rulebase caching does speedup rule system bootstrapping. Furthermore, matching optimization with conjunct ordering of the most constrained variables, AlphaNode hashing, and BetaNode indexing improve rule inference throughput. Specifically, both the left tuple and right fact node should be evaluated with indices. Rule firing is optimized well with default implementation. Rule parallelization such as OR parallelism and AND parallelism helps performance speedup. For rule optimization, it is very critical to create definite clauses without functions in policy ontology to avoid costs of resolution since a Modus Ponens or lifted version Modus Ponens inference rule applies to definite clauses directly.

For large rule management, states of Rete network reduce the recomputation of partial matching. To avoid irrelevant fact conclusions, it is suggested to optimize rule specification without drawing irrelevant conclusions. Another formal method is to restrict forward chaining to a selected subset of rules. Specifically, a magic set is used to speedup inference. In addition, horizontal rule partition and distribution are proposed to the above finite state classification. The rule can be local fact partition and distribution across multiple versions of working memory. This means that multiple working memory and the software processes are loaded with partitioned rules. If rule management is the major performance consideration, horizontal rule partition on a single host will result in a gain factor.

Storage fact and aspect systems require dynamic memory allocation; hence, aggressive software tuning is critical for performance optimization. The proposed memory allocation formula gives a guideline of heap sizing with estimation of GC control information.

For instrumentation, virtual machine, agentlib, and heap tools are effective to optimize rule system throughput. In addition, Solaris built-in mpstat, prstat, vmpstat, and iostat do help too. The Sun M5000 is an adequate system for storage fact management and policy aspect discovery. Aspect-based policy discovery is one of the feasible tools for large policy spaces.

3.6 Closure

Policy concerns emerge over time. Due to dynamics of programming calculus and derivation of policy life cycle management, storage, and data management software engineering processes experience a definite structure of change events E. The processes are going through difference time intervals t with a predicate T. To continuously model processes of derivation, event calculus is utilized. To specify the continuous nonchange, state is introduced to map to an invariant as it is addressed earlier in formulation. Solving policy-aspect discovery with uncertainty is one of the critical future topics to explore.

References

[1] Colyer, A. and A. Clement. Aspect-oriented programming with aspectJ. *IBM Systems Journal*, 2005.

[2] Kellens, A. et al. A survey of automated code-level aspect mining techniques. Transactions on Aspect-Oriented Software Development Iv. *Lecture Notes in Computer Science*, 4640:143–162, 2007.

[3] Sampaio, A. et al. EA-miner:towards automation in aspect-oriented requirements engineering. *Lecture Notes in Computer Science*, 4620(4):4–39, 2007.

[4] Henderson-Sellers, B. *Object-Oriented Metrics: Measures of Complexity.* Edition: 1(1995–12–04). Prentice Hall-Gale, PTR, NJ, 1995.

[5] Marin, M. et al. Applying and combining three different aspect mining techniques. *ACM Transactions on Software Engineering and Methodlogy*, 17(1), 2007.

[6] Ceccato, M. Applying and combining three different aspect mining techniques. *Software Quality Journal*, 14:209, 2006.

[7] Ganter, B. and R. Wille. *Formal Concept Analysis: Mathematical Foundations.* Springer Berlin/Heidelberg, 2004.

[8] Bruntink, M. On the use of clone detection for identifying crosscutting concern code. *IEEE Transactions on Software Engineering*, 31(10):804–818, 2005.

[9] Zhang, C. and H.-A. Jacobsen. Efficiently mining crosscutting concerns through random walks. *AOSD 07*, 2007.

[10] Pollock, K. L. Introducing natural language program analysis. *PASTE'07*, 2007.

[11] Charfi, A. and M. Mezini. Aspect-oriented web service composition with ao4bpel. *Springer*, 3250, 2004.

[12] Charfi, A. and M. Mezini. Hybrid web service composition: Business processes meet business rules. In *Proceedings of the 2nd International Conference on Service Oriented Computing*, 30–38, 2004.

[13] Cibran, M. A. and B. Verheecke. Dynamic business rules for web service composition. In *Dynamic Aspect Workshop*, 2005.

[14] Rosenberg, F. and S. Dustdar. Towards a distributed service-oriented business rules system. In *Proceedings of the 3rd IEEE European Conference on Web Service*, 2005.

[15] C. Courbis and A. Finkelstein. Towards aspect weaving applications. In *Proceedings of the 27th International Conference on Software Engineering*, 69–77, 2005.

[16] Baligand, F. A concrete solution for web services adaptability using policies and aspects. *ISOC'04*, 2004.

[17] Georg, G. Using aspects to design a secure system. In *Proceedings of International Conference on Engineering Complex Computing Systems*, 2002.

[18] Verhanneman, T. Implementing a modular access control service to support application-specific policies in caesarj. *AOMD'05*, 2005.

[19] Ray, I. An aspect-based approach to modeling access control concerns. *Information and Software Technology*, 2003.

[20] Fradet, P. and S. Ha. Aspects of availability. *GPCE'07*, 2007.

[21] Baresi, L. and S. Guinea. A dynamic and reactive approach to the supervision of bpel processes. *ISEC'08*, 2008.

[22] Liu, H. and M. Parashar. Dios++: A framework for rule-based autonomic management of distributed scientific applications. In *Proceedings of the 9th International Euro-Par Conference*, Springer-Verlag, 2003.

[23] Petri, C. A. Kommunikation mit automaten. *PhD Thesis, University of Bonn*, 1926.

[24] Warren, D. H. D. An abstract prolog instruction set. *Warren, Technical Note 309 SRI International*, 1983.

[25] McDermott, J. R1: A rule-based configure of computer system. *Artificial Intelligence*, 19:39–88, 1982.

[26] Forgy, C. Rete: A fast algorithm for the many pattern/many object pattern match problem. *Artificial Intelligence*, 19:17–37, 1982.

Chapter 4

Stabilizing Read–Write Throughput of Transactional Memory for Contention Management

4.1 Introduction

4.1.1 Background

Software transactional memory (STM) has gained momentum as an alternative to lock-based programming and has received considerable discussion in the literature. STM systems simplify the complexity of low-level task and memory management of modern operating systems.

4.1.2 Why STM performance is important

The issue of performance improvement for lock-based STMs is noteworthy. A goal of operating systems on multicore hardware is to allow parallel operations without conflicts in accessing memory to proceed concurrently. As concurrent programming becomes ubiquitous, STM systems are viable candidates and are needed to use transactional memory today. However, coherent read operations are expensive for write transactions and mixed transactions, so they may limit performance and scalability.

Achieving scalable performance is feasible in STM. Transactional memory has gained momentum as an alternative to lock-based programming. Hardware transactional memory (HTM) support is a long way from being available. Specifically, the hardware support for transactional memory needs to be as ubiquitous as multiprocessors. Hence, STM provides an interim solution. In addition, single-chip systems are rapidly taking over a large proportion of desktop computing space. The cost of coherence on multi-core systems drops to the amount of making design of lock-based STM viable.

4.1.3 What has been done

In regard to performance assessment of lower synchronization and coherence costs, researchers discussed the consensus in the literature. Researchers proposed evaluation of existing invisible readers [1–4]. There are also methods to reduce synchronization overhead of detecting visible readers [5]. A recent study [6] proposed to assess performance of visible-reader based STMs.

The common practice of evaluating performance of STMs has been through micro-benchmarks [1–4, 6]. This method uses the standard-concurrent tree structure of STM micro-benchmarks. Micro-benchmarks verify transactional memory implementations with varying workloads and bottlenecks. Short and ordinary transactions of micro-benchmarks are valid for testing the mechanics of the STM itself and comparing low-level details of different implementations, but they have high overhead on the single-memory address accesses. The low-level overhead has the most negative effect in micro-benchmarks.

In the context of multicore systems, existing STM systems often do not appear to have scalable performance [7]. Transactions read and write shared objects. Two transactions conflict if they access the same object and one tries to write to the object. STM allows only one transaction to acquire an object for writing to the object at a time. Contention management must decide which transaction may proceed and which must wait or abort to determine if a second transaction requires an object currently in use. In STM, contention management refers to the mechanisms used to secure further progress to avoid livelock and starvation. Researchers propose a number of contention manager strategies [8, 9], ranging from a primary one (exponential backoff) to an enhanced one (different priority-based strategies). Experiments have shown that contention control algorithms can affect transaction throughput. In some cases, the effect is substantial. Contention management improves throughput and fairness. On fairness, specifically, a livelock-dominated problem, researchers studied contention management [10, 11]. For throughput, an investigation suggested priority schemes [11] using a fair resolution of conflicts in an STM with invisible reads.

4.1.4 Open issues

Unfortunately, researchers [11–13] designed contention management approaches for obstruction-free STM frameworks, and introduced unusual constant-time overheads. While empirical analysis will always be necessary for evaluating contention manager designs, researchers [11] proposed to develop a more systematic theory of contention management. The research seeks to understand the general solution for contention management schemes to provide optimal performance [10]. The related research question is whether other benchmarks might exhibit different characteristics from those characteristics studied earlier. Researchers also want to see whether better prioritization can be effective for transactions. In addition, researchers need to consider if and how different contention management schemes might affect a heterogeneous workload. Furthermore, researchers need to understand if the overhead of contention management can be made to adapt to different policies.

The above studies have succeeded in interpreting the detailed structure of the excited transactions of complex memory systems. Observation of levels of throughput requires precise information concerning millions of memory locations, while all structures may become random. In states of such a large ensemble, only transactional spin (phase) and parity (commit or abort) remain faithful. The excited transactions require a method of performance management at throughput levels. The performance method will not predict the detailed sequence of throughput levels in any transactional memory location, but the method will describe the appearance and the degree of irregularity of the transactional-level structure. The appearance and irregularity may occur in any transaction, which is too complicated to be understood in detail. Hence, this research focuses on a general method of stabilizing transactional throughput as states transit. As systems evolve, this research predicts system behavior without exact knowledge of resembled states. Subsequently, this research proposes dynamic optimization of transaction observation and feedback control in the purpose described by costs and functions of transactional memory during transaction processing.

4.2 Problem Statement and Goal

This section gives a precise formulation of the problem.

4.2.1 Problem formulation

This section analyzes STM as a chaotic system by representing a transactional state through its basis expansion. This section represents a state with the geometric intuition. In addition, this section proposes the algebraic representation and physical interpretation. For complexity, this chapter formulates a transactional space. This chapter studies an optimal contention control to stabilize transactional throughput.

(1) *Transactional Chaos:* Input to a transactional memory location is dependent on its arrival streams. Output from the memory location is dependent on the load. The data stream is independent of rate of transmission, such as throughput. Throughput is independent of acceleration of throughput. In addition, the load is dependent on data as transactions are processing the data. Hence, throughput of transactional

memory and load of the location are dependent as an equation

$$m\nabla^2 u + r\nabla u + f(u) = f(t) \tag{4.1}$$

where $\nabla^2 u$ is the rate of throughput changes. ∇u represents throughput. $f(u)$ represents the volume of data that a transaction is processing. $f(u)$ includes both soft-spring and hard-spring forces. $f(t)$ denotes the load, which is dependent on time t.

For simplicity, let's assume $f(t)$ is a harmonic-forcing function such as $F_0 \cos \omega t$. F_0 is the load of a memory location. Equation 4.1 represents a classic duffing equation

$$\begin{bmatrix} u' \\ y' \end{bmatrix} = \begin{bmatrix} 0 & 1 \\ f(u) & -r \end{bmatrix} \begin{bmatrix} u \\ y \end{bmatrix} \tag{4.2}$$

where $y = u'$ represents throughput of a transactional system.

The dumping factor [14] introduces a transactional-jump phenomenon associated with Equation 4.2, whereby a continuous variation of arrival rate can lead to discontinuous changes in the throughput. Contention control adjusts the load of the memory location. Throughput transits from harmonic and subharmonic oscillations to random motions with infinite loops. The throughput evolution is the Butterfly effect. This transactional behavior admits periodic solutions and aperiodic ones, which are sensitive to initial conditions. It is exponentially sensitive to minor perturbations. A small change in the initial state will change system states with larger changes of complex orbit structure. Because initial states are seldom known explicitly in real-world systems, the ignorance limits transactional predictability [15].

(2) *State Representation Using Momentum Basis:* This section expands a transactional memory system by a pair of read-write momentum. Specifically, a transaction for a memory location can be described in terms of its read-write eigenbasis, that is, the set $\{\mathbb{R}, \mathbb{W}\}$. $\{u\}$ can be written in any orthogonal basis, corresponding to different physical observables. A discrete representation of read-write momentum is up to the constant $-i * \hbar$, the rate of changes of the throughput state vector from one point to the following. The generalized momentum relationship [16] can be represented by the following equation

$$M(u) = -i * \hbar * \frac{u(s + \delta s) - u(s)}{\delta s} \tag{4.3}$$

$M(u) = b * Ops/s$ represents the read-write momentum of transactional memory. b is the bandwidth utilization of a read-write channel. Ops/s is the number of read-write operations per second. s represents the state on the integral curve using transactional memory. Hence, for a single phase transaction on a memory location, the rate of throughput changes is proportional to the read-write momentum. The equation gives the concrete dynamics, which determine the evolution of a transactional system. After one solves the equation with some initial conditions, one determines the read-write momentum over state changes whenever one can specify the rate of the changes.

(3) *State Representation Using Orthogonal Basis:* A directional angle is another observable. A transactional state can be written in an orthogonal basis relative to the angle. Hence, a transactional memory system can be expanded by a discrete angle eigenbasis.

Mathematical Representation: Each transaction can be represented as a physical quantity with its magnitude and a direction by two-dimensional geometrical intuition. The magnitude is the performance measurement of the transaction whereas the direction $\theta_i \in [0, 2\pi)$ is the identifier of the transaction. If one sets the initial point of the transaction at the origin, a vector $V_i = (r, \theta_i)$ represents the transaction for a memory location. Hence, the restart or failure of a transaction represents a corresponding class of transactions with the direction of $\theta_i \in [2\pi, 2k\pi]$.

In algebraic interpretation, a complex number $a + bi \mapsto (a, b)$ represents a transaction. The complex number is nothing more than an ordered pair of ordinary real numbers. There are several properties of the components of each transaction. All real numbers excluding 0 from a group with respect to ordinary multiplication. The addition identity is $(0, 0)$ and the multiplication identity is $(1, 0)$. Every element has its inverse. Hence, a transaction group is a field. The transaction field contains all solutions for any of its polynomial equations. So the transaction field is algebraically completed. The completeness guarantees obtaining solutions to ensure system progresses. The field isomorphism ensures a one-to-one correspondence between a memory location and a transactional group.

The above two-dimensional transactional representation can be extended in a three-dimensional geometric way. The canonical representation [17] of a transactional vector space has only two real numbers (θ and ϕ)

$$\rho = \cos\theta \; C + e^{i\phi} \sin\theta \; R \tag{4.4}$$

where C represents the state of commit and R represents the state of abort. θ is half the angle that a transaction makes with the z axis. ϕ is the angle that a transaction makes from the basis x axis along the equator. The standard parameterization of the three-dimensional representation is

$$x = \cos\phi \sin 2\theta \tag{4.5}$$

$$y = \sin 2\theta \sin\phi \tag{4.6}$$

$$z = \cos 2\theta \tag{4.7}$$

The physical interpretation of the above three-dimensional model relies on the two physical parameters. In Equation 4.4, $e^{i\phi}$ is the phase parameter. θ controls the probability of collapsing transactional commit to abort. A performance measurement decomposes a transaction as the probability of commit and abort.

From parameter z, the probability of a transaction terminating at commit mode C depends exclusively on θ. The angle θ controls the strength of terminating at C mode or R mode. It indicates the prediction of a transactional termination. The changes of ϕ without θ do not alter the probability but phase $e^{i\phi}$. This parameter is a phase state that represents periodic transactional motions with classic states of C or R.

(4) *Transaction Vector Space:* Two transactional vector spaces of the same dimension over the same field are isomorphic. N-tuples are the prototypes of the vectors. This means we can restrict attention to n tuples without loss of generality. The metric of Hilbert space [18] may not be derived from a physical principle. It is rather a consequence of inferring an optimal statistical procedure. The distance between two vectors is proportional to the angle between the two vectors with arbitrary distinguishable criteria. The distance does not depend on the position of the vectors. In a two-dimensional Hilbert space, we compute the distance as Equation 4.8

$$W(\theta_1, \theta_2, n) = |\theta_1 - \theta_2|\sqrt{\frac{2n}{\pi e}} \tag{4.8}$$

where θ is the direction of the vector in the plane from some reference directions spanned by the two vectors. n is the number of equivalent states in a sample space.

Equation 4.8 shows that the number of distinguishable states in the interval of angles $[\alpha_1, \alpha_2]$ depends on the length of the interval and the square root of the number of identical states with a rigorous notion of distinguishability. It does not depend on the position of the arcs comprising the range of the unit circle.

The result can be generalized for the N-dimensional Hilbert space of states of a system [19]. The number of distinguishable states is

$$W(n, \Omega) = \Omega(cn)^{\frac{N-1}{2}} \tag{4.9}$$

where n is the number of copies of identical states. c is a constant.

That means that the number of distinct states depends only on the area Ω of the domain on the sphere from which states can be chosen, but does not depend on the shape and position of the domain. The uniform distribution is optimal over the domain in a polar-orthogonal basis.

(5) *System Evolution:* In addition to state revolution, an ensemble of systems represents the behavior of transactional memory when the system changes. Gaussian ensemble is the most convenient one in practice. However, Gaussian ensemble cannot define a uniform probability distribution on an infinite range. Orthogonal ensemble is a valid one to apply under different circumstances, but researchers [20] reported that orthogonal ensemble is always appropriate for even-spin systems with time-reversal invariance and a system invariant under space rotation. Orthogonal ensemble is the space of symmetric unitary matrices. Transactional memory is symmetric with respect to time. STM has characteristics of space rotation, but for odd-spin systems, orthogonal ensemble does not apply. A much simpler ensemble is unitary ensemble. Unitary ensemble applies only to systems without invariance under time reversal. Unitary ensemble is the space of a Hamiltonian, which may be not restricted to be symmetric or self-dual. A general ensemble proposed by Dyson is a symplectic ensemble that applies to both spin systems. The symplectic group can be expressed in terms of quaternion

$$[r_1] = \begin{bmatrix} 0 & -i \\ -i & 0 \end{bmatrix} \quad [r_2] = \begin{bmatrix} 0 & -1 \\ 1 & 0 \end{bmatrix} \quad [r_3] = \begin{bmatrix} -i & 0 \\ 0 & i \end{bmatrix} \tag{4.10}$$

As shown, symplectic ensemble is the space of self-dual unitary quaternion matrices. The symplectic ensemble represents the notion of uniforming a priori probability in the space. The dimension of the general ensemble space is $[2N^2 - N]$ where N is the dimension of the symplectic group.

(6) *Performance Controls:* A transactional state is a sufficient coordinate not only for closed throughput (input controls, output observations, and feedback) but also for open (open to observation and feedback control) and unstable throughput of transactional memory. An unstable transactional system can be approximated by the Markov approximation. However, a differential equation with high or infinite dimensionality needs to be solved if N grows hyper-exponentially. Nevertheless, the Bellman principle can be applied as traditional states [21].

(a) *Costs of Control:* As researchers pointed out [21], unstable controls allow continuous measurement. For conditional states, a dynamic programming method optimizes transactional controls with concave cost function and convex constraints. With the three-dimensional model, the cost becomes the expected value. Researchers have derived Bellman equations and the corresponding Hamilton–Jacobi equations for a wider class of cost functions than classic cost functions.

The optimal average cost on the interval (t, τ) is $S(t, \rho)$. Researchers define the minimum concave cost to function by the path integral in

$$S(t_0, \rho_0) = \int_{t_0}^{\tau} [< q_\tau, p_\tau > -H(q_\tau, p_\tau)]dr + S[\rho(q_\tau)] \qquad (4.11)$$

where state ρ starts from 0 to q_τ. dr represents derivation of the control path. p is the tangent element of the state space and q is the cotangent element of the state space. The control force is represented as $[< q_\tau, p_\tau > -H(q_\tau, p_\tau)]$. $S[\rho(q_\tau)]$ is the initial cost.

The optimal control starts in state ρ at time t. Bellman's optimality principle holds in Equation 4.11. This leads to the Hamiltonian boundary value problem

$$q_t - \nabla_p H_v(q_t, p_t) = 0, \quad q_0 = a \qquad (4.12)$$
$$p_t + \nabla_q H_v(q_t, p_t) = 0, \quad p_\tau = b \qquad (4.13)$$

where $H_v(p, q)$ is a Hamiltonian transform, which solution defines for $a = 0$ if $\rho^0 = \rho_0$, $b = \nabla_\rho S[\rho]$. ∇H_v is a gradient of a scalar transform.

(b) *Costs of Erasing Information*: Landauer's erasure principle [22] states that the erasure of information incurs an energy cost. Recent research [23] discovered that the energy cost in Landauer's erasure principle is incurred because of the use of a thermal reservoir. The reservoir can be replaced by a statistical ensemble of energy degenerate spin-$\frac{1}{2}$ particles. Equation 4.14 gives the total spin cost of the whole process. It includes the spinning of the initial state

$$\triangle J_z^{'} = \sum_{n=0}^{\infty} \frac{e^{-n\hbar\beta}}{1 + e^{-n\hbar\beta}} \qquad (4.14)$$

where $0 <= \alpha <= 1$. $\hbar$ is a constant. n represents nth cycle of spin. $\beta = \frac{1}{\hbar} ln(\frac{1-\alpha}{\alpha})$ z is the z component of spin angular momentum of each particle as the logical states *Commit* or *Abort*.

With this replacement, the erasure of information incurs a physical cost in terms of spin angular momentum only. Furthermore, the above sum in Equation 4.14 can be approximated by

$$\beta^{-1} ln(2) < \triangle J_z^{'} < \beta^{-1} ln(1 + e^{\hbar\beta}) \qquad (4.15)$$

where β has the same units as $\hbar$.

4.2.2 Statement of problem

Given a steadily running chaotic STM, how can one improve or keep its time averaged performance?

- Given a steadily running STM, how can one increase or maintain its time averaged performance?
- What is the joint distribution of the eigenvalues in a transactional ensemble?
- What is the cost function for optimal controls with the lowest costs?
- What determines the arrival rate (driving frequency) results in aperiodic and random throughput?
- What is the asymptomatic expression of the frequency and configurations?
- What is the orbit evolving from its current state to a different target location?
- What are the quantitative performance characteristics?
- Under optimal controls, how can one reduce contentions?
- How to assess the proposed method empirically?

The first, second, and third problems relate to orbit structures. The fourth and fifth problems have connections with sensitivity and stability. Given Equation 4.11 and Equation 4.14, we need to obtain a cost function for optimal control of transactional performance with the minimal costs. Transactions may be entangled with nested or multiple phase transactions. The planning history of one transaction may be uncertain. One is not sure of the current transactional state. We need to derive a discrete method to control the statistical state of transactional memory. An information theoretic scheme is required to increase transactional performance.

4.3 Brief Review of the Literature

4.3.1 Fourier analysis

Continuous relations can be represented by Taylor series. For periodic phenomena, infinite Fourier series are universally used to present general periodic (both continuous and discontinuous) functions. The Fourier method represents a complex ordinary differential equation (ODE) or partial differential equation (PDE) as a superposition (linear combination) of ordinary periodic (sine and cosine wave functions). The presentations write the solution as a linear combination of the corresponding eigensolutions. The Fourier series is this superposition or linear combination. Fourier integrals and Fourier transforms extend techniques of Fourier series to nonperiodic functions. Discrete Fourier transforms (DFT) and fast Fourier transforms (FFT) work with sampled values rather than with functions

$$\mathbb{U} = [e^{(-2\pi i/N)(nk)}]u \tag{4.16}$$

where n, $k = 0, \ldots, N-1$.

When one obtains measurements (sample values), a desired memory throughput state can be computed by an arbitrary initial state. Hence, discrete Fourier analysis depends on large amounts of equally spaced data. Both Fourier and Laplace transforms depend on time variables.

4.3.2 Wave equation

A wave equation $\frac{\partial^2 u}{\partial t^2} = c^2 \nabla^2 u$ [24, 25] is a prominent second order linear partial differential equation. A wave equation presents the propagation of a variety of waves. It can represent small throughput vibrations of memory transactions. The problem is to determine the vibrations of the data stream, which is to achieve its throughput $u(x, t)$ at any given transaction x and any time $t > 0$. One can specify the eigenfunctions as follows:

$$u(x,t) = \sum_{n=1}^{\infty} u_n(x,t) = \sum_{n=1}^{\infty} (B_n \cos \lambda_n t + B_n * \sin \lambda_n t) \sin \frac{n\pi}{L} x \tag{4.17}$$

where eigenvalues are $\lambda_n = \frac{cn\pi}{L}$. L is the length of service time. The scalar vector $\{\lambda_i\}$ is the spectrum. For discontinuity or nonanalytic functions, one requires a discrete method. Even when a wave equation has a characteristic method for discontinuity, the limitation of continuity requires stability analysis. The wave equation has the disadvantages similar to Fourier analysis.

4.3.3 Vector calculus

Fundamental in scalar and vector field theory are differential operators. One needs to evaluate the quantity of the throughput field that an operator measures. To know more intuitively the physical content of the basic equations of transactional memory, let $\mathbb{T}$ be defined in a memory region R. The physical nature of $\mathbb{T}$ is immaterial here, but for definiteness let us think of $\mathbb{T}$ as a rate of operations field. Focusing attention on a memory location $\mathbb{P} = (x, y, z)$ in the data flow, let us introduce a control volume around the memory location $\mathbb{P}$ and denote it as a potato shape $\mathbb{B}$. A control volume is only a mathematical region rather than a physical presence of storage capacity. We introduce it so that we can keep track of the flux of quantities: memory read-write operations. If, at a given memory location in the memory region, the following relation holds

$$I(P) = lim_{d(R)\to 0} \frac{1}{V(R)} \iint_{S(R)} n \cdot v dA \tag{4.18}$$

where V is the volume of region R. S is the boundary surface of V. $|v \cdot ndA|$ represents fluid crossing R.

Next, let us divide the volume flux integral in Equation 4.18 by the volume, then we define the divergence of v at the memory location P as

$$div\ T = \nabla^2 f(u) \tag{4.19}$$

Thus, dotting ∇ into a throughput vector field produces a scalar field associated with throughput. If we consider the action of ∇ to a scalar field of throughput u, the operation suggests its physical significance of divergence measuring outflow and inflow. This evaluates effects of both read-write operations and abort operations. However, the divergence theorem requires a twice continuously differentiable scalar transactional function or a continuously differentiable vector transactional function. The application of the divergence theorem in potential theory needs the continuity.

Vector expansion method: The difference Equation 4.3 can be solved by the eigenvector expansion method. Within vibration phases, the eigenvectors of A as transactional basis can be used but not as any basis for the N tuple.

$$(\mathbb{A} - \lambda \mathbb{M})\mathbf{x} = 0 \tag{4.20}$$

The idea is that the vector Ae_j is simply $\lambda_j e_j$ if e_j is an eigenvector of A, whereas it is a linear combination of all the base vectors if one uses some other basis. The eigenvalues are the natural frequencies. The eigenvectors are the mode and configuration of solutions. Hence, memory locations become a degree of freedom. If there are n memory locations and n degrees of freedom $x_1(t), \ldots, x_n(t)$, then read-write motions of each memory location consist of a linear combination of n eigenmodes of one $n \times n$ matrix. There will be a solution only if the forcing vector F does not excite that particular eigenmode, or F is orthogonal to e. Therefore, read-write momentum can be further expanded with its natural frequencies and amplitude.

$$x_n(t) = a_n \sin \omega t + r_n \cos \omega t \tag{4.21}$$

However, singular points occur when driving frequencies are equal to natural frequencies or forcing vector F is not orthogonal to e. In addition, the expansion method does not give a practical presentation to the aperiodic behaviors and randomness.

4.3.4 Ordinary statistics

Statistical methods rely on exact knowledge of a system. The ordinary method assumes that all states have equal probability in a large ensemble [20]. One obtains relevant information about overall system behavior when it is complex or impractical to observe of all states of the system. However, this statistical method is not adequate for discussion of transactional throughout levels since the detail of the throughput structure cannot be obtained for representing states. However, studies on an ensemble of systems reported that the ensemble average of many-body systems with strong interactions was hard to compute. In addition, there is no proof that an ensemble average accurately represents system behavior.

4.3.5 Random matrices

A random matrix is a matrix-valued random variable. With multiple concurrent transactions, the physical-transactional memory may have sequence conflicts. The corresponding matrices get random. The mathematical properties of matrices determine the physical properties with random elements selected from random matrices. For random matrices, the eigenvectors and eigenvalues are critical. Quantum chaos is an application of random matrix theory (RMT). The theory of random matrix starts from a series of researches [20]. This chapter applies RMT to evaluate system evolution and throughput structure partitioning.

4.3.6 Qualitative analysis

Real-life nonlinearity may not be solvable analytically. Simulation methods provide a quantitative model. Using auxiliary variable y, the higher-order relations $p(x)$ can be transformed into a first order differential equation $p(x, y)$ with a single integration constant. With conservational law, the constant becomes the total energy. If we take it as the result and study it by a (x, y) plane, the energy parameter gives a family of curves or surfaces representing possible throughput activities resulting from the consequence of transactional trajectories.

Any explicit reference to t can be suppressed by dividing one equation by the other and obtaining

$$\frac{dy}{dx} = \frac{P(x,y)}{Q(x,y)} \tag{4.22}$$

Instead of obtaining transactional solutions, the qualitative and topological nature of nonlinear solutions can be partitioned by geometric approaches. The distinctive relationship exists in some open intervals containing t_0. One can classify the types of equilibrium points by qualitative characteristics. The stability of throughput trajectories can be further studied in the transactional phase plane.

Qualitative methods evaluate singularity types and stability of a transaction throughput where jump points cannot be observed either in a physical transaction or its simulation. However, qualitative methods are usually proposed in a real plane. Qualitative methods have difficulties for representing higher-dimension relations.

4.3.7 Lattice models

As opposed to continuous-space or space-time, lattice models can be applied. Lattice models are often an approximation of continuous methods for giving a cutoff to prevent divergences or perform numeric computation. The quantum chromodynamics (QCD) lattice model, discrete QCD, is one of widely studied continuum theories. In addition, lattice gauge theory and lattice field theory are active areas. However, the physical parameters of a lattice require computation of the dynamical matrix, which represents the particle-particle interactions.

4.3.8 Controlling chaos

A unstable periodic orbit (UPO) control algorithm controls chaos. After one identifies a suitable UPO embedded within the attractor, one can specify how the small controls execute. The control keeps the system orbit on the selected UPO. Researchers [15] propose controls to place the orbit on the UPO. The control also keeps it close to the stable manifold of the preferred UPO. The study discusses a control technique using pole placement. Researchers studied the methods to implement UPO control. The proposed methods use a single-scalar state variable with only time-series measurements. A study shows a technique to control fast dynamics such as lasers. However, the chaotic methods are hard to evaluate.

4.3.9 KAM theorem

In this theorem, there are three boxes linked together. R, which represents a classic, basic system, P, which denotes a classic chaotic system, and Q, which describes a quantum system. The connectivity between R and Q models Bohr's correspondence principle, which claims that quantum mechanics contains a classic mechanism where an object is larger than the size of atoms. The primary transition between R and P is the Kolmogorov-Arnold-Moser (KAM) theorem. The KAM theorem is a utility to determine how much of the structure of a stable system survives when a minor perturbation applies. The theorem can find controls that result in a regular system to sustain chaotic states. Quantum chaos is to establish the relation between boxes P and Q. KAM theorem requires a bridge between R and P.

4.4 Approach

4.4.1 Physical assumption

To make a statement about the details of the throughput level structure, we visualize a complex STM system as a black box in which many transactions are interacting according to unknown laws. In a mathematical approach, we assume to define an ensemble of STM systems where all interaction laws have equal probability.

4.4.2 Information-theoretical description

To complete the extension to generalized-transactional ensemble, we reverse the cart and the horse by evaluating the properties of transactional respect to the level of axioms and performance characteristics. The ensemble describes the behavior of a singular object such as a transaction, a memory location, or STM.

(1) *Reversibility:* Researchers [26] have discovered that erasing information is an irreversible, energy-dissipating operation but writing information is reversible.

$$A * A^{+} = A^{+} * A = I_n \tag{4.23}$$

Hence, a transaction can be aborted. It is a unitary operation. The evolution of transactional memory is symmetric with respect to time.

(2) *Long Transactions:* Long-run transactions or read-write operations may be tangled and not separable. Hence, there are long transactions for these activities. In addition, these activities can be nested with writing and erasing information. Since erasing information is not reversible, they are irrevocable transactions.

(3) *Non-blocking:* Most transactions are reversible. The abort operation is a symmetric-unitary operation.

(4) *Deadlocks:* Intensive or inappropriate exclusive locking can lead to the deadlock position between two locks. The locks can be released. The locks attempt to obtain resources mutually from each other. The deadlocks represent singularity of the system. There is no solution curve to determine the oscillations. Transactional memory has a fail safe procedure and will automatically abort one of the locks releasing the resource to jump out of the cycle. A transaction is a reversible operation. Hence, processes or transactions involved in the deadlock can be aborted.

(5) *Livelocks:* When a transaction is executing another transaction may suspend its actions. The two transactions may end up swaying from one to another without any progress. The states of the transactions have livelock without progress. Livelock is probable for some algorithms detecting and recovering from deadlocks. If more than one transaction requires execution, the deadlock detection can be constantly triggered. Livelock can be avoided by executing one random or precedent transaction at a time. Transactional associativity helps to determine the

randomness or priority. The canceled actions represent decoherence of transactional performance.

(6) *Progress Guarantee:* With methods of resolving deadlocks and livelocks, transactional memory does not face external, driving frequency to excite oscillation with natural frequency. By avoiding approaching singularity, there will be infinite solution curves to transactional state changes.

(7) *Associativity:* Separable transactions do not have precedence. For separable transactions such as all single phase transactions, transactions can be decomposed as a tensor pair of transactions $A \otimes B$. The tensor product is associative.

$$A \otimes (B \otimes C) = (A \otimes B) \otimes C \tag{4.24}$$

For separable transactions, there is no conflict in distributing the transactions to individual cores. Because of associativity, transactional memory can be assembled incrementally to build a larger and larger system to achieve horizontal scalability.

$$V_0 \otimes V_1 \otimes \cdots \otimes V_k \tag{4.25}$$

(8) *Distributivity:* Transactional activities are multiplication states with action matrices.

$$1 * V = V \tag{4.26}$$

The invariant operation shows transactional performance is kept indifferent without external forces. In addition, it ensures transactional privacy.

$$c_1 * (c_2 * V) = (c_1 \times c_2) * V \tag{4.27}$$

The incremental multiplication indicates that performance improvement upon a single transaction can be done progressively without interruption of external transactions. This also reproduces the results of associativity, which means performance improvement can be done by incrementally adding workload or optimizing each transaction individually.

$$c * (V + W) = c * V + c * W \tag{4.28}$$

where c is a scalar. The multiplication distribution over addition equation shows that a load to multiple cores results in the same contention to each individual memory location without load balancing. This also indicates the importance of a load balancing scheme for contention management

$$(c_1 + c_2) * V = c_1 * V + c_2 * V \tag{4.29}$$

where $c_1 \neq c_2$ are scalar. The scalar distribution equation demonstrates that a strength or load can be distributed among different transactions. The load to each memory location can be balanced. This also proves the correctness of parallelization of transactional memory, which means performance improvement can be done by assigning transactions to different memory locations according to the contention.

(9) *Noncommutativity:* The order of executing each transaction is sensitive. For separable transactions such as all single phase transactions, transactions can be decomposed as a tensor pair of transactions $A \otimes B$.

$$A \otimes B \neq B \otimes A \tag{4.30}$$

In general, although they are not equal, they do have the same entries, and one can be transformed to the other with a change of rows and columns. The configuration change is to alter the eigenbasis. Entangled transactions, such as multiple phase transactions or nonfactorized distributed transactions (broadcasting communication), are not separable and cannot be written as the tensor of vector pairs. But they can be written as the nontrivial sum of such tensors. The orthogonal basis is linearly independent. Hence there is no order of execution. They can be distributed equally to different cores. However, for each tensor pair, the order is critical.

(10) *Coherence:* Matrix operations respect addition. This means two transactions can be added together to create a larger or nested transaction (constructive interference). Or a transaction can be decomposed into smaller transactions (destructive interference), depending on their relative service time. Transactions are said to be coherent if they have a constant relative service time. The degree of coherence is measured by interference visibility, a measure of how perfectly the transactions can be canceled due to destructive interference.

(11) *Parallelization:* Separable transactions, such as all single phase transactions, can be decomposed as a tensor pair of transactions $A \otimes B$.

$$(A \otimes B) * (V \otimes V') = A * V \otimes B * V' \tag{4.31}$$

If A acts on V and B acts on V', then we define the action on their tensor product. This is action parallelization. Separable transactions are parallelizable.

(12) *Load Balancing or Multiplexing:* Contention can be specifically reduced by distributing the weight of load on each memory location. This keeps the overall throughput of STM.

$$c(\dot{V_j} \otimes V_k) = (c\dot{V_j}) \otimes V_k = V_j \otimes (c\dot{V_k}) \tag{4.32}$$

(13) *Additivity and Multiplicative Transactions:* Researchers [27] studied the highest purity of outputs of additive and multiplicative channels of communications

$$v_H(\phi_1 \otimes \phi_2) <= v_H(\phi_1) + v_H(\phi_2) \tag{4.33}$$

where ϕ represents different channels. p is a probability distribution to an arbitrary state ρ.

The additive inequality has proved the conjecture that classical capacity or the maximal purity of outputs cannot be increased by using entangled inputs of the communication channels. As communication channels, transactions transform a set of system states to another set of states. Hence, one cannot improve transactional performance by entangling activities or nesting transactions into a long transaction

$$v_p(\phi_1 \otimes \phi_2) >= v_p(\phi_1)v_p(\phi_2) \tag{4.34}$$

where ϕ represents different channels. v_H represents the maximal output purity of a channel.

Similarly, the multiplicative inequality indicates that multiple phase commit schemes decrease transactional performance.

(14) *Privatization (Implicit, Proxy):* Since each transaction represents an orthogonal basis, they are linearly independent. The independence provides an isolation level to ensure its privacy.

(15) *Throughput Observables:* As established in the transactional memory literature [1–4, 28], both *Ops/s* and *Abort/s* are the physical observables to measure transactional throughput.

4.4.3 Evaluation

The action of carrying out observation on STM is specified by a measurement operator. Transactional state evolution is computed with dynamic operations and systems transit with a general ensemble. Throughput structures are evaluated from a correlation function and a density function. The correlation function is used to evaluate a group of throughput continuities. The density function calculates values of a throughput group. For the same group of continuities, a method of continuous tuning can be used. For transactions with discontinuous throughput, a dynamic method is proposed to evaluate STM evolution. The associated costs are used to control performance. Finally, an experiment is proposed to show whether employing this method can make a STM system run stably.

(1) *Measurement Operator:* A physical transactional memory system can be specified by a double list. The list is composed of a state space and a set

of its observables. The observables, such as service time Ω_s, throughput Ω_p, and arrival rate Ω_a, are physical quantities that can be observed in each state of the state space. Hence, they are three 2×2 hermitian operators. Since observation $\Omega\mathbb{T}$ is not a scalar multiplication, it modifies the transactional states. Thus the result does not represent the same physical state.

$$\begin{pmatrix} 1 & 0 \\ 0 & -1 \end{pmatrix}$$

For a transaction system, the operators are not commutative. Hence, the order of observation is critical. But there is a limit for the differences of a simultaneous measure of any two observables (see Section 4.5).

For the C^n domain, the trace of a system state holds as: $Trace(A^+, B) =< A, B >$. For a squared operator C, $Trace(C) = \sum_{i=0}^{n-1} C[i,i]$. It is the sum of all diagonal elements of the matrix. It is the basis of the throughput measurement. Hence, with two measurements (λ_1, λ_2), we can define the throughput operator as

$$y = \begin{bmatrix} \lambda_1 & x_1 \\ x_2 & \lambda_2 \end{bmatrix} \tag{4.35}$$

What is left is to derive the other two elements.

(2) *Correlation Function:* We consider a spectrum of N throughput levels $x_n, n \in [1, N]$ with values on the entire axis. An transactional ensemble of infinitely many such spectra is specified in terms of a normalized probability density $P_N^{(E)}(x_1, \ldots, x_N)$. This implies that $P_N^{(E)}(x_1, \ldots, x_N)$ is invariant under the permutations of arguments. The correlation functions [20] describe the statistical properties of the ensemble. The k-point correlation function is obtained by integrating the probability density over $N - k$ arguments,

$$R_k(x_1, \ldots, x_k) = \frac{N!}{(N-k)!} \int_{-\infty}^{+\infty} dx_{k+1} \ldots \int_{-\infty}^{+\infty} dx_N P_N^{(E)}(x_1, \ldots, x_N) \tag{4.36}$$

Let H denote a Hamiltonian defined in a Hilbert space. We focus on H with finite dimension N with $N \gg 1$. The spectrum of H contains N levels and is given by the trace of the imaginary part of the Green function. The ensemble is defined by a probability density $P_N(H)$ and a measurement in matrix space. The $k-$point correlation functions can be defined as

$$R_k(x_1, \ldots, x_k) = \frac{1}{\pi^k} \int P_N(H) \prod_{p=1}^{k} Imtr \frac{1}{x_p^- - H} d[H] \tag{4.37}$$

where the measure $d[H]$ is the Cartesian volume element of H. With jumping and discontinuity of throughput, transactional memory is a system with broken time-reversal invariance, H is a complex Hermitian, irrespective of whether rotation invariance holds or not. However, read-write behavior does represent the rotation invariance of the system. Thus, H can be viewed as an $2N \times 2N$ matrix.

Due to computational complexity, a general conjecture states a partitioning rule to compute the discontinuity (see Equation 4.46).

4.4.4 Dynamics

Rather than measurement, state evolution is computed by its dynamic mechanics. For any 2×1 transaction, every 2×2 matrix operation can be visualized as a way of manipulating the sphere. Then X, Y, and Z Pauli matrices are transaction policies of rotating π in the three orthogonal directions. Hence, the transactional read or write operations perform the following operations upon the same data sets. For example, flipping along X, the operation is represented as a negation of an original operation

$$\begin{pmatrix} 0 & 1 \\ 1 & 0 \end{pmatrix}$$

Lock is a phase change operation. It can be represented by a phase shift matrix.

$$\begin{pmatrix} 1 & 0 \\ 0 & e^{\theta} \end{pmatrix}$$

Hence, rollback performs the following operation on an arbitrary transaction.

$$\begin{pmatrix} \cos\alpha \\ e^{\theta} e^{i\phi} \sin\alpha \end{pmatrix}$$

where $e^{i\phi}$ is the phase parameter.

A read operation performs rotation to the current state. The rotation action is applied to a state vector by the matrix multiplication. The rotation matrix R is

$$\begin{pmatrix} \cos\theta & -\sin\theta \\ \sin\theta & \cos\theta \end{pmatrix}$$

where θ is a counterclockwise angle in the three-dimensional model.

The rotation does not change the probability of state transition. It keeps the transaction in the same physical state. Hence, the new state of the transaction will remain unchanged. Only the phase of the transaction will change.

A write operation performs translation to the current state. The translation matrix T is a column vector as state vector u. The translation rule is

$$u' = u + T \tag{4.38}$$

where T is the write operator. u' is the transformed state vector.

There are times, such as performance tuning for a specific parameter, when we want to rotate a particular number of degrees around the $x_{throughput}$, $y_{service-time}$, $z_{arrival-rate}$ axis. The following matrices will perform the task:

$$\begin{pmatrix} \cos\frac{\theta}{2} & -i\sin\frac{\theta}{2} \\ -i\sin\frac{\theta}{2} & \cos\frac{\theta}{2} \end{pmatrix}$$

To improve overall transactional performance, a $D = (D_x, D_y, D_z)$ can be a three-dimensional vector of size 1 from the origin. The rotation matrix is given as

$$R_D(\theta) = \cos\frac{\theta}{2}I - i\sin\frac{\theta}{2}(D_xX + D_yY + D_zZ) \tag{4.39}$$

As shown, the unit sphere geometric representation is a good tool to understand a single transaction and its associated operations. For multiple transactions, it is hard to visualize what happens when multiple transactions are manipulated at once. A single phase committed transaction is a spin particle. Two phase commit is two spin particles. And a multiple phase commit is k spin particles. The transaction becomes a full joint combination of k transactions. It has a 2^k dimension.

$$u_1^2 \otimes u_2^2 \cdots \otimes u_k^2 \tag{4.40}$$

4.4.5 Discrete control

The global energy of an isolated system is preserved throughout its evolution. Energy is an observable. Therefore, for a concrete transactional system it is possible to obtain a specific hermitian matrix representing the system. This observable is the hamiltonian of the system. Hence, given a concrete transactional system, the system change lies in the Schrodinger equation.

$$\frac{u(t+\delta t) - u(t)}{\delta t} = -i\frac{2\pi}{\hbar}H|u(t)| \tag{4.41}$$

The equation states that the rate of variation of the throughput state vector $u(t)$ with respect to time at the instant t is equal to $u(t)$ multiplied by the operator $-i * H$. By solving the equation with some initial conditions one is able to determine the evolution of the system over time whenever its hamiltonian is specified. Hence, the eigenvalues of the ensemble should be determined.

Researchers obtain a formula to compute the joint distribution function of the eigenvalues in the transactional ensemble [20]. The formula states the probability for finding eigenvalues $[exp(i\phi_j)]$ of S with an angle ϕ_j in each of the intervals $[\theta_j, \theta_j + d\theta_j]$, $j = 1, \ldots, N$, is given by $Q_{N\beta}[\theta_1, \ldots, \theta_N]d\theta_1 \ldots \theta_N$

$$Q_{N\beta}(\theta_1, \ldots, \theta_N) = C_{N\beta} \prod_{i<j} |e_i^{i\theta} - e_j^{i\theta}| \tag{4.42}$$

where $\beta = 1$ for the orthogonal, $\beta = 2$ for the unitary, and $\beta = 4$ for the symplectic ensemble.

The most obvious consequence of Equation 4.42 is the repulsion of throughput levels. The probability of finding an unusually small separation $\triangle = (\theta_i - \theta_j)$ between two levels tends to zero with $\triangle$ like $\triangle^\beta$.

A series of N eigenvalues taken from a transactional ensemble can carry only a reduced amount of information

$$I(\beta) = I_0 + S(\beta)[N/ln2] \tag{4.43}$$

This loss of information content is a direct measure of the statistical regularity of the eigenvalue series of the transactional ensemble.

4.4.6 Cost inner product

There is a correlation relationship between the concave cost function 4.11 and the cost of erasing information 4.14. Hence, a inner product of the two cost functions represents a general cost function. The gradient of the product is computed as the vector of cost changes. The direction represents increasing or decreasing of the changes.

4.4.7 Throughput convergence

Two observables (read-write operations and abort operations) are measured in this research. Divergence operation of the two observables is computed to evaluate the throughput quantity.

4.4.8 Experiments

To test whether the proposed transaction ensemble and performance method work well, an experiment is proposed. The experiment is the red-black tree test presented in Figure 4.1 of a research [6]. It will evaluate the throughput and abort ratio during a 10-second test cycle.

The test will be executed with 75% put operations and 35% delete operations when tree size is set to 2K. This is a classic contention case designed for performance evaluation. For two distinct TL2 targets, the tests will be separated with parameter GV4 and GV6 on each hardware platform. The tests will evaluate performance effects by increasing contention from 25% to 75% and decreasing contention from 75% to 25%.

The experimental setup for this critique will be made of a pair of disconnected multicore servers. One server will be a single chip 8-core system (SunFire T5120) with 64 virtual processors. Another server will be a four chip 8-core system (SunFire T5240), which has 256 virtual processors. They both utilize the UltraSPARC T2 Plus processors.

In addition to two servers, the resources used will be profiling tools, Oracle Solaris™Studio Performance Analyzer and Solaris Dynamic Tracing (DTrace) utility. All tests will run independently on each server. Results will be collected from test statistical output, analyzer, and DTrace utility.

(1) *Test Procedure:* The test program is executed with the following sequences in a single test cycle:

- Setup key range [0, 63].
- The main program allocates memory. The umem_alloc and umem_cache are created and initialized.
- Solaris p threads are created, then each thread calls pollsys to wait to warm up and prepare for the tests.
- Each thread repeats: three lookups, one insert, one delete. First, a worker thread puts a key/value pair into the tree. Then the put operation does insertion to the tree. Afterward, the delete routine is invoked.
- The put operation is an insertion. It gets a node and starts a transaction: transactional write and store the value. Then it calls TxCommit and ReleaseNode at the end. If it fails, the TxAbort routine is invoked.
- Other operations apply similar transactional routines.
- Aggregate number of successful operations, aborts for the test.
- Measure duration of the test.

The selected performance metrics, analysis upon decomposed transactional operations, read-black tree micro-benchmark, and tests against real application are appropriate because they are established in the STM literature. They are suited for SMT algorithm design criteria and validation.

(2) *Test Results:* In addition to 2 servers, the resources used are profiling tools, Oracle Solaris Studio Performance Analyzer and Oracle Solaris Dtrace utility. All tests were run independently on each server. Results are collected from test statistical output, Performance analyzer, and Dtrace utility. They are presented in the following sections, respectively.

As illustrated in Figure 4.1, performance of TL2 is labeled as 64-libumem on the single chip system. On the four-chip system, the test throughput of TL2 is labeled as 256-libumem. The curves without GV6 flag are the tests ran with GV4 flag for each TL2 test. The tests for TLRW-IOMux and TLRW-ByteLock are labeled with the names of the algorithms.

As can be seen, the results in Figure 4.1 recapitulate the findings represented in the Figure 4.1 of the target research. The performance of TL2 and TLRW-ByteLock are about the same, with similar scalability curve. On both systems, TL2 outperformed TLRW-ByteLock and TLRW-IOmux in terms of throughput Ops during the 10-second test cycle.

That is completely normal and expected. TL2 does not provide implicit or proxy privatization whereas the TLRW forms both do. TLRW-IOMux is just a form used for reference to compare the other transactional algorithms. It uses a relative simple RW lock, with the only concession to scalability being that instead of using a single counter of the number of extant readers we use two counters, one that reader threads atomically increment on ingress and another that readers increment on egress.

TLRW-ByteLock performed as well as TL2-Ref4 under 40 threads. ByteLock was even better between 40 and 48 threads. At most 48 threads use the bytelock at any one time, the remainder use a locking protocol similar to that of TLRW-IOMux. Again, that's in no sense a surprise.

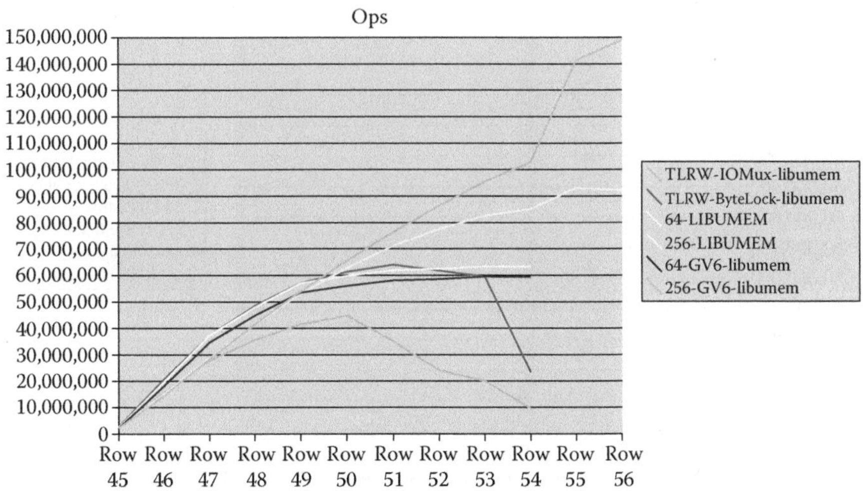

FIGURE 4.1: Throughput of red-black tree with 25% puts and 25% deletes when tree size is 2K.

It seems multiple chip coherence overhead is significant for TL2-Ref4 to run on a four-chip system with lower contention less than 32 threads. That is why the test compared against both the "GV4" and the "GV6" forms in this critique.

As TL2-Ref4 runs with more than 32–40 threads, specifically more than 40 threads, the coherence overhead is less significant than the contention of throughput processing. A four-chip system starts to outperform a single-chip system for TL2-Ref4. The centralized counter in GV4 constitutes a well-known issue for TL2 when we have off-chip coherency latency. In translocational locking read write (TLRW) we also have communication hotspots for writers, particularly for "triangular" data structures such as the red back (RB) tree, where traversal (readers) start at a root node.

Abort is to avoid deadlock. Figure 4.2 shows TL2-GV4 has lower abort rate than TL2-GV6. This is partial because TL2-GV6 admits more false aborts. But TL2-GV4 generates more read-write traffic. TLRW-IOMux has the lowest abort rate. TLRW-ByteLock has similar abort rate to support the property of stronger guarantee of progresses. The higher rates of aborts indicates that HTM support maybe valuable to eliminate unnecessary aborts. The conclusion is that both TL2 and TLRW-ByteLock provide scalable performance for transactional operations. Specifically, TLRW-ByteLock is a good candidate for transactional implementation on single-chip multicore systems.

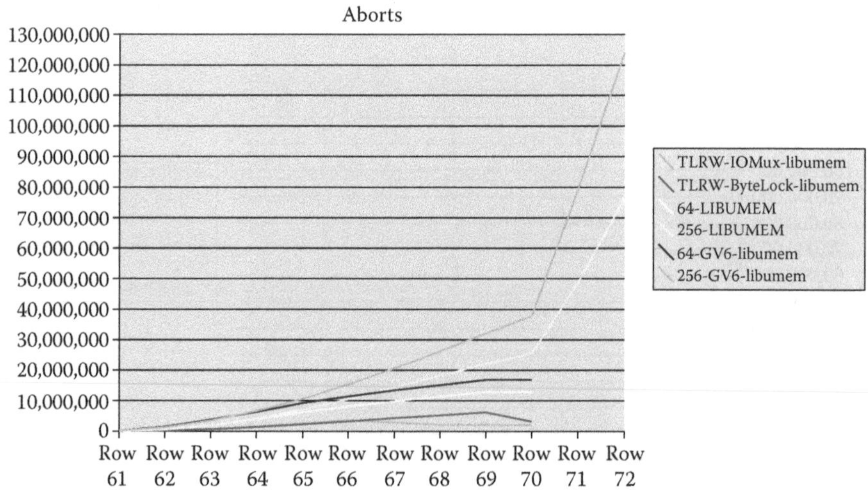

FIGURE 4.2: Aborts of red-black tree with 25% puts and 25% deletes when tree size is 2K.

4.5 Barriers and Issues

To achieve throughput optimization, there are difficulties for contention management.

4.5.1 Errors of simultaneous measurement

The expected value of observing a single throughput observable, such as *Ops/s* or *Abort/s* repeatedly on the same state is a real number. However, a simultaneous observation of the two observables leads to an error due to noncommutativity of the operations. According to Heisenberg's uncertainty principle [29], concurrent measurement of any two observable results in errors that are dependent on energy. The error is computed as

$$Error >= \frac{1}{4}| < \Omega_1, \Omega_2 > |^2 \tag{4.44}$$

where $< \Omega_1, \Omega_2 >$ is the commutator of two simultaneous measurements of two observables.

The evaluation demonstrates that there is a lower bound of measurement error as the noncommutativity exists. For a one-phase commit, the commutativity of each transaction holds. Hence, there is no order for each transaction. However, for a multiple phase commit scheme, transactions may not be commutative. Hence, a transaction group under a multiple phase commit scheme is not albelian.

4.5.2 Conjecture of partition function

There is no general direction calculation of partition function [12].

$$A_N(\beta) = (2\pi)^{-N} \int \cdots \int_0^{2\pi} \prod_{i<j} |e^{i\theta_i} - e^{i\theta_j}|^\beta \times d\theta_1 \cdots d\theta_N \tag{4.45}$$

Only a conjecture leads to a public statement on partitioning.

$$\psi_N(\beta) = \Gamma\left(1 + \frac{1}{2}N\beta\right) \Big/ \left[\Gamma\left(1 + \frac{1}{2\beta}\right)\right]^N \tag{4.46}$$

where β is the constant to represent a type of an ensemble.

The presumption states explicitly the statistical properties of a finite system of N particles. To represent the statistical properties of eigenvalues of complex systems, we are interested in $N \to \infty$.

4.5.3 Error detection of entangled states

For contention management, it is critical to decide whether a transactional state ρ is an entangled or separable state. This is especially true for multiple phase commit schemes. Formally a given state is composed in the convex envelope of product states and it can be decomposed as a tensor product of two vectors. If so, it is a separable state. Otherwise it is entangled. Researchers suggested [30, 31] a number of separability criteria. The most recent report [32] proposed covariance matrix criterion (CMC) for separability. If the relation below holds, it is a separable state, otherwise it is an entangled state.

$$2\sum_{i=1}^{d_A^2} |C_{i,i}| <= [1 - \mathrm{tr}(\rho_A^2)] + [1 - \mathrm{tr}(\rho_B^2)] \tag{4.47}$$

where A and B are two subsystems with dimensions d_A and d_B, respectively. $C_{i,j} =< A_i \otimes B_j > - < A_i >< B_j >$.

If the *Ops/s* and *Aborts/s* can be selected so that C is diagonal, CMC can be calculated from trace $\mathrm{tr}(\rho^2)$. Evaluation of CMC shows detection methods failed even in low dimensional spaces, such as 3×3 and 2×4 systems. Hence, the error detection of state entanglement in multiple phase transactional schemes will reduce the throughput of transactional memory. For entanglement distribution, there is a research report [33] on utilizing classic feedback to support reverse coherent information to improve performance. This could be applied to transactions across multiple cores. The result is based on successful entanglement detection and distribution.

References

[1] Fraser, K. Practical lock freedom. *Technical Report UCAM-CL-TR-579, Cambridge Computer Laboratory*, 2003.

[2] Ennal, R. Software transaction memory should not be obstruction-free. *Technical Report Nr. IRC-TR-06-052, Intel Research Cambridge Tech Report*, 3, 2007.

[3] Luchangco V. Y., M. Moir, and D. Nussbaum, Y. Lev. Anatomy of a scalable software transaction memory. In *Proceedings of the 14th International Conference on Architectural Support for Programming Languages and Operating Systems*, 2009.

[4] Shavit, N and D. Dice. Transactional locking ii. In *Proceedings of the 20th International Symposium on Distributed Computing*, 2006.

[5] Lev Y., V. Luchangco, and F. Ellen. Snzi:scalable nonzero indicators. In *Proceedings of the 26th Annual ACM Symposium on Principles of Distributed Computing*, 3, 2007.

[6] Shavit, N. and D. Dice. Tlrw: Return of the read-write lock. *4th ACM SIGPLAN Workshop on Transactional Computing*, 2009.

[7] Shavit, N. and D. Dice. What really makes transactions faster? *First ACM SIGPLAN Workshop on Languages, Compilers, and Hardware Support for Transactional Computing*, 2009.

[8] Herlihy, M. et al. Software transactional memory for dynamic-sized data structures. In *Proceedings of the 22nd Annual Symposium on Principles of Distributed Computing*, 92–101, 2003.

[9] Scherer, III and M. Scott. Contention management in dynamic software transactional memory. In *PODC Workshop on Concurrency and Synchronization in Java Programs*, 2004.

[10] Scherer, W. and M. L. Scott. Advanced contention management for dynamic software transactional memory. In *Proceedings of the Annual ACM Symposium on Principles of Distributed Computing*, 240–248, 2005.

[11] Scott, M. et al. A comprehensive strategy for contention management in software transactional memory. In *Proceedings of the 14th ACM SIGPLAN Symposium on Principles and Practice of Parallel Programming*, 141–150, 2009.

[12] Herlihy, M., B. Pochon, and R. Guerraoui. Toward a theory of transactional contention managers. In *Proceeding of the 24th ACM Symposium. on Principles of Distributed Computing*, 258–264, 2005.

[13] Attiya, H. Transactional contention management as a nonclairvoyant scheduling problem. In *Proceedings of the 25th Annual ACM SIGACT-SIGOPS Symposium on Principles of Distributed Computing*, 3–9, 2006.

[14] Wiggins, S. *Application to the dynamics of the damped, forced duffing oscillator. 1.2e in introduction to applied nonlinear dynamical systems and chaos.* Springer-Verlag, New York, 5–6, 10, 23, and 153–175, 1990.

[15] E. Ott. *Chaos in Dynamical Systems.* Cambridge University Press, New York, 2002.

[16] Schrdinger, E. An undulatory theory of the mechanics of atoms and molecules. *Physics Review*, 28(6):1049–1070, 1926.

[17] Chrus'cin'ski, D. Geometric aspect of quantum mechanics and quantum entanglement. *Journal of Physics Conference Series*, 39:9–16, 2006.

[18] Wooters, W. K. Statistical distance and hilbert space. *Physics Review, D,* 23:357–362, 1049–1070, 1981.

[19] Levitin, L., Toffoli, T., and Walton, Z. Information and distance in Hilbert space. *Quantum Communication, Computing, and Measurement*, 3(I):19–25, 2002.

[20] Dyson, F. J. Statistical theory of the energy levels of complex systems, i,ii,iii. *Journal of Mathematical Physics*, 3, 1962.

[21] Belavkin, V. P. Quantum filtering and control in example:unstable qubits. *Ninth International Conference on QCMC. AIP Conference Proceedings*, 1110:57–62, 2009.

[22] Landauer, R. Irreversibility and heat generation in the computing process. *IBM Journal of Research Letter*, 67:661, 1961.

[23] Barnett, S. M. and J. A. Vaccaro. The cost of erasing information. *Ninth International Conference on QCMC. AIP Conference Proceedings*, 1110:37–40, 2009.

[24] Zavada, P. Relativistic wave equations with fractional derivatives and pseudodifferential operators. *Journal of Applied Mathematics*, 2(4):163–197, 2002.

[25] Jeffreys, B. and H. Jeffreys. *Methods of Mathematical Physics*, 3rd ed. Cambridge University Press, Cambridge, 289–300, 1993.

[26] Bennett, C.H. Quantum filtering and control in example:unstable qubits. *Logical Reversibility of Computation IBM Journal of Research and Development*, 17:525, 1973.

[27] Amosov, G. G. and A. S. Helevo. Additivity/multiplicativity problems for quantum communication channels. *Fifth International Conference on QCMC. AIP Conference Proceedings*, 3–9, 2001.

[28] Lev, Y., M. Moir, D. Nussbaum, and D. Dice. Early experience with a commercial hardware transactional memory implementation. *Fourteenth International Conference on Architectural Support for Programming Languages and Operating Systems*, 2009.

[29] Sitaram, A. Uncertainty principle, mathematical, In Hazewinkel, M. (Ed.). *Encyclopaedia of Mathematics*. Springer, New York, 2001.

[30] Yu, X. and Liu, N. Entanglement detection by local orthogonal observables. *Physical Review Letters*, 95:1515, 150504, *American Physical Society*, 10/2005.

[31] Zhang, C-J., Zhang, Y-S., Zhang, S., and Guo, G-C. Entanglement detection beyond the cross-norm or realignment criterion. *Physical Review A*, 77, 060301(R), 2008.

[32] Gittsovich, O., P. H., Ghne, and J. Eisert. Covariance matrix criterion for separability. In *Ninth International Conference on QCMC AIP Conference Proceedings*, volume 1110, 63-66, 2009.

[33] García-Patrón, R., Pirandola, S., Lloyd, S., and Shapiro, J. H. Reverse coherent information. *Physical Review Letters*, 102:210501, 2009.

Chapter 5

Parallel Search Optimization for Storage Virtualization

5.1 Introduction

Storage virtualization proposes presentation methods of logical abstraction of classes of storage resources such as disks, blocks, tape systems, file systems, files, and records. It encapsulates the complexity and implementation of hosts, storage arrays, switches, storage area network (SAN)-attached appliances, and networks. Hence, virtualization applied to storage resources conveys the ubiquity of connecting, filing, and storing functions.

Most recent advances in high-throughput computing such as chip multi-threading (CMT), transaction memory management, and parallel file systems are proposing challenges for storage management to expose parallelism. In addition, system biology and information pathway simulation motivate storage virtualization with autonomic and biological personality. Intuitively, data management operations, such as snap-shot, data replication, and backup depend on a search utility to determine initiators and targets for pervasive storage data management.

For storage virtualization strategies in the settings of problem solving and reasoning, pervasive search problem formulation represents many combinatorial optimization problems of approximation with action control. All aspects of the search-task environment represent various classes of applications, such as routing, scheduling, and intrusion-detection pattern matching, in addition to storage management.

Given a directional graph G with distinguished starting state S_{start} and a set of goal states $\overrightarrow{S}_{goal}$, search means following the edges to visit vertices and locating the set of state-action sequences with least-cost or maximized reward to go from S_{start} to any element of $\overrightarrow{S}_{goal}$. A search process is the executable form of a collection of program files designed to solve search problems.

Within the operating system kernel, a virtual address space is created by the fork() system call as a search program is executed on the user land. Virtual addresses are assembled from a series of memory mappings. The search executable instructions reside in text mapping. The initialized variables in the search executables are located in the data mapping. In addition to heap space, the stack is allocated from anonymous memory and is mapped to read/write.

During the execution of programming texts, data-driven procedures take data and perform actions determined by the form of data in the case of a language processing system. Intuitively, the semantics, or the meaning of programming language features, is one of the influential factors of search optimization.

The rest of the chapter is organized as follows. Section 5.2 illustrates the significance of complexity problems and convergence issues in the search community and proposes a formal optimization method from core programming calculus as the research goal. Section 5.3 formulates the search problem and associated properties. Section 5.4 briefly reviews the solution space in search literature. Section 5.5 proposes a set of optimization strategies, including exposing parallelism, data distribution, and aggregation comprehension for stochastic systems. Section 5.6 presents performance evaluation and analysis of the proposed optimization method. Section 5.7 introduces experimental studies and discusses simulation results of the proposed search optimization. Finally, Section 5.8 draws conclusions.

5.2 Significance of Research

The most influential search study is sequential algorithm optimization and proof. Informed searches use problem-specific knowledge to exploit heuristic information [1]. The most commonly used informed search strategies are variants of A^* search [2], best-first search [3], and its variant of greedy best-first search. In addition, local search provides an optimal solution with or without gradient information [4]. Variants of hill-climbing algorithms were proposed for nonlinear-programming numeric methods, such as gradient descent with finite differences and tabu search [5]. Simulated annealing is one of the active optimization research areas. Furthermore, genetic algorithms [6] have evolved for the search optimization. In another thread of studies on state space searches for problem solving, uninformed search strategies are the central topic. Some of the well-known algorithms are breath-first search [7], method of dynamic programming [8], uniform-cost search [9], depth-first search (DFS), depth-limited search, and iterative deepening search. Dynamic programming (DP) formulated optimization guarantees search optimality. However, state enumeration is restricted due to large-state transitions or high-dimensional feature extraction during search computation. In addition to the DP paradigm, search optimization was studied with a theory of gaming for the best-response dynamics in noncooperative task settings.

Search optimizations are proposed with parallel algorithms [10–12]. Variants of parallel techniques were applied to search optimization in these studies, such as parallel genetic algorithm, simulated annealing, tabu search, and greedy random adaptive search procedures. In addition, an application framework [13] was suggested for a large-scaled tree search with application design and implementation. In previous research, parallelism and index structure were proposed for large and high-dimensional state spaces. However, the parallel optimization method attempted to break through from traditional algorithmic optimization stand points of view.

Within theoretical settings, quantum theory has been proposed for bound analysis and design of traditional algorithmic complexity with local search [14–17].

In general, a common issue is that search procedures may be trapped into local optimum instead of global optimum. Most search methods also share the common space complexity and computation complexity with traditional optimization techniques. Moreover, learning-based methods may require supervised training for search optimization. Furthermore, search function approximation may result in issues of error convergence. This is one of the major constraints of existing search methods.

Hence, this research extends the previous work on parallelization and suggests language-based search optimization with a core calculus of programming that abstracts data type, induces syntactic category, reduces variables, and exposes parallelism. It proposes search optimality with complexity reduction and sufficient parallel resources such as multicore processors and shared memory structures.

5.3 Problem Formulation

Pervasive search within a virtual storage task environment is a stochastic process generating random state changes with dynamic optimization in which the goal is to find an optimal action for each state visited during state transitions. Intuitively, an adaptive search is a state-action control optimization problem. Hence, search actions and associated state changes form a stochastic decision process resulting in search-state transitions, which is usually probabilistic. Search is a problem of dynamic computation optimization.

In previous work, a dynamic search process is modeled by a quadruple (S, A, R, T) consisting of

- A finite set of states $S, s \in S$
- A finite set of actions $A, a \in A$
- A reward function $c : S \times A \times S \rightarrow \Re$
- A state transition function: $T : S \times A \rightarrow PD(S)$ that maps current states and actions into a set of probability distribution

It formalizes the dynamic characteristics of the search-task environment but misses programming properties, specifically, language and concurrency attributes.

Theoretical work has been done on parallelism in functional languages [18]. COBWEB is an architecture that was studied in the research. Given a functional program that consists of reducible expressions, all subexpressions can be spawned off as autonomous processes that are reducible in parallel. All arguments $e_1 \ldots e_n$ are required to be computed in parallel. Consequently, the parallel evaluation of a function application is illustrated as

$$f e_1 \ldots e_n \tag{5.1}$$

With core programming calculus, λ calculus [19] is one of the influential factors contributing to search function and application formalization. It takes a functional view of search algorithms. However, λ calculus is a formal language processing system that was designed for the purpose of analyzing computability such as function execution and evaluation. Consequently, sequentiality and serial mode are well established in model theory, which is available in language research. This is the root foundation of inductive search method formalization in well-known programming languages with the limitations of sequential execution and evaluation. Intuitively, λ calculus can formulate sequential programs and it is hard to formalize parallel search optimization with λ calculus and traditional functional programming languages.

Predicate calculus [20] is the foundation of deduction model theory. Unlike natural languages, it uses a formal language interpreted by mathematical structures. Predicate calculus is a system of deduction that extends propositional logic so that quantification over individuals of a given domain is allowed. Similarly, predicate calculus is limited to formalize dynamic searches to expose parallelism.

However, π calculus [21] is a model of computation for parallel systems in literature. π calculus specifies semantics for a high-level parallel or distributed programming language. With π calculus, nonterminal states can be induced as processes, parallel composition of processes, synchronous communication between processes through channels, creation of fresh channels, replication of processes, and nondeterminism. A process is an abstraction data type of an independent thread of controls. A channel is an abstraction data type of the communication links between two processes. Hence, π calculus is a formulation of parallel programs.

Let P denote a set of parallel search processes. Then concurrent search behavior can be formalized with the programming constructs in Figure 5.1. As specified in Figure 5.1, P denotes a search thread context composed of K threads in parallel. Different search threads can be executed concurrently. For communications between threads, any thread can wait to read a value from a channel and transit to the next state upon receiving the value. In addition, a thread can wait to send a value along a channel and transit to the next state when the value has been acknowledged by the counter party. Moreover, a fresh

$$
\begin{aligned}
P ::= \; & x(y).P \\
& |\overline{x} < y > .P \\
& |P|P \\
& |(\mu x)P \\
& |!P \\
& |\emptyset
\end{aligned}
$$

FIGURE 5.1: Core calculus of parallelism.

$$
\begin{aligned}
p &::= \overrightarrow{d}\, e \\
d &::= td \\
& \quad |od \\
fd &::= f[[\overrightarrow{\alpha \textbf{ extends } N}]](\overrightarrow{x : \tau}) : \tau = e \\
td &::= \textbf{trait } T[[\overrightarrow{\alpha \textbf{ extends } N}]] \textbf{ extends } \overrightarrow{\{N\}} \overrightarrow{fd} \textbf{ end} \\
od &::= \textbf{object } O\ [[\overrightarrow{\alpha \textbf{ extends } N}]](\overrightarrow{x : \tau}) \textbf{ extends } \overrightarrow{\{N\}} \overrightarrow{fd} \textbf{ end}
\end{aligned}
$$

FIGURE 5.2: Core calculus of fortress program constructs.

channel can be created within a thread. A thread can be replicated with k copies. There could be a NIL thread to represent a thread that is completed or stopped. Hence, this research defines π calculus as the core calculus to formalize parallelism for search optimization in this research.

With the above formalization of parallel search processes, a search program can be further formulated as a set of syntactic categories by nonterminal p, which is referenced by any sentential form as Figure 5.2.

Figure 5.2 is a Fortress [22] program, which is a type system specified with a list of evaluating expressions e with the descriptions of object denoted by od and trait represented as td. A trait specifies a collection of functions as fd. An expression could be a subexpression of any expression that contains it recursively. One trait can be extended by others. Intuitively, the defined trait is the subtype of the trait extended. An object denoted by od is a value object, a reference object, and a function object. Functions are values that have arrow types. Each function takes one argument,which may be a data type, and returns one result, which may be a data type. Evaluation of an expression yields a result with the modification of a program. Intermediate expressions representing transitional states are generalizations of ordinary Fortress expressions. Within an execution environment, lexical binding is used to denote the variables.

5.3.1 Task environment formulation

In the case of language processing systems, an environment maps the names to values and locations. A Fortress program starts executing with an empty environment. Environments are extended with new mappings by variables, functions, object declarations, and functional calls. All search tasks have the property of representation independence. Search programs are independent of the particular representation used to implement an abstract data type. Intuitively, an environment is a function whose domain is a finite set of variant field names or keys, and whose range is the set of all target nodes who hold the target values. The interfaces define the constructors that build elements of data types; observers extract information from values of the data types. The environment properties are

- A search process that has a discrete set of percepts and actions
- A deterministic search setting where the next state is completely dependent on the current state and the action, which will be taken further
- A discrete event with a set of state transitions and environmental feedback signals
- A set of ordered pairs, which are sets of the form $\{(s_1, v_1), ..., (s_n, v_n)\}$

5.3.2 Goal formulation

(1) *Goal Properties*:

- State: A goal state is specified by s_{goal}, however, the goal state might be unknown or hard to formulate within a dynamic or partial observable task environment. In addition, there are program features associated with the goal state: the steps of thread execution and a set of memory locations accessed by search procedures. Here, normally completed thread executions and converged memory consumption are the goal definition.
- Performance:
  - Unknown objective functions
  - Search program speedup with parallelism
  - Search program parallel slack

(2) *Problem Formulation*: As specified in previous work, problem properties are enumerated as

- States: A set of system properties $\overrightarrow{S}$ reachable from an initial state specified as $s_i = In(s_i)$. For a finite state space, the total count of states,

$count[S] = M$. The state of an executing search program is extracted by two features: thread and memory. A thread is executed by steps. There are four states of a thread: not started, executing, suspended, normally completed, or abruptly completed. A memory consists of a set of locations.

- Initial state: $In(s_{start})$. Search starts from the location with $s_1 = In(s_{goal})$. The initial Fortress run process and top level variable memory allocation also define the initial state.

- Goal state: May or may not be formulated with simple presentation.

- Actions: Commonly formulated as a successor function to generate states with actions. Actions form a set of action-state pairs. Both state-action and value-action mapping are defined in Section 5.4

$$\begin{aligned} AS_i = &\{< Go(s_i, a_i), In(s_i, a_i) >, \ldots, < Go(s_{goal}, a_{goal}), \\ &In(s_{goal}, a_{goal}) >\} \end{aligned}$$

- *Goal Test*(): It may be hard to formulate the goal evaluation equation but may approximate the optimal policy.

- $Go(s_i; a_i)$: Represents the action expending function from state s_i with action a_i.

- Policy: It is a control mechanism. For n state decision process, it is formulated as n tuple, π specifies the action to be selected in the state associated with that element.

- Path: In state space, a set of states S are connected by a set of actions A.

- N = $\{S\}$ denotes the number of elements in the state decision states.

- A: A finite set of action state spaces where Ai is an element of action vector associated with state s_i.

- Search decision value function: Stored in a finite set of vectors.

- Search Cost: Cost function assigning numeric cost to each path as a performance measure specified in Section 5.5 as the negative forms of scalar value computed by reward function.

Consequently, the parallel search problem is formulated as a combinational optimization of data locality, distribution, reduction, and an environmental control.

5.4 Review of Literature

Programming calculus is one of the influential threads on parallelism. λ calculus consists of the essential features of functional computation. In addition, other foundations for functional computation, such as Turing Machines, share the same expressiveness. The limitations of λ calculus result from the constraint that a functional computation is to yield specific results when presented with different input values. However, the significant difference of π calculus is the characteristic to pass channels as data with other channels. Hence, process mobility can be expressed, which in turn causes the changes in process structures to be expressed. Consequently, the process mobility model is meaningful to analysis of how parallel processes communicate with each other across different regions on memory systems.

Exposing parallelism through parallel data structures is another thread of studies on parallelization. The Paralation Model [23] and Connection Machine Lisp [24] ensure data parallelism with high-level control operations on paralleled data structures. The common operations are iteration and reduction. Since this approach defines parallelism solely in terms of a particular data structure, these operational controls are not general solutions to the problem of specifying parallelism in explicitly parallel programs.

Functional programming in turn is known for its minimization of side effects. λ functions or expressions may modify a global or a static variable and modify one of its arguments, and then write data to external routines. λ functions do not produce a side effect since states are not modified but values are returned. Fortress is an imperative programming language that employs side effects to make programs function. Fortress has its own calculus. There are a couple of reasons for this: *OO* languages have formal semantics, but they're invariably unreadable, but the unreadable semantics allow us to do type soundness proofs.

As far as parallel computational model evolves, λ calculus and π calculus are both side-effect-free, and thus strictly less expressive than Fortress. It is hard to model a parallel heap in λ calculus as a sequential language does. The denotational semantics are nearly useless for parallel languages. But if Fortress programs are written with no side effects, two things are hard to predict. One is λ calculus with call-by-value semantics. Another thing is parallel argument evaluation.

Cilk [25] is a general-purpose programming language designed for parallel programming. But Cilk does not offer library-level support for parallel iterations. It requires either compiler support or a higher-order language (or, as in Fortress, both). Cilk adds work stealing to C, along with some memory model support. There are about 15 years of research on Cilk. Fortress supports work stealing in a similar (but not identical) way on top of the Java virtual machine (JVM). Fortress does not look like C code or have sequential erasing semantics as the goals of Cilk. Cilk researchers are thinking about some library-level support for parallel iterations as Fortress has.

With user library support in Fortress, program constructs such as tuple expression, also do blocks, method invocations, and function calls, for loops, compression, sums, generated expressions and big operators, extremum expressions, and test are implicitly parallel. An implicity thread does not need to be scheduled fairly. Parallelization of a program Q is guided by a mapping of the data space of Q to the processors and disks. The data space A is the set of declared arrays of Q. Let A $\in$ Q denote an arbitrary array. $p \in P$ is a processor array.

An array has a unique geometry in which a vector is an array of dimension one, so the vector is considered to hold a set of objects in parallel. One component at each index is denoted as O_i. The value of OA at index i is that of variable O at the index given by the evaluation of expression A at index i. The convention of subscription rule corresponds to a π channel: Evaluating a subscripted variable is the same as fetching the value of this variable on the processor p of set P. Then the distribution of data to processor array is defined as

$$\mu_p^A : I^p \rightarrow \phi(I^p) - \{\emptyset\} \tag{5.2}$$

where $I^A = [l_1 : \mu_1, ..., l_n : \mu_n]$.

At each active index of i, component O_i is updated with a local binding of the value of expression E. The special case of the channel communications is the getter. It is denoted as $X : Y_A$. On the termination of the last action of sequencing of iterations, the execution of the action set of T is initiated. Specifically, the active indices where the test predicate evaluates to $FALSE$ become idle during the execution of vector O. The state is denoted as

$$State = (Env \times Ctx) \cup \{\perp\} \tag{5.3}$$

where $\perp$ denotes the unspecified state. The other elements remain active. At each active index, an environment env is a function from names to vector values

$$[[O : e]](env, c) = (env', c) \tag{5.4}$$

where the new environment $env' = env[O \leftarrow V]$. The initial activity context and the final result are restored on the termination of the O. e is a parallel expression. Then the semantics $[[p]]$ of a program p is a function of a state to a state. For iterations, the action set of O is repeatedly executed with the current extent of parallelism, until the Boolean expression evaluates to $FALSE$ at each currently active index.

Predicates are first order formulated. For every predicate on a vector variables Var

$$env \models V[e/O] \tag{5.5}$$

the predicate test expression denotes the new context

$$[[test]](env, c) = (env', c) \tag{5.6}$$

with $[[A]](env, c \wedge env(B)) = (env', c')$.

The semantics of the sequencing comprehension is a functional composition of

$$[[O : Y]](env, c) = [[Y]]([[A]](env', c)) \tag{5.7}$$

In addition to calculus, data structures, and user library, parallel work scheduling is a significant related work in literature. The Cilk scheduler uses Work-Stealing policy to divide procedure execution efficiently among multiple processors. Fortress inherits this Work-Stealing model to schedule paralleled work items across multiple cores. With multiple processors, each processor maintains a stack on which it places each frame that it has to suspend to handle a procedure call. The suspended states can be removed from either end of a stack. A processor can still remove states only from its own stack from the same end where work is inserted on the stack. However, any processor that has completed its own work or has not been assigned any work will pick another processor randomly. Through the scheduler, the processor attempts to steal work from the other end of its processor stacks. Specifically, the stolen states are the states that the originating processor would execute last. By acquiring those suspended states, the stealing processor starts to execute the work.

A Java^{TM}version of Work-Stealing framework [26] is implemented and maintained as part of $JSR166b$. Originated from divide-and-conquer algorithmic techniques in sequential programming, the Fork-Join algorithms are parallel versions in parallel design and analysis (Figure 5.3). Implementation techniques were proposed to efficiently construct task queues and management

---

FORK-JOIN(problem)

Description: Parallel Fork-Join Algorithm
INPUT: problem state
OUTPUT: solution result to the problem
if(*problem is small*)
    COMPUTE(*problem*)
else
    DECOMPOSE(*problem*)
    for each $sub - task$ **in** *problem* **do**
    FORK − SOLVE($sub - task$)
    JOIN($sub - task$)
    COMPOSE($sub - result$)
return result

FIGURE 5.3: A parallel Fork-Join algorithm.

of queues and worker threads. In the study on Work-Stealing framework, the basic tactics from the Cilk work-stealing scheduler were summarized as

- Every worker thread uses a scheduling queue to keep all runnable tasks.
- Queues are implemented as double-ended queues supporting both last-in-first-out (LIFO) push and pop operations, as well as a first-in-first-out (FIFO) take operation.
- Subtasks decomposed from tasks running within a given worker thread are pushed onto that thread deque.
- Worker threads process their own deques in LIFO order by popping task queues.
- When a worker thread has no local tasks to run, it attempts to steal a task from another randomly chosen worker in a FIFO order.
- When a worker thread encounters a join operation, it processes other tasks until the target task is noticed to have completed (via is Done). Otherwise, all tasks complete execution with nonblocking mode.
- When a worker thread has no task and fails to steal work from other threads, it yields, sleeps, and/or engages priority adjustment. Or it tries again later unless all workers are known to be similarly idle, in which case they all stay in block mode until another task is invoked from the top level.

Fortress joins $JSR166b$ parallelization with enhanced Work-Stealing library. Tasks are Fortress parallelization cores with multiple task queues per thread. The internals of Fortress parallelism design are distributions, generators, and arrays. Fortress has a tiered parallelism approach. On the top, the library allocates locality-aware distributed arrays and implicity parallel constructs such as tuples, comprehension, sum, and loops. Synchronization is accomplished by atomic sections. In addition, there are distributions of libraries which allow locality and data distribution to be specified explicitly. The at expression requests the computation to take place in a particular region of a host. Finally, there are mechanisms to construct new generators via recursive subdivision into tree structures.

Concurrent computation may not be orderly. Different specifications of what can be observed may be varied for different circumstances. Different notations are specified when two concurrent systems have the consistent responses. If one wishes to observe or ignore the degree of parallelism of a system, under some circumstances it may deadlock. The distribution of its π process among processors is resilient to various kinds of failures. Moreover, concurrent systems can be described in terms of many different constructs for creating π processes such as fork/wait, cobegin/coend, futures, and data parallelization. However, exchanging information between shared memory, rendezvous, message-passing, and dataflow manages their use of shared atomic resources such as semaphores, monitors, and transactions. The atomic section specified by the Fortress language resolves the conflicts. Within Fortress program constructs, data and loop iterates are distributed. Shared location update should be performed only with atomic expressions.

5.5 Methodology

The optimization of a search process is to tune an initial computation network with arbitrary parameters architecture. The objective is to obtain the approximate optimal parallelism with a certain input vector for specific search keys. The number of resulting targets depends on the thread group optimization and the data region of hosting machines within the computational graph. Both online and incremental methods can be used to optimize the traditional parallel techniques. The tuning is a data distribution, reduction, and comprehension problem for optimizing computation procedures. Hence, exposing parallelism by data distribution, data reduction and aggregation comprehension is the major characteristic of research methodology of this research. With the formulated data locality and parallel control problem, the following characteristics are critical in this research for search optimization.

- Data Distribution: Mapping each element of an abstract data type into a subset of processor arrays. A specific element can be run on a designated target region of the host. For distribution by local data computation, the data request by a search program should be read/write from the best suited location. Data should be requested from local memory as much as possible.

- Strength Reduction: An inductive function of some systematically changing variable is calculated more efficiently by using previous values of the function and reordering of computing operations.

- Dynamic: Since search optimization is formulated as a stochastic task environment, it has dynamic search properties.

- Parallelization: With sufficient parallel resources, time complexity is further optimized with thread and parallelism.

- Concurrency: Operations are performed simultaneously on shared objects. To synchronize data accesses, data lock expression is applied.

The physics of computation represents the independence of the analytic model of each element within the universe. The analytic model of parallel computing is to derive the instruction execution stream with the above principle. The scheme of the proposed level computing engine exposing parallelism is enumerated as following

- Define the work specification for the entirety of data.
- Specify the computational topology that it is the kernel of thread control context.
- Schedule to apply the work unit for each stream execution.

5.5.1 Data abstraction

An abstract node is an abstract data type that represents a set of quantities within a pervasive graph. The proposed abstract node has values and operational procedures that manipulate the quantities. Data type abstraction divides a data type into interface and implementation. The interface shows what the data represents, what the operations are on the data type, and what properties these operations may be relied on to have. The implementation provides a specific representation of the data and code for the operations that make use of the specific data representation. The implementation is representation independent. The most important part of an implementation is the specification of how the data is represented.

The concise notation of the Backus normal form (BNF) rule definition for a graph data type is shown in Figure 5.4.

The proposed graph search utility has the associated procedures corresponding to the above grammar's nonterminals. The proposed graph utility also defines the following auxiliary procedures:

- Evaluate node procedure.
- Apply node procedure.
- Make initial graph procedure.

The specification of the abstract data type does not indicate how the nodes are to be represented. It requires only these procedures to produce the

```
< graph >::= ()
      node ::= node|(< node >< child >)
< child >::= node| < graph >
< node >::= (< key >< value >)
< key >::=< symbol >
< value >::=< datum >
```

FIGURE 5.4: A concrete syntax tree for graph.

specified behavior.

$$isLeaf = \begin{cases} 0 & \text{if it is not a leaf node} \\ 1 & \text{if It is a leaf node} \end{cases}$$
$$node = \lceil node \rceil \;; successor\ proceeder \tag{5.8}$$

The specification defines the elements of a graph as BNF format. To manipulate values of this data type, we need

- A constructor that allows us to build each kind of graph
- A predicate that tests to see if a value is a representation of a graph
- Some way of determining, for a given graph, whether it is a leaf or an interior node, and of extracting its components

With the above defined aggregate data type, an element is named as a field and selected by field name.

5.5.2 Data parallelism

An algebra is a mathematical structure with a set of values and a set of operations on the values. These operations enjoy algebraic properties such as commutativity, associativity, idempotency, and distributivity. In a typical process algebra, processes are values and parallel composition is defined to be a commutative and associative operation on processes. To model the parallelism of search, the following function is run on a region of a host. A parallel search process returns the target node on the graph with a key:

$$search(node, key)\ return\ node; \tag{5.9}$$

First, we model the search function as a process in p calculus as follows

$$!search(node, key).node < key > \tag{5.10}$$

The π expression specifies a node channel that accepts two inputs: one is the name of the node channel, node, which we will use to return the result of searching from a specific root node, and the other is the argument, search key, which will be located in a target node with its satellite data upon a discrete client call. After the call, the search process will send back the result of the attributes of the target on the node channel. The use of the replication operator !, in the above π expression means that the search process will happily make multiple copies of itself, one for each client interaction.

Similarly, the calling process can be formalized with the following assignment statement, the result of calling search π with a node n gets bound to the node variable k:

$$k := search(n, key) \tag{5.11}$$

Hence, a parallel π process is modeled as follows in p-calculus:

$$(.node)(search < node, key > |node(k)) \tag{5.12}$$

As search is modeled with π processes in parallel, the parallelism can be further numerated as follows:

- Search on the node channel both the channel n for passing back the target node and the key.
- Receive on the node channel the result k.
- The use of the . operator guarantees that a private node channel of communication is set up for each search iteration with the search computation.

By deriving search processes in parallel together we get the final process expression, which expresses search iteration.

$$!search(node, key).node < k > |(.node)(search < node, key > |node(k)) \tag{5.13}$$

Executing a Fortress program consists of evaluating the body expression of the run function, the initial-value expression of all top-level variables, and a singleton object field in parallel. In a Fortress program, the distribution of large data structures is defined in the Fortress standard library. The primitive elements of the formal presentation can be specified by the following disjoint set:

- F, a finite set of function names
- FB, a finite set of function descriptions
- A, a finite set of variable names

A method is formalized as a partial function mapping a single method name with a partial method body

$$a \longmapsto m \tag{5.14}$$

where $a \in N$ and $m \in B$.

The method dictionary $d \in D$ is a total function, which maps the finite set of method names to bodies $d : N \in B^*$, where $d^{-1}(\top) = \emptyset$.

With the trait, $t \in T$, is a formulated as function $t : N \to B^*$. The trait methods are formalized in Figures 5.5 and 5.6.

Fortress recursively traversing algorithms, such as List and Purelist, are proposed for child node expansion. Specifically, a finger tree balances and supports nearly any operation in optimal asymptotic time and space. A finger tree is a functional data structure used to efficiently develop other functional

$selfSends : 2^B \rightarrow 2^N, selfSends(\mu) = \cup_{m \in \mu} selfSends(m)$
$superSends : 2^B \rightarrow 2^N, superSends(\mu) = \cup_{m \in \mu} selfSends(m)$

FIGURE 5.5: Function definition.

$selfSends : \Gamma \rightarrow 2^N, selfSends(t) = \cup_{l \in N} selfSends(l)$
$superSends : \Gamma \rightarrow 2^N, superSends(t) = \cup_{l \in N} selfSends(l)$

FIGURE 5.6: Trait definition.

```
node Generator Parallelism extends Generator[[object]]
generate [[R extends Monoid [[R, ⊕]], opr⊕]]
          while true do
            r : R = Identity[[⊕]]
            r := r ⊕ body(i)
          end
    end
    throw Unreachable Code
end
```

FIGURE 5.7: Generator-parallelism algorithm with fortress.

data structures, such as strings. A finger tree has the amortized constant access time to the fingers, which are usually the leaves. Hence, cons, reversing, and cdr have the time complexity of amortized O(1) . In addition, append and split are computed with O(logn). They can be adapted to be indexed or ordered sequences which are optimal for the problem solver such as Sudoku search presented in the following sections.

Parallelism is expressive with a generator list that binds a series of variables to the values produced by a series of objects with the generator trait. Defined by the Fortress library, generators manage parallelism and the assignment of threads to processors. Recursive subdivision is the technique used for exposing large parallelism proposed by this research. It adjusts easily to varying hardware platform architectures and is dynamically load balanced. The generator-based parallelization algorithm is illustrated in Figure 5.7.

A monoid is a set of values with an associative binary operator that has an identity. It is suggested to perform computation locally to reduce the synchronization in the middle of the loop. Hence, a reduction operation should apply to the variables, which are accumulated in the loop body but not read.

```
Search Block Distribution
        while true do
          if node.isShared then node.copy() else node end
          Blocked(n, n, 1)
        end
   end
   throw Unreachable Code
end
```

FIGURE 5.8: Algorithmic distribution of parallel search block with fortress.

```
label Atoimic Search Block
   while true do
        try
             result = try atomic search − body
             exit Atomic Search Block with result
          catch e
             AtomicFailed()
          end
        end
   end
   throw Unreachable Code
end Atomic Search Block
```

FIGURE 5.9: Algorithmic atomicity of parallel search block with fortress.

If chunk arrays are co-located or search iterations of the search loops exist, data and locality control need to apply. To map threads and arrays to regions, the distribution is designed with the following algorithmic operations. It lays out the node array with the same distribution in the same way in memory. The iteration will be kept to execute with the same distribution. Specifically, the target node population will be blocked into the equal chunks as in Figure 5.8.

With syntactic labeling, parallel search in Fortress program constructs can be associated with the integer labels. The atomic algorithm is illustrated in Figure 5.9. Variables of nodes mutated in the search loop body without reduction must be accessed within an atomic search block.

5.6 Evaluation

In programming literature, probabilistic wp-calculus [27, 28] was proposed as a proof system to evaluate correctness of imperative programming languages. The probabilistic wp-calculus is an extension of wp-calculus [29] to reason about programs containing probabilistic choices. The probabilistic wp-calculus contributes to the following factors in this research.

- The proposed parallel search contains a probability of reaching some results. The method is not deterministic ones to identify if a search achieves some desired outcome.
- Probabilistic wp-calculus provides formal semantics other than natural languages.
- Probabilistic wp-calculus provides a set of predicate rules for search analysis.

The fundamental property of the value function is used throughout entire study of data distribution, reduction, and comprehension for parallelism tuning. This can produce accurate estimation. Moreover, this estimation is represented as a tabular with a set of tuples, which are states or search-action pairs. A wp-calculus rule is defined in Figure 5.10. It represents the assignment rule, sequencing rule, condition rule, and partition rule evaluation of the proposed search optimization on the basis of programming calculus and parallelization techniques.

The observation of parallel search expansion uses a probabilistic assignment. A simple case would be a variable x takes the value of E with probability p and the value F with probability $1 - p$.

Hence, a generalized probabilistic assignment has the form

$$x := E_i@p_i \tag{5.15}$$

where $0 <= i < N$ and $\sum_{i=0}^{N-1} p_i = 1$.

For the parallel search (Figure 5.11) program p and postcondition $post$, $wp(p, post)$ represents the search wp from which p is guaranteed to terminate and result in a state satisfying post. The wp-calculus assignment rule for the parallel search is given by

$$wp(x := E, post) = post[x := E] \tag{5.16}$$

Hence, the wp-calculus rule for a set of sequential search composition is given by

$$wp(p_1; p_2, post) = wp(p_1, wp(p_2, post)) \tag{5.17}$$

$$\begin{aligned} x := {} & E@p \\ & F@(1-p) \end{aligned}$$

FIGURE 5.10: A probabilistic assignment.

Init
do C **times**
    body
end
Result

FIGURE 5.11: A parallel search loop.

Taking probabilistic search assignment into consideration, a simple assignment rule is

$$wp(x := E_i@p_i, 0 <= i < N, post) = \sum_{i=1}^{N-1} p_i \times post[x := E_i] \tag{5.18}$$

For a simple parallel search loop, formalize $wp(Result, S = x_0)$ for state s_0

$$wp(Result, S = x_0) = \sum_{i=1}^{N-1} p_i \times (x_0) \tag{5.19}$$

Formalize $wp(body, p_s)$ for probability of occurrence of s

$$wp(body, p_s) < \frac{1}{N} \tag{5.20}$$

Formalize $wp(Init, p_s)$ for probability of occurrence of s

$$wp(Init, p_s) = \frac{1}{N} \tag{5.21}$$

5.7 Experimental Study

5.7.1 Analysis

Among well-known published search algorithms, the A^* algorithm is selected to experiment a proposed search optimization. A multinode wide search population will be considered for testbed design and implementation.

The A^* search algorithm is formulated with numerous variants. It is a graph search algorithm that finds a path from a specific initial node to a given goal node. It proposes a heuristic estimation of $h(x)$ that ranks each node by an estimate of the optimal route that goes through the node. It visits the nodes in order of the heuristic estimation. Well-known DFS, breadth-first search (BFS), and Dijkstra's algorithm are special cases of A^* algorithm.

For this research, an application A^* algorithm is to solve a logic-based number placement puzzle, Sudoku [30], meaning single number. The objective is to fill a 9×9 grid so that each column, each row, and each of the nine 3×3 regions contains the numbers from $\{1, 2, 3, 4, 5, 6, 7, 8, 9\}$, only one time each (that is, exclusively). The puzzle setter provides a partially completed grid. There are several reasons to select a Sudoku problem to evaluate the proposed search methods in this research.

- Solving Sudoku has become a classical search problem for evaluation since 2005. Among those variants, the 9×9 grid with 3×3 regions is by far the most common test problem.
- The Sudoku has been adopted as one of the instruments that computer researchers use to test a new search algorithm. Hence, the proposed methods for optimal or approximated optimal decisions for solutions can be validated by benchmark results.
- A Sudoku puzzle may not be a real-life problem but a simplification of the problem definition and constraints. Hence, an exact description of the problem is possible, and factors that affect the problem are deterministic. Therefore, with problem abstraction, it is a problem that can be solved efficiently with search optimization.
- There are processors and memory requirements for state-action value function mapping. A sufficiently large-state space with space complexity is required to evaluate proposed search methods. The results can demonstrate the parallelism and reduction performance with core systems.

5.7.2 Testbed setup

A single CMT server is considered to set up a test environment for this research. It is a SunFire™T2000 server with 24×1 Ghz Ultra scalable processor architecture (UltraSPARC) T1™processors, 8 GB RAM, 2×68 GB disks, and 4 Gigabit Ethernet ports. The T2000 servers were optimized with CMT and Ultra-SPARC T1 technology, firmware, and hardware cache design. In contrast to traditional processor design, which focuses on single hardware thread execution, the T1 processor provides instruction level parallelism instead of thread level parallelization. It has multiple physical instruction execution pipelines and several active thread contexts per pipeline. In addition, improved hardware design with masking memory access reduces memory latency for a processor spending most of its time stalled and waiting for memory. There is a 12-way associative unified L2 on chip cache. Double Data Rate 2 memory reduces stall. Furthermore, each board has switch chips to connect to on-board components. Hence, the T2000 server has sufficient processors to demonstrate parallel processing for this research.

Fortress software packages (v.0.1 ALPHA) were deployed on the SunFire™ T2000 server. In addition, Java™2 Software Development Kit 6 Update 4 was installed on the system. During test cycles, execution time was collected from test scripts and central processing unit (CPU) utilization was sampled by a Solaris^{TM}built-in utility tool: cpustat with a 3-second interval. To produce reproducible experiment test results, this research adopts the Sudoku solver reference implementation from the Fortress packages. Discussion and test results on parallelism are presented in following sections.

5.7.3 Discussion on parallelism

- isConsistent() procedure: A forward propagation strategy is implemented; Within the Sudoku solver, parallel loops are utilized. Four loops are nested, all are running in parallel, one for each axis and one for each 3×3 grid. Each loop nest runs over all $9 \times 9 \times 9$ entries in parallel. It exits early if an inconsistency of Sudoku rules is discovered . Hence, $9{\times}9{\times}9{\times}4$-fold parallelism is achieved in theory. This indicates too much parallel slack. In practice this code runs until we test that $best.isComplete()$ is true. The four SUM operations are added together; each runs in parallel with the others.

```
while props < 81 AND keepTrying do
    options : ZZ32 := 0
    keepTrying :=
        (BIG OR [i<-0#9, j<-0#9] do
            k' : ZZ32 := -1
            s = SUM [k<-0#9]
                if state[i,j,k].working() then k' := k; 1
                else state[i,j,k].candNum() end
                atomic if s > options then
                        options := s
                        iMax := i
                        jMax := j
                    end
                chk(s,k',i,j,k')
            end) OR
            (BIG OR [i<-0#9, k<-0#9] do
                j' : ZZ32 := -1
                s = SUM [j<-0#9]
                    if state[i,j,k].working() then j' := j; 1
                    else state[i,j,k].candNum() end
                chk(s,j',i,j',k)
        end) OR
        (BIG OR [j<-0#9, k<-0#9] do
            i' : ZZ32 := -1
            s = SUM [i<-0#9]
                if state[i,j,k].working() then i' := i; 1
                else state[i,j,k].candNum() end
```

```
            chk(s,i',i',j,k)
        end) OR
        (BIG OR [i0<-0#3, j0<-0#3, k<-0#9] do
            i' : ZZ32 := -1
            j' : ZZ32 := -1
            s = SUM [i<-(3 i0)#3, j<-(3 j0)#3]
                if state[i,j,k].working() then i':=i;
                    j':=j; 1
                else state[i,j,k].candNum() end
            chk(s,i',i',j',k)
        end)
            updated := updated OR keepTrying
end
```

With the atomic expression, interactions of parallel executions are controlled to store the MAX number of candidates. Variables mutated in the loop body without reduction must be accessed within an atomic block. An atomic expression is executed in the manner that all other SUM threads observe either that the computation of MAX has completed, or that it has not yet started. No other thread observes an atomic MAX computation only partially completed.

- *children*() function: The parallelism provided by a particular generator is specified by its definitions for the methods of the Generator trait. In general, the Fortress library code for a generator dictates the parallel structure of computations involving that generator. It invokes $Array3.indexValuePairs()$, and ArrayList.filter. It results in a parallel task for each point in the $9 \times 9 \times 9$ grid. Of these, only those points whose value is "Perhaps" are nontrivial; the search attempts a move in each of those, which involves a grid copy which is fully parallel and presently gratuitously slow. In addition, it has invalidation of entries along the three axes and in the 3×3 grid. For n "Maybe" entries search gets $n \times (9 \times 9 \times 9)$-fold parallelism.

```
getter children(): Generator[\Sudoku\] =
    if isConsistent() then
        incons : Sudoku = Sudoku(0,props+1,state)
        <| if state[iMax,jMax,k].working() then
            child = self.copy()
            child.fillState(iMax,jMax,k)
            child
    else
            incons
    end
            | k <- 0#9 |>.filter(fn (s) => s.cands >= 81)
```

```
    else
        emptyList[\Sudoku\]()
end
```

- Search constructs the new portions of the priority queue in parallel, and merges them in parallel. But that gives only this search $O(n) - fold$ parallelism. The heap merge operations should be $O(1)$. The total parallel work is $O(n)$. The critical path of the merge is $O(lgn)$ because we're combining heaps in pairs.

```
aStar[\T extends SearchInstance[\T,C\],C\](root: T):
        Maybe[\T\] =
    label succeed
        q : Pairing[\C,T\] := singletonPairing[\C,T\]
                (aStarPair[\T,C\](root))
        while NOT q.isEmpty() do
            (c,best,q') = q.extractMin()
            if best.isComplete() then
                exit succeed with Just(best)
            end
            q := q'.merge(heap(best.children().map[\(C,T)\]
                (aStarPair[\T,C\])))
        end
        Nothing[\T\]() (** Search Failed. **)
end succeed
```

The major sequential bottleneck is $q : extractMin()$, which is $O(lgn)$ for an n-entry queue. But I believe that the lgn is a work bound, and the merge in parallel proceeds, so the actual serial time is $O(lglgn)$. In any case, it's not a problem in practice, mostly because everything else is so slow right now. More time may be spent on setting up and tearing down the other parallel works than the time complexity of $extractMin()$.

- To be nonsequential, entries need to be extracted rather than the minimum value from the heap. But note that we can parallelize this function retrieving and tweak the search strategy independently of the problem we're trying to solve,which is the goal of writing a generic search function.

- The code from Heap to show merge parallelism provides lgn reduction for the sequential looping. Pairing heaps are used. Splay heaps are not implemented yet. For pairing heaps it's actually $O(1)$ merge, and $O(n)$ worst-case, but $O(lgn)$ amortized extractMin. My test code actually cross-checks these bounds and seems to be accurate in practice. The worst case is actually proportional to the number of deferred merge operations performed directly with the minimum node of the heap.

Here's the extractMin for NodeP:

```
extractMin(): (K,V,Pairing[\K,V\]) = (k,v,kids.emk(empty()))
emk(e: EmptyP[\K,V\]): Pairing[\K,V\] = sibs.ems(e,self)
ems(e: EmptyP[\K,V\], leftSib: NodeP[\K,V\]): NodeP[\K,V\] =
    merge(e,leftSib).merge(e,sibs.emk(e))
```

- Here emk merges a node with its siblings, with ems acting as a helper function. We can compare this to pattern matching in a functional language, where we might write (this is actual Haskell code for the same data structure):

```
data Sib a = R a !(BTree a)
data BTree a = L | N a !(BTree a) !(BTree a)
    extractMin (P t) = return (mergePairs t)
    mergePairs (R r0 c0) = (r0, mp0 c0)
        where mp0 L = EP
              mp0 n = P (mps n)
mps :: (Ord a) => BTree a -> Sib a
mps (N r1 (N r2 s c2) c1) =
    jmp (joinT (R r1 c1) (R r2 c2)) s
mps (N r L c) = R r c
mps L = error "mps L should not happen"
jmp :: (Ord a) => Sib a -> BTree a -> Sib a
jmp n L = n
jmp n s = joinT n (mps s)
```

The helper function ems in the Fortress version essentially does the nested pattern match that it is seen in the first clause of mps in the Haskell code.

5.7.4 Initial states

There are six 9×9 matrix test seniors as initial states:

Initial State 1

$$\begin{bmatrix} 0&0&0&0&0&0&0&1&2\\ 0&0&8&0&3&0&0&0&0\\ 0&0&0&0&0&0&0&4&0\\ 1&2&0&5&0&0&0&0&0\\ 0&0&0&0&0&4&7&0&0\\ 0&6&0&0&0&0&0&0&0\\ 5&0&7&0&0&0&3&0&0\\ 0&0&0&6&2&0&0&0&0\\ 0&0&0&1&0&0&0&0&0 \end{bmatrix}$$

Initial State 2

$$\begin{bmatrix} 0 & 0 & 0 & 0 & 0 & 0 & 0 & 1 & 2 \\ 0 & 0 & 5 & 0 & 4 & 0 & 0 & 0 & 0 \\ 0 & 0 & 0 & 0 & 0 & 0 & 0 & 3 & 0 \\ 7 & 0 & 0 & 6 & 0 & 0 & 4 & 0 & 0 \\ 0 & 0 & 1 & 0 & 0 & 0 & 0 & 0 & 0 \\ 0 & 0 & 0 & 0 & 8 & 0 & 0 & 0 & 0 \\ 9 & 2 & 0 & 0 & 0 & 0 & 8 & 0 & 0 \\ 0 & 0 & 0 & 5 & 1 & 0 & 7 & 0 & 0 \\ 0 & 0 & 0 & 1 & 0 & 3 & 0 & 0 & 0 \end{bmatrix}$$

Initial State 3

$$\begin{bmatrix} 0 & 0 & 0 & 0 & 0 & 0 & 0 & 1 & 2 \\ 3 & 0 & 0 & 0 & 0 & 0 & 0 & 6 & 0 \\ 0 & 0 & 0 & 0 & 4 & 0 & 0 & 0 & 0 \\ 9 & 0 & 0 & 0 & 0 & 0 & 5 & 0 & 0 \\ 0 & 0 & 0 & 0 & 0 & 1 & 0 & 7 & 0 \\ 0 & 2 & 0 & 0 & 0 & 0 & 0 & 0 & 0 \\ 0 & 0 & 0 & 3 & 5 & 0 & 4 & 0 & 0 \\ 0 & 0 & 1 & 4 & 0 & 0 & 8 & 0 & 0 \\ 0 & 6 & 0 & 0 & 0 & 0 & 0 & 0 & 0 \end{bmatrix}$$

Initial State 4

$$\begin{bmatrix} 0 & 0 & 0 & 0 & 0 & 0 & 0 & 1 & 2 \\ 4 & 0 & 0 & 0 & 9 & 0 & 0 & 0 & 0 \\ 0 & 0 & 0 & 0 & 0 & 0 & 0 & 5 & 0 \\ 0 & 7 & 0 & 2 & 0 & 0 & 0 & 0 & 0 \\ 6 & 0 & 0 & 0 & 0 & 0 & 4 & 0 & 0 \\ 0 & 0 & 0 & 1 & 0 & 8 & 0 & 0 & 0 \\ 0 & 1 & 8 & 0 & 0 & 0 & 0 & 0 & 0 \\ 0 & 0 & 0 & 0 & 3 & 0 & 7 & 0 & 0 \\ 5 & 0 & 2 & 0 & 0 & 0 & 0 & 0 & 0 \end{bmatrix}$$

Initial State 5

$$\begin{bmatrix} 0 & 0 & 0 & 0 & 0 & 0 & 0 & 1 & 2 \\ 5 & 0 & 0 & 0 & 0 & 8 & 0 & 0 & 0 \\ 0 & 0 & 0 & 7 & 0 & 0 & 0 & 0 & 0 \\ 6 & 0 & 0 & 1 & 2 & 0 & 0 & 0 & 0 \\ 7 & 0 & 0 & 0 & 0 & 0 & 4 & 5 & 0 \\ 0 & 0 & 0 & 0 & 3 & 0 & 0 & 0 & 0 \\ 0 & 3 & 0 & 0 & 0 & 0 & 8 & 0 & 0 \\ 0 & 0 & 0 & 5 & 0 & 0 & 7 & 0 & 0 \\ 0 & 2 & 0 & 0 & 0 & 0 & 0 & 0 & 0 \end{bmatrix}$$

Initial State 6

$$\begin{bmatrix} 1 & 2 & 3 & 4 & 5 & 6 & 7 & 8 & 9 \\ 0 & 0 & 0 & 0 & 0 & 0 & 7 & 8 & 9 \\ 0 & 0 & 0 & 0 & 0 & 0 & 0 & 0 & 2 \\ 0 & 0 & 0 & 0 & 0 & 0 & 0 & 0 & 5 \\ 0 & 0 & 0 & 0 & 0 & 0 & 0 & 0 & 8 \\ 0 & 0 & 0 & 0 & 0 & 0 & 0 & 0 & 3 \\ 0 & 0 & 0 & 0 & 0 & 8 & 9 & 7 & 6 \\ 0 & 0 & 0 & 0 & 0 & 3 & 2 & 1 & 9 \\ 0 & 0 & 0 & 0 & 0 & 0 & 6 & 5 & 4 \end{bmatrix}$$

5.7.5 Goal states

There may be one optimal goal state for each test case. However, for illustration, only the goal state 1 associated with the initial state 1 is presented in a 9×9 matrix below. The attached data file includes detailed results for other initial states.

Goal State 1

$$\begin{bmatrix} 3 & 4 & 6 & 7 & 9 & 5 & 8 & 1 & 2 \\ 2 & 5 & 8 & 4 & 3 & 1 & 6 & 9 & 7 \\ 9 & 7 & 1 & 8 & 6 & 2 & 5 & 4 & 3 \\ 1 & 2 & 9 & 5 & 7 & 6 & 4 & 3 & 8 \\ 8 & 3 & 5 & 2 & 1 & 4 & 7 & 6 & 9 \\ 7 & 6 & 4 & 3 & 8 & 9 & 2 & 5 & 1 \\ 5 & 1 & 7 & 9 & 4 & 8 & 3 & 2 & 6 \\ 4 & 9 & 3 & 6 & 2 & 7 & 1 & 8 & 5 \\ 6 & 8 & 2 & 1 & 5 & 3 & 9 & 7 & 4 \end{bmatrix}$$

5.7.6 Data samples

To conduct data analysis, wall time (nanoTime) of A search to expand child nodes from a root to reach a goal state was collected during each test cycle. Wall time is used to calculate speed up and efficiency in later sections. In addition, CPU statistics at three second intervals were monitored and gathered to verify parallelism through CPU utilization.

5.7.7 Performance metrics

The performance speedup and parallel stack are two major measurement of the search optimization. There's currently no easy way to do this, because there is no way to measure critical path length. To measure critical path, it is required to instrument the FJTask library.

$$Parallel\ Slack = \frac{t_{infinity}}{t_1} \tag{5.22}$$

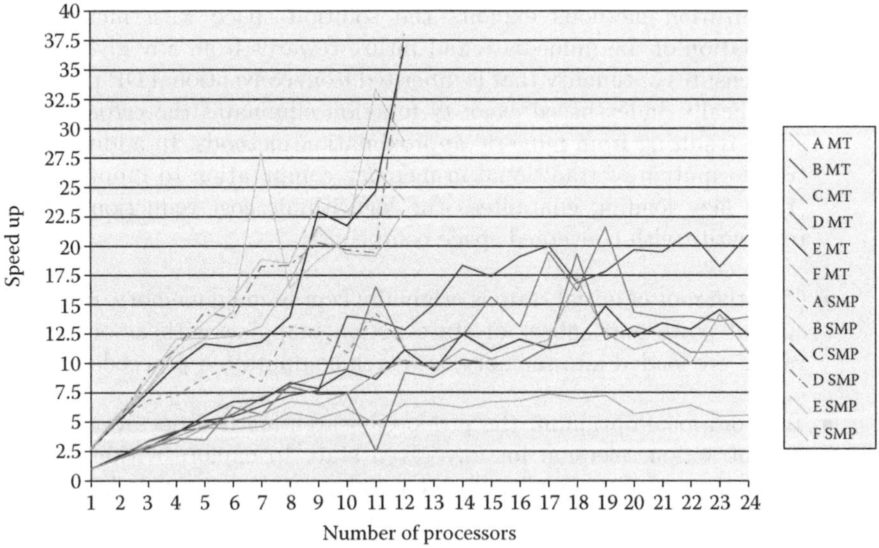

FIGURE 5.12: A simulation scenario with parallelization speedup.

where $t_{infinity}$ = critical path length = ideal time on infinite number of processors and t_1 = total work done = ideal time of sequential execution.

But it's possible to compute either speedup or efficiency. The data processing results are enclosed in a spreadsheet and graph. Basically speedup is computed against $1 - thread$ Niagara. Higher is better.

$$Efficiency = \frac{p}{speedup} \tag{5.23}$$

The results are illustrated in Figure 5.12. As the results show, the above experiment achieved from 2.5× to 20× speedup on 24 core processors for six initial states through exposing parallelism. CPU processing power was fully utilized from 70% to 90%. In addition, the results show 2.5× to 37.5× speedup on symmetric multiprocessing (SMP) (12 way) processors. Furthermore, the SMP system holds about 70% CPU utilization, which indicates more workload can be shipped to different processors. Hence, both efficiency and correctness of the proposed parallel search optimization are proved from the experiment results on CMT and SMP processors.

5.8 Discussion

General findings from this chapter are itemized below:

- The above search computation illustrates that the proposed Q learning-based search algorithm rooted from reinforcement learning (RL) optimization methods exploits the solution space with incremental calculation of the immediate and future rewards from any given state. This ensures optimality that is inherited from conventional DP methods. Specifically, index-based exact Q function eliminates the error convergence resulting from numeric approximation methods. In addition, the transformation of traditional in-memory computation to input/output (I/O) lazy loading guarantees the logarithmic cost reduction of disk read/write with converged space complexity.

- Only the root of initial state is originally kept in main memory. However, current state and subset of state action mapping with associated Q values are loaded into memory as search computation proceeds.

- To avoid local optimum, the proposed search method does randomization of action selection for any given state to explore within a large solution space. Specifically, state enumeration does not terminate until the threshold of search iterations is exceeded.

- Simulation plays a critical role in the proposed search optimization. To obtain the entire solution space, the proposed search method is optimized by simulation. As shown, simulation does not enumerate the state space for Q function mapping but for search optimization to obtain optimal action policy and expected state transition costs. This is different from traditional simulation experiments.

- Stochastic exploration tends to result in a BFS tree if the maximum iteration is sufficiently large and simulation does a possible long run. This indicates the optimality of the proposed search methods. However, performance degradation within a limited episode is reduced by randomization instead of expansion of BFS nodes. In addition, for any known goal state, a monotonically converged Q value indicates the approximation to the goal state. Intuitively, unless the goal state is unknown, the simulation is normally halted at the goal states.

- For unknown goal state search, optimality is obtained by possible long run of the entire state space. However, this generates an index-based BFS tree which is located on the secondary storage to reduce space complexity. A Q function does index I/O based lazy loading.

- Within a routine of local path discovery, the proposed search methods show the depth-first search (DFS) similar logic to expand the single path of state transition. The upper bound of iterations could be the maximum threshold of iterations or terminated at a local goal state if the goal state is known. However, to avoid trapping into the local optimum, randomization is required to conduct further state via simulation as BFS type of enumeration to ensure the global optimality.

- Q factor provides an indication of optimal path search as heuristics based search does. This could reduce search time complexity. However, to avoid trapping into local optimum, randomization is required to conduction further state via simulation as BFS type of enumeration to ensure the global optimality.

- A genetic algorithm could be applied to the proposed search optimization. However, a genetic algorithm is an evolutional approximation to the traditional memory bound problem for large-state spaces and solution spaces. The proposed search optimization is an incremental learning search. In addition, it does online learning that is different from genetic algorithms. Traditional genetic algorithms depend on clearly defined objective functions with supervised training. This is prohibitive in dynamic search optimization problems.

- Unlike conventional local search methods such as tabu search, gradient descent, hill climbing, and simulated annealing techniques, the proposed search optimization enhances conventional dynamic programming techniques for optimality. With Q function exact mapping, the proposed search optimization resolves error convergence problem resulting from traditional function approximation problem.

- Data parallelization is critical for system parallelism and pipelined processors. Time complexity is reduced by the speedup derived from parallelized search computation and simulations. In addition, each randomized initial state is searched with indexed value function mapping without the risk of data hazard.

- The proposed index data structure is a simple lookup pointer structure to locate the target states on the secondary storage devices. At any time, only a single root node, which owns the pointers to the disk based states, loads an initial state to begin the search. Afterward the pointers of search-state transition for action space A logically construct the search tree with state simulation.

5.8.1 Conclusion

This derives the conclusion that the proposed dynamic search with adaptive index structure provides a parallelized formal framework with data parallelization to reduce time complexity and resolve the memory bound and convergence problems existing in AI search community.

References

[1] Bagchi, A. and A. Mathanti. Search algorithms under different kinds of heuristics-a competitive study. *Journal of ACM*, 30(1):1–21, 1983.

[2] Hart, P. E., N. J. Nilsson, and B. Raphael. A formal basis for the heuristic determination of minimum cost paths. *IEEE Transactions on Systems Science and Cybernetics*, 4(2):100–107, 1983.

[3] Pearl, J. *Heuristics: Intelligent Search Strategies for Computer Problem Solving.* Addison-Wesley, Reading, MA, 1983.

[4] Brent, R. P. *Algorithms for Minimization Without Derivatives.* Prentice-Hall, Upper Saddle River, NJ, 1973.

[5] Glover, F. Tabu search 1. *ORSA Journal on Computing*, 1(3):190–206, 1989.

[6] Goldberg, D. E. *Genetic Algorithms in Search, Optimization and Machine Learning.* Kluwer Academic Publishers, Boston, MA, 1989.

[7] Moore, E. F. The shortest path through a maze. In *Proceedings of an International Symposium on the Theory of Switching, Part II*, 285–292, Aug. 1959.

[8] Bellman, R. and S. E. Dreyfus. *Applied Dynamic Programming.* Princeton University Press, Princeton, NJ, 1962.

[9] Dijkstra, E. W. A note on two problems in connexion with graphs. *Numerishe Mathematik*, 1:269–271, 1959.

[10] Grama, A. and V. Kumar. State of the art in parallel search techniques for discrete optimization problems. *IEEE Transactions on Knowledge and Data Engineering*, 11(1):28–35, 1999.

[11] Clausen, J. *Parallel Search-based Methods in Optimization.* Springer Berlin/Heidelberg, 1999.

[12] Mavridou, T. et al. Parallel search for combinatorial optimization: Genetic algorithms, simulated annealing, tabu search and grsp*. In *Workshop on Parallel Algorithms for Irregularly Structured Problems*, 1995.

[13] Clausen, J. Alps: *A Framework for Implementing Parallel Tree Search Algorithms.* Springer Berlin/Heidelberg, 2005.

[14] Grover, L. Quantum mechanics helps in searching for a needle in a haystack. In *Harvard Computer Science Technical Reports for 1988*, 1997.

[15] Ambainis, A. Quantum lower bounds by quantum arguments. In *Proceedings of the 32nd Annual ACM Symposium on Theory of Computing*, 636–643, 2000.

[16] Zhang, S. New upper and lower bounds for randomized and quantum local search. In *Proceedings of the 38th Annual ACM Symposium on Theory of Computing*, 634–643, 2006.

[17] Aaronson, S. Lower bounds for local search by quantum arguments. In *Proceedings of the 36th Annunal ACM Symposium on Theory of Computing*, 403–413, 2004.

[18] Treleaven, P. C. et al. Towards a parallel architecture for functional language. In *Future Parallel Computers, Series Lecture Notes in Computer Science*, 272, Springer Berlin/Heidelberg, 270–285, 1987.

[19] Kleene, S. A theory of positive integers in formal logic. *American Journal of Mathematics*, 57(1):153–173, 1935.

[20] Shapiro, S. Classical logic. *Stanford Encyclopedia of Philosophy*, 2007, http://plato.stanford.edu/entries/logic-classical/

[21] Milner, R. *Communicating and Mobile Systems: The Pi-calculus.* Cambridge University Press, New York, 1999.

[22] Allen, E. et al. *The Fortress Language Specification 1.0 Beta.* Sun Microsystems, Inc., 2007.

[23] Sabot, G. W. An architecture-independent model for parallel programming. *Harvard Computer Science Technical Reports*, 1988.

[24] Hillis, D. New computer architectures and their relationship to physics or why CS is no good. *International Journal Theoretical Physics*, 21(3/4):255–262, 1982.

[25] Agrawal, K. et al. Nested parallelism in transactional memory. In *Proceedings of the 13th ACM SIGPLAN Symposium on Principles and Practice of Parallel Programming*, 2008.

[26] Lea, D. A java fork/join framework. In *Proceedings of the ACM 2000 Conference on Java Grande*, 36–41, 2000.

[27] Morgan, C. Proof rules for probabilistic loops. In *BCS-FACS Refinement Workshop*, Springer Berlin/Heidelberg, 1996.

[28] Morgan, C. et al. Probabilistic predicate transformers. *ACM Transactions on Programming Language and System*, 18(3):325–353, 1996.

[29] Dijkstra, E. *A Discipline of Programming.* Prentice-Hall, Prentice, NJ, 1976.

[30] Brian, H. Unwed numbers. *American Scientist*, 94:12, 2006.

Chapter 6

Finite Automata for Evaluating Testbed Resource Contention

6.1 Introduction

6.1.1 Background

Next-generation Internet and wireless telecommunication networks suggest the setting of a pervasive computing graph abstracted with a set of large-scale distributed systems, small and resource constrained devices, and communication edges or links. Nodes share the same physical media. The data-link layer manages link resources and coordinates medium access among peers. The network layer maintains communication paths. Mobility and the degree of adaptation may vary from application awareness to agnostic.

The properties of the graph hold a partially observable and stochastic task environment due to incomplete environmental data collection, input, and uncertainty of future states. In addition, the environment is a dynamic and sequential task since a current load can influence test performance and consequently have impact on future testbed sizing and capacity planning. Moreover, divergent vendor specific architectures and implementations pose a challenge to a finite experimental environment in performance instrumentation. An infrastructure for the above fixture is referred to as a testbed.

Testbed strategy can be a combination of full-scale tests, simulation, and emulation. Exploratory actions with a real-test environment such as production probing and tracing are limited by the period of execution and overhead of management traffic. In addition, implementation may involve system level programming and deployment of a large-scale testbed. However, scientific methods such as simulation models [1] require low-level implementation and development of programs and validation against a probabilistic distribution of job or task workloads. Emulation [2] provides a middle ground between the above simulation and full-scale experimental capabilities with reproducible results.

The problem of architectural issues in developing a scalable Internet and wireless testbed is synchronizing access to shared computational resources such as vertices, edges, and links, using locking primitives and techniques. A lock is a single byte location in RAM. It has two mutually exclusive states: free (0×00) or acquired ($0 \times FF$). Implementing a locking scheme that does only one or the other can severely affect scalability and performance. The numbers and types of locks need to be deterministic and comply with the lock hierarchy and rules of acquiring locks toward resource usage and data manipulation. Hence, contention, the time spent to access resources, is important to estimate total response time.

6.2 Problem Analysis

A next-generation testbed is different from the conventional classes of a concurrent environmental model in terms of uncertainty and independence with dynamics of processors, topologies, input, and locality. Within the preceding environmental setting, a set of computing resources was located at nodes within a network graph, $G = (V, E)$. A vertex is a virtual environment identified within the directed graph, which is a book keeping data structure. An edge is an attack path or link to another vertex. The edge between a pair of vertices v and u will be u, v, where $u, v \in V$. A testbed is denoted to represent a finite set of processes for targeted resources.

Finite automaton [3] is a useful model for many important kinds of hardware and software to verify systems that have a finite number of distinct states. A next-generation testbed is composed of many systems or components and viewed as being at all times in one of a finite number of states. It is further formulated as a finite automaton with a set of execution states of test plans with state transactions in response to input Σ originated from external actions such as load generation and administrative commands. Self-organization and resource allocation are considered as internal actions, which may affect state changes. The final states of testbed automaton are denoted as a set F.

(1) *Problem Formulation*: A testbed automata (shown in Figure 6.1) is defined as

$$A_{testbed} = \left(Q, \sum, \delta, q_0, F\right) \tag{6.1}$$

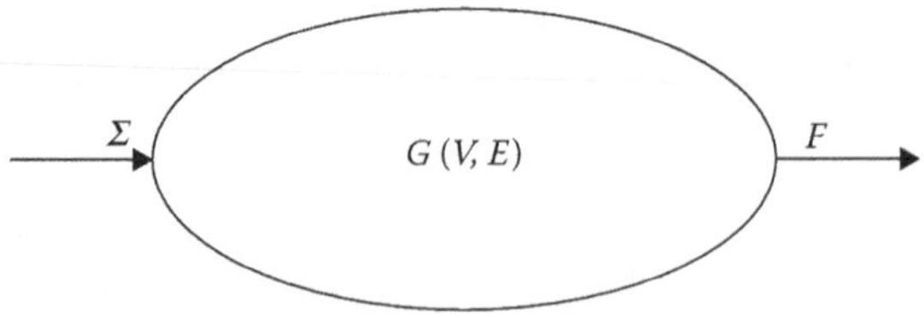

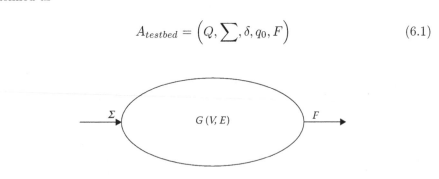

FIGURE 6.1: Testbed automaton.

States: Each state represents a situation that a testbed could be in. The state abstracts the specific important events, which have taken place as a sequence of actions. In addition, the state records the relevant portion of the testbed history. Since testbed automata have only a finite number of states and the pervasive state history generally cannot be stored, the next-generation testbed must be designed carefully to remember what is important and neglect the unimportant. Moreover, the major advantage of adopting a finite number of states is to implement a testbed with a finite set of automata elements and computational resources. The state container is specified as a structure with the following properties:

- The set of vertices existing in $A_{testbed}$
- The set of channels (edges and links) existing in $A_{testbed}$
- The set of lock automata existing in $A_{testbed}$

Initial State: For simplicity, a testbed is constructed with physical vertices, edges, and links but without an initial contention property. In each state management of testbed automata, both the external state and internal controls organize the computational resources before the execution of next automata input.

$$vertices[A_{testbed}] \leftarrow N \tag{6.2}$$

$$channles[A_{testbed}] \leftarrow N \tag{6.3}$$

Transition Function $\delta(q, a)$: As state transition illustrated in Figure 6.2, transaction functions are internal controls to allocate testbed computation resources.

However, even for a self-organized testbed, external interactive administration controls could be automata input to justify the state manipulation.

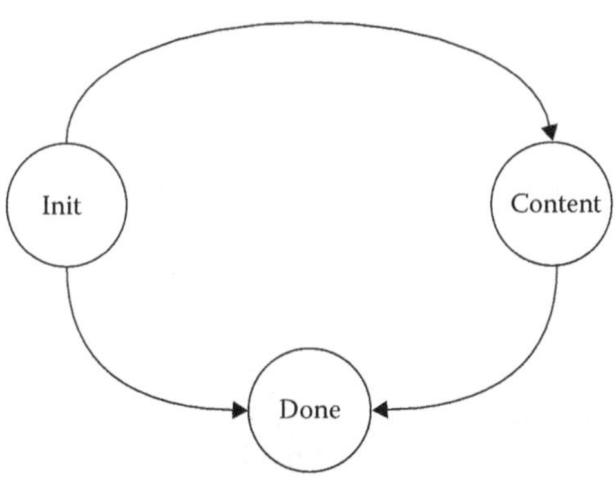

FIGURE 6.2: Testbed automaton state transition.

Input Σ: Testbed automata input could be quantified as deployment of a test matrix, simulation packages, and emulation software artifacts.

Output F and Goal Test: The success of state transitions is measured upon the fairness of execution of test plans, contention reduction, and responsiveness of test results.

Cost: If the bound of test duration is the step time $O(t_i)$ then the time measurement of testbed automata complexity is the discrete summation of $\Sigma_{0<k<n}\, a_k$ as the time assigned to a specific input Σ.

This process is one of the most fundamental abstractions provided by testbed automaton. It is an instance of a program running on each vertex. Since each process is an executable form of file associated with exclusive resource utilization within the testbed, resources required by processes are abstracted for execution time on processors and allocation of physical memory, as well as to perform authorized services, such as network and disk input/output (I/O). Specifically, within the same instance of an operating system, a process state can be maintained in kernel address space for the occupied pages of physical memory, which hold specific memory segments with computational components such as instructions, stack space, data space, and other necessities for execution. Therefore, a concrete formulation of testbed automaton is a summation of finite process automaton as $\Sigma_{n\geq k\geq 1,t>0}\, a_{k,t}$.

Hence, a contention automata is defined as

$$A = \left(Q, \sum, \delta, q_0, F\right) \tag{6.4}$$

States Q: Each contention state represents a situation in which locks could exist. Similarly, the state indicates that specific contention events have taken place. The contention state is designed to record every critical portion of contention history. Since there is only a finite number of contention states, the entire contention histogram is generally not necessary, so the contention automata must store what is important and must neglect what is not. The major advantage of adopting a finite number of states is that we can implement the system with a finite set of resources. The properties of a contention state are defined as

- The number of lock contentions that exist
- The duration of sleep time for blocking contentions
- The number of spin counts for nonblocking contentions

Initial State q_0: At any given time the number of locks is dynamic. Locks can be created dynamically during normal operations. For instance, kernel threads and processes are created, file systems are mounted, files are created and opened, network connections are made. The starting state is the "init" state. To support concurrent test plans, multiple initial states could exist in automaton A.

Transition Function $\delta(q, a)$: In state transition as illustrated in Figure 6.3, transaction functions are internal controls to allocate testbed computation resources.

The internal controls are managed by the kernel scheduler or generic resource management daemon processes as automata input to manipulate contention state transitions.

Input Σ: Contention automata input is the source of data information resulting in resource contentions.

Output F and Goal Test: The success of state transitions is measured upon the fairness of execution of contented processes or kernel execution threads. The releases of lock events are the exiting stages of lock contentions.

Cost: If the bound of a contention resolution is the step time $O(t_i)$ then the time measurement of contention automata complexity is the discrete summation of $\Sigma_{0<k<n}\ a_k$ as the time assigned to a specific lock hold event from contention occurrence to the releases of locks.

6.2.1 Contribution

The purpose of this chapter is to provide an apparatus and method for a resource organization within the next-generation Internet or wireless network infrastructure and associative task environment. To construct real large-scale tests, simulation and emulation tests within a next-generation test environment, one needs to depict and reason about the capacity and configuration of vertices, edges, and links within a testbed computational graph. Deterministic finite automata (*FDA*) theory [3] is applied. Specifically, testbed and contention automata are suggested. The automata models are proposed to simplify the resource organization and prediction. To explore

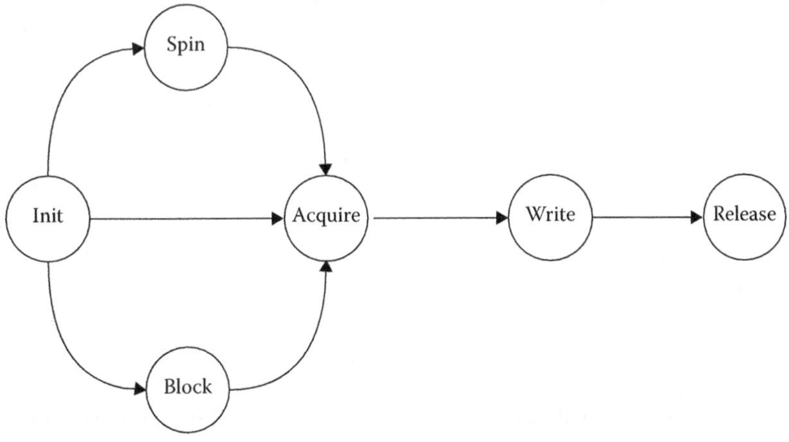

FIGURE 6.3: Contention automaton state transition.

the interactions of automata, a product automaton is formed to represent contention within a concurrent test environment. In addition, a set of testbed algorithmic operations are proposed to resolve lock contentions and self organization of resource allocation. Furthermore, an empirical testbed is advocated with self organization in terms of resource partition, allocation, constraints, and virtualization for public access.

6.3 Review of Literature

The main threads of conventional testbed researches fall into three categories: real tests, simulation, and emulation. The most influential testbed strategy is simulation-focused study [1]. Simulation requires less physical resources involved in the small-scale test. However, an experiment has a dependency on simulation test input distribution. This distribution is normally built upon design and test hypothetical assumptions about traffic, failure patterns, and topology.

Another thread of testbed research is to expose experiments to a real-task environment. A real-world test environment ideally was proposed to construct a protocol evaluation [4] for ad-hoc networks. The techniques are designed to achieve scalable and reproducible experiments over large-scale networks. However, real large-scale tests require distributed design and implementation rather than massive deployment and configuration with the complexity of nodes, transport protocols, middleware, and applications. Moreover, real experiments with distributed sensor networks could become troublesome if the nodes grow and exceed a dozen. Self-organization of testbeds remains as an open research issue. Hence, it was limited to large carrier practices. Among the above approaches, emulation [2] was in the middle. Emulation increases the experimental realism with acceptable reproducible results. Another thread of study [5] on testbeds was initially discussed on the combination of the above three-test strategies within a distribution task environment. The study suggested adaptation to wireless networks from layer 2 to layer 7 to provide an execution framework for both remote and local end users. This research augments the hybrid test strategies to propose a self-organized testbed with adaptation, virtualization, partitioning, and dynamic resource allocation.

From automata literature, an extension of the probabilistic I/O automata framework [6] has been studied to support modeling and verification of security protocols. However, there is no existing discussion on automata and related resource contention within a testbed state space. This research proposes testbed and contention automata for experiments within next-generation Internet and wireless networks.

6.4 Methodology

As a generalized view of next-generation testbed automaton, the detailed implementation and deployment aspects are abstracted. To reduce complexity, a general goal-based finite automaton model is developed to abstract out some complexities of platform and software implementation of real tests, while retaining those essential to meet the service objectives.

To map a user land application execution into a kernel scheduling and execution unit with associated physical resource utilization, one can abstract the complexity of an appliance system as three interconnected blocking and spin locks of operating system kernel resources and underlining hardware processors. The automaton model can be applied to analyze a workload density or a set of discrete input events with a given transaction arrival Σ of service data or content traffic. The instance of automaton in kernel space can abstract out physics of contention elements such as disk, network, and memory contributions to the potential performance degradation of good-put within the testbed environment.

In addition, resource partitioning and isolation of execution environments of $\Sigma_{0<k<n,0<j<n}\ env_{k,j}$ could share a single instance of the host operating system and multiple instances of guest operating systems with associated kernel resources. Kernel tunable, kernel built-in resource management module, and networking open system interconnection model (OSI) reference implementation provide congestion and administrative controls on the bounds of resource utilization. Hence, both user land processes and kernel threads are explicitly considered as automata elements. Pertaining to blocking primitives, fair scheduling, priority scheduling, first in first out (FIFO) scheduling, and lock implementation are generalized as a generic queue, which abstracts the detailed queue implementation such as the direction of the queue for inbound and outbound packets, and number of queues.

For mutual exclusion, lock primitives ensure concurrency as a thread attempts to acquire a mutex lock that is owned by another thread. The calling thread can either spin or block to wait for available resources. A spinning thread enters a tight loop to acquire the lock in each pass of the algorithmic operation. On the other hand, a blocked thread is placed on a sleep queue as another thread holds the intended lock. The sleeping thread will wake up when the lock is released. The blocking locks require context switching to get the waiting threads off the processors and a new runnable thread onto central processing units (CPUs). In addition, there is a little more lock acquisition latency.

There are spin locks and adaptive locks for most operating system implementations. Adaptive locks are the most common type of lock used and are designed to dynamically either spin or block when a lock is being held, depending on the state of the holder. Selection of a locking scheme that only

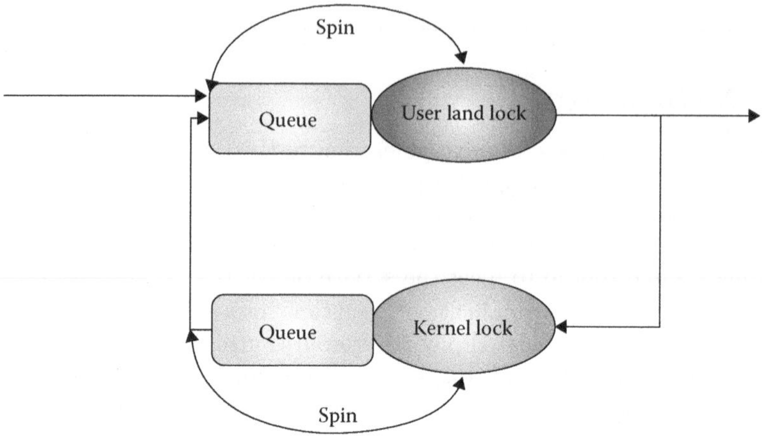

FIGURE 6.4: Contention automaton.

does one or the other can severely affect scalability and performance. Only spin locks can be used in high-level interrupt handlers. In addition, spin locks can raise the interrupt level of the processor when the lock is acquired.

Rather than kernel space generalization, user land activities need to be abstracted. Specifically, tested application specific lightweight processes, software threading model, and scheduling implementation are included in the automaton qualification to simplify the abstraction. A process is stopped, either by a job control signal or because it is being traced. Internal actions are the self-organization of testbed automaton (see Figure 6.4).

To observe the behavior of automaton state transitions, the event-driven probe algorithm described in Figure 6.5 is used to discover the asynchronous subsequences consisting of all the actions.

6.5 Performance Evaluation

The testbed architecture was composed of a VLAN configuration. A single point of dual interface is configured to act as an Internet gateway. Within this private network, Sun N1™Grid Engine provides uniform job submission and scheduling service interfaces for test plan execution within a testbed. In addition, the grid engine has public accessible web user interfaces for job submission via hypertext transfer protocol (HTTP). Sun N1 Service Provisioning System evaluates the proposed performance model. A Gigabit switch provided point-to-point connection between the preventive appliances with a load generator. The software packages were deployed on four SunFire™T2000 servers with 32× 1 Ghz UltraSPARC T1™processors, 8 GB random access memory (RAM) and 2 × 68 GB disks, 4 × Gigabit Ethernet ports.

```
PROBE-CONTENTION(event, no, time)

  if(type[event] == USER-LAND)
    case BLOCK
      spins ← no;
      lock++;
    case SPIN
      spins ← no;
      lock++;
    case READ-WRITE-BLOCK
      sleep ← time;
      lock++;
  end if
  if(type[event] == KERNEL)
    case ADAPTIVE-SPIN
      spins ← no;
      lock++;
    case ADAPTIVE-BLOCK
      spins ← no;
      lock++;
    case SPIN-SPIN
      spins ← no;
      lock++;
    case READ-WRITE-BLOCK
      sleep ← time;
      lock++;
  end if
```

FIGURE 6.5: Contention probe function.

The T2000 servers were optimized with chip multithreading (CMT) and UltraSPARC T1™ technology, firmware and hardware cache design. In contrast to traditional processor design, which focuses on single hardware thread execution, the T1 processor provides instruction level parallelism instead of thread level parallelization. It has multiple physical instruction execution pipelines and several active thread contexts per pipeline. In addition, improved hardware design with masking memory access reduces memory latency for a processor spending most of its time stalled and waiting for memory. There is a 12-way associative unified L2 on the chip cache. Double Data Rate 2 memory reduces stall. Furthermore, each board has switch chips to connect to on-board components.

Even more, the Solaris™ 10 operating system was configured with optimal tuning parameters from kernel core modules to device drivers. Three key parameters of the internet protocol (IP) module needed to be specified to dispatch the worker threads to different processors (ip_soft_rings_cnt=32, ip_sequence_bound=0, ip_sequence_fanout=1) to execute the interrupt handlers to increase processor utilization and throughput. The critical transmission control protocol (TCP) module tunable (tcp_conn_req_ max_q,

```
pool testbed_resource_pool
    boolean pool.default false
    boolean pool.active true
    int pool.importance 1
    string pool.comment
    string pool.scheduler FSS
    pset batch
pset testbed_pset
    int pset.sys_id 1
    string pset.units population
    boolean pset.default true
    uint pset.min 2
    uint pset.max 4
    string pset.comment
    boolean pset.escapable false
    uint pset.load 0
    uint pset.size 0
    string pset.poold.objectives locality tight; utilization < 40

cpu
    int cpu.sys_id 5
    string cpu.comment
    string cpu.status on-line
cpu
    int cpu.sys_id 7
    string cpu.comment
    string cpu.status on-line
```

FIGURE 6.6: Script for resource pool configuration.

tcp_conn_req_max_q0) and the backlog of the user land process were set to 8K to reduce the error rate and improve throughput. At user land, both listening backlog and listener threads were configured as optimal values. Service provisioning plan for resource pool configuration were listed as a segment of script as shown in Figure 6.6.

6.6 Implementation

Zone configurations are defined to implement resource partitioning. Resource pools are specified for dynamic resource allocation with constraints. Hardware virtualization provides a heterogeneous test environment with both SPARC and ×86 platforms. A public grid scheduler is enabled from web interfaces. Dynamic tracing tasks are scripted with D Language [7] to probe contention events at runtime as shown in Figure 6.7.

For adaptive-block events, the probe fires after a thread, which has blocked on a held adaptive mutex lock, has reawakened, and has acquired the mutex

```
PROBE-USERLAND( )
   plockstat:::mutex-block
   {
     lock = arg0;
     @locks["mutex-block"] = count();
   }
   plockstat:::mutex-spin
   {
     lock = arg0;
     @locks["mutex-spin"] = count();
   }
   plockstat:::rw-block
   {
     lock = arg0;
     @locks["rw-block"] = count();
   }
PROBE-KERNEL( )
   lockstat:::adaptive-spin
   {
     spins = arg1;
     @locks["adaptive-spin"] = count();
   }
   lockstat:::adaptive-block
   {
     sleep = arg1;
     @locks["adaptive-block"] = count();
   }
   lockstat:::spin-spin
   {
     spins = arg1;
     @locks["spin-spin"] = count();
   }
   lockstat:::rw-block
   {
     sleep = arg1;
     @locks["r-w-block"] = count();
   }
```

FIGURE 6.7: Script to probe contention events at runtime.

lock. Either adaptive-block or adaptive-spin will fire for a lock acquisition. For adaptive-spin events, the probe invoked has successfully acquired the mutex as a thread that has spun on a held adaptive mutex. A spin-spin contention-event probe is triggered to acquire the spin lock after a thread that has spun on a held spin lock. A read-write contention event fires as a thread is reawakened and has acquired the lock soon after the thread that has blocked on a held readers/writer lock.

In Figure 6.8, a lock contention snapshot resulting from a web service integration server shows the top ten calls at user land, which led to CPU contention within the testbed.

Rank	Self (%)	Accum (%)	Count	Trace	Function
1	31.04	31.04	1713	300293	DataFactory.create
2	30.14	61.18	1663	300216	PlainSocketImpl.socketAccept
3	12.25	73.43	676	300328	TestGetDocument.getDocument
4	6.80	80.23	375	300288	createReader
5	3.01	83.24	166	300277	Thread.setPriority0
6	2.90	86.14	160	300337	RecordToDocumentService. recursiveToDocument
7	2.08	88.22	115	300363	lookup
8	1.72	89.94	95	300331	getCursor
9	0.92	90.87	51	300223	readDoc
10	0.83	91.70	46	300280	start0

FIGURE 6.8: Samples on Tue Dec 12 13:13:15 2006.

6.7 Conclusion

Dynamic tracing, resource allocation, partitioning, virtualization, self-healing, and kernel resource constraints are proven critical characteristics to provide self-organization to a next-generation testbed. Simulation, emulation and real large-scale test plan can be achieved with simplification. Future work is considering conducting a further study on the semantics of testbed and contention automata within a large-state space.

References

[1] Kelton, W. D. and A. M. Law. *Simulation Modeling and Techniques*, 3rd ed. McGraw-Hill, New York, 2000.

[2] Chien A. A. and X. Liu. Traffic-based load balance for scalable network emulation. In *The Proceedings of the ACM/IEEE Conference on Supercomputing*, 2003.

[3] McCarthy, J. and C. E. Shannon. *Automata Studies*. Princeton University Press, Princeton, NJ, 1956.

[4] Lundgren, T. et al. A large-scale testbed for reproducible ad hoc protocol evaluations. In *The Proceedings of Wireless Communications and Networking Conference*, 2002.

[5] Ishizu, S. et al. Adaptive wireless-network testbed for cognitive radio technology. In *The Proceedings of the 1st International Workshop on Wireless Network Testbeds, Experimental Evaluation & Characterization*, 2006.

[6] Canetti, R. et al. Time-bounded task-pioas: A framework for analyzing security protocols. In *The Proceedings of 20th International Symposium on Distributed Computing*, 2006.

[7] Shapiro, M. W., A. H. Leventhal, and B. M. Cantrill. Extreme software scaling. In *The Proceedings of USENIX Annual Technical Conference*, 2004.

Chapter 7

Adaptive Buffer Tuning for Data Intensive Algebraic Operations

7.1 Introduction

7.1.1 Background

In research literature, buffer management limits the number of buffers used to make main-memory-specific computing resources available to database-specific processes such as queries and other database actions. Many earlier researches [1] on buffer management focused on the double paging problem. However, the research efforts [2] have been shifted to discover buffer management policies. This paper studies the primary factors contributing to buffer management design and analysis for database algebraic algorithm executions.

Architectural decisions could be one of the influential factors on buffer management design and implementation. In practice, two modes of buffering are in common use. Many relational databases adopt buffer management involving direct main memory access control, whereas virtual memory (VM) based control deferred to underlying operating systems (OS) is implemented by many main memory relational databases and object oriented databases. Direct main memory buffer management allocates main memory buffers but VM buffer management allocates VM buffers. VM buffer management leaves the main memory buffer allocation to the underlying OS. Hence, VM-based buffer management is impacted by OS kernel scheduling policies.

Algorithm analysis and design techniques impact buffer management solutions. Dynamic programming (DP) design and analysis can be applied to initialize a single pool of buffers to achieve a global optimal solution for each algebraic operator. Originated from greedy design techniques, buffer pools can be isolated and partitioned for different purposes. However, not every local allocation decision results in a global optimal buffer replacement. To amortize the time spent waiting for input/output (I/O) processing, buffers are allocated and replaced not just for one or a few items but on a per page basis.

Finally, algorithmic evaluation methodology concludes the final assessment of a buffer management design and implementation. Researchers suggested conducting intensive tests in a multiuser environment to evaluate buffer management solutions instead of a limited simulation environment [2].

Hence, the physics of online buffer tuning on real-world systems is one of stochastic optimal control problems with continuous states and discrete actions serving stochastically arriving workloads.

The objective that buffer tuning focused on is $\bar{t}_{wait}$ the average squared waiting time, which is the duration of each algebraic operator waiting for data processing. The goal is to keep the queuing time low, while ensuring the fair sharing of a buffer pool.

7.2 Significance of Work

The most influential buffer management strategies were combinational strategies of buffer allocation and buffer replacement algorithmic operations. The limitations of more traditional VM allocation were in connection with page replacement strategies, which were argued not to be suitable for the database environment [2]. These buffer replacement strategies may cause invulnerable or nonguaranteed buffer allocation. The most commonly used buffer replacement strategies are least recent used (LRU), most recent used (MRU), first-in-first-out (FIFO), clock algorithm (CLOCK), optimal page replacement algorithm (OPT) [3], random algorithm (RANDOM), worst algorithm (WORST) and system control.

One of the main threads is the best-known dynamic VM allocation algorithm [4], which is a working-set algorithm (WS). WS keeps the pages forming the working set of a transaction in the buffer and makes all pages not belonging to any working set available for replacement. Since WS identifies only whether a certain page in the buffer is available for replacement, it has a dependency with buffer replacement algorithms. Therefore, the combinational operations of buffer allocation and replacement algorithms may impact the optimal decisions of buffer management solutions.

In another thread of study on buffer allocation, a domain separation algorithm [5] was suggested to partition pages with associated buffer management algorithms. Within each domain, the least recent used algorithm (LRU) discipline is utilized for managing buffers. However, this algorithm failed to reflect the dynamics of page references that varied in different queries due to the static domain isolation. To find a better algorithm, a new algorithm [6] was advocated to subdivide and allocate buffer pools on a per-relation basis. However, the "new algorithm" failed to improve the performance of an experimental study on buffer allocation with LRU replacement. In addition, most recent used algorithm (MRU) is only adjustable in limited cases. A Hot set algorithm (HOT) was proposed to provide predictability on future reference behavior [7]. But it was evaluated by limited simulation results without insight in overall system performance. However, a DBMIN algorithm (1985) was suggested on the basis of a query locality set model (QLSM). In addition to forecasting future reference behavior, the DBMIN algorithm was proposed for the separation of the modeling of reference behavior with buffer replacement algorithms.

Moreover, conventional proposed buffer management methods are based on relational query behavior. The dependencies of algorithmic operations on buffer allocations may require adaptive buffer replacement algorithms. Sorted-based algorithms are possible to adapt to changes in buffer allocations. However, hash-based algorithmic design cannot respond to the dynamic characteristics of buffer replacement.

From reinforcement learning (RL) literature, a provable convergent approach has been developed for learning optimal policies in continuous state and action spaces under average rewards [8]. This technique has been applied to research [9] with nontrivial configurations. However, there is no existing discussion on RL and function approximation within buffer management state and action space. This research proposes combined RL and fuzzy rulebase approximation for buffer allocation and replacement with next-generation data intensive algebraic computational networks.

7.3 Problem Analysis

A stochastic optimal buffer prediction and control problem results in large-state and action spaces with quantified continuous features. It poses a challenge to traditional buffer management methods for complexity analysis and convergent proof such as DP and value interactions.

Problem Formulation: Buffer tuning is a stochastic process generating random state changes with dynamic optimization in which the goal is to find an optimal action in each state visited during state transitions. Intuitively, an adaptive tuning is a state-action control optimization problem. Hence, buffer management actions and associated state changes form a stochastic decision process resulting in buffer state transitions, which is usually probabilistic. Buffer tuning is a problem of dynamic computation optimization.

Buffer management is a memoryless process. Specifically, each state transition probability is dependent only on the current state but not on previous states. In addition, state transition time is not a unity time step. Hence, it is a semi-Markov decision problem (SMDP). However, in real-world systems, state transition probabilities and reward discount factors are unknown or hard to compute. Without transition probability matrices (TPM), transition reward matrices (TRM), and transition time matrices (TTM) as the foundation of the theoretical model, adaptive buffer tuning is hard to formulate as a traditional Markov decision problem (MDP), which can be solved by DP algorithms.

In addition, buffer objective functions may have high-dimensional random decision variables in large-state spaces. The objective function may have difficulty obtaining the probability mass or distribution function of these parameters. Furthermore, given a distribution function, it may not be solved in closed forms. With distribution of system inbound random decision variables, estimated transition probability and reward matrices could generate TPMs and TRMs via simulators. However, the solution does not scale-up to large-state and solution spaces. For large-state spaces, state-aggregation is required to approximate models with a manageable number of states.

Traditional buffer learning is explicitly computed in the space of state-action along the edges to vertices. Approximation, such as explorations or revolutionary methods, would climb policy space for state generation and evaluation to obtain policy improvements. In general, by direct searching, entire policy spaces are formulated and evaluated with scalar quantities. Intuitively, fixed policy is held with practices many times which could result in biased local optimum. Buffer policy against large-state spaces or high dimensional task environment is also hard to resolve as an explicit search approximation problem.

With RL optimization, search costs and rewards can be assigned or computed as environmental feedback treated as state values learned by interactions. Therefore, with RL methods, optimal policies can be reached without an explicit search over the possible sequence of entire states and actions. Hence, buffer tuning is a dynamic problem, which can be resolved with large and even infinite spaces.

Formulation of classical control theory cannot be used to address the scheduling problem within the utility accrual (UA) paradigm. The objective can be handled by optimal control theory. The discrete time optimal control problem is a well-known MDP, which can be solved by DP algorithmic techniques. However, the real-world system may not be able to abstract from a known system model with a small number of possible state spaces. It does not satisfy the interest of constraints to apply DP approaches.

A buffer state is defined as an MDP for a single agent can be illustrated by a quadruple (S, A, R, T) consisting of

- A finite set of states $S, s \in S$
- A finite set of actions $A, a \in A$
- A reward function, $R : S \times A \times S \rightarrow \Re$
- A state transaction function, $T : S \times A \rightarrow PD(S)$

which maps the agent's current state and action into the set of probability distribution over.

States Q:

- x_1, number of blocks in buffer pool
- x_2, number of page faults
- x_3, number of pages allocated for a file
- x_4, maximum number of pages to allocate for a file
- x_5, maximum rate of page I/O, so that I/O can be queued by the expected cost of page in and page out

Initial State Q_0: For simplicity, a buffer pool is constructed with physical vertices, edges, and links but without an initial contention property. In each state management of a buffer pool, both external state and internal controls organize the computational resources before the execution of next automata input.

Action: The learning agent needs to make a few simple decisions, which are the allocation and replacement of the buffer slots for waiting physical operator processing.

Transition Function: As in state transition illustrated in Equation 7.2, transaction functions are internal controls to allocate buffers as computation resources.

Consequently, the dynamic buffer tuning problem is formulated as an RL-and DP-based SMDP problem.

$$R_t = \int_0^{\infty} e^{-\beta\tau} r_{t+\tau}\, d\tau \tag{7.1}$$

The extension of the state action value function mapping is evolved as

$$\begin{aligned} Q(s,a) \longleftarrow\ & Q(s,a) \\ & + \alpha \left[\int_{t_1}^{t_2} e^{-\beta(\tau - t_1)} r_\tau\, d\tau + e^{-\beta(t_2 - t_1)} \operatorname*{argmax}_{a'} Q(s', a') - Q(s,a) \right] \end{aligned} \tag{7.2}$$

7.4 Contribution

The purpose of this work is to provide an adaptive learning apparatus and method for buffer management within a next dynamic network infrastructure and associative task environment. To serve a large eigenspace, fuzzy rulebase function approximation is proposed to provide generalization. To construct features of large-state and action spaces, one needs to depict and reason about the capacity and configuration of buffer management. MDP theory is applied. Specifically, value and cost functions are suggested. Fuzzy rulebase function approximation is proposed to simplify buffer organization and prediction. In addition, a set of learning algorithmic operations is proposed to attain optimal resource allocation.

7.5 Methodology

With the formulated SMDP and DP problem, "Memoryless," "Parallelization," "Dynamic," and "Adaptive" are critical in the context.

- Each state transition probability is independent of previous states but not of the current state. Hence, it is a memoryless process.
- Since buffer tuning optimization is formulated search as a stochastic DP problem, it owns the properties of dynamics.
- To handle large-state space and unknown objective functions, the DP problem is transformed into an RL-based adaptive learning problem. Adaptiveness means that search is conducted interactively with converged resources.
- With data parallelization, time complexity is optimized by algorithmic parallelism from system and pipelined processors.

Dynamic programming algorithms require computation of a theoretical model of a system on transition probabilities, transition rewards, and transition times. These quantities are unknown or hard to evaluate. Specifically, to obtain transition probabilities, multiple integrals with the probability distribution functions of many random variables are involved in the calculation on a complex stochastic system.

Both DP and RL algorithms have a dependency with $\Sigma_{x \leq t} p_x(x)$, the distributions of the random variables that govern the system behavior for a time interval t. For continuous random variables, $\int_{-\infty}^{x} f(x)dt$ is applied. However, RL does not need the above theoretical model quantity evaluation or estimations but simulates the system using the distributions of the governing random variables. For adaptive buffer tuning, one needs the distribution of random decision variables.

Value function and state mapping can be done directly by table lookup. However, the lookup results in a memory bound problem due to large-state transitions. Hence, value state mapping was proposed generalized by function approximation to reduce time and space complexity in the literature. But function approximation introduces error convergence problems to achieve the approximated state value mapping. To resolve the time and space complexity of value mapping without the approximation error convergence issue, this work proposes value state mapping based on a storage based index structure for the exact mapping function. The index structure is a logarithm space reduction data structure with algorithmic operations to map the state and solution space.

However, reinforcement learning techniques provide near optimal solutions without evaluation of the above quantities. Similarly with DP techniques, one element of the value function vector is associated with each state variable. RL buffer learning associates each element of the value mapping vector with a given state-action pair (i, a) as $Q(i, a)$ for a search cost or reward evaluation to derive optimal policies.

Value iteration calculations do not compute the system of linear equations. However, value iteration for MDP poses difficulties for Bellman optimality equation computation with unknown value of the average reward (ρ^*). SMDP in the average reward context gets into the approximation solution space. However, a regular DP value iteration becomes unbounded for an average reward MDP. Hence, relative value iteration keeps the bound operation. Due to the discounting factor, the computation is hard to measure in the real world, so average reward tends to be a more popular performance measure.

- Traditionally, value action function computation is done by in-memory table form lookup. This is limited to small-state and solution spaces. With large-state and solutions spaces or high-dimensional state space, table-based lookup is prohibitive because of limited computational resources due to space complexity such as memory constraints. Rather than table based exact function computation, value action function approximation uses additional numeric methods to fit the possible state and value mapping. However, function approximation introduces a classic error convergence problem in information theory. With unknown dynamic task environment and partial observable decision variables, the error propagation will be hard to predict. Hence, convergence is hard to obtain from a formal proof with approximation methods. This is the root cause of the convergence problem to resolve in this work.

The rationale of learning is to locate a stationary policy that optimizes a state transition ($\pi : S \rightarrow A$) to maximize the expectation of either a discounted sum of future rewards or the average reward per time step starting from any initial state. For an advanced version of RL learning, there may not be received discounts nor distinctly divided episodes with finite returns.

For an estimation policy π, in the long run the average reward is the same. The transient value function is defined by the average expected reward per time step under this policy.

$$\rho^{\pi} = \lim_{n \to 0} \frac{1}{n} \sum_{1 <= k <= n} E_{\pi}[r(s_t, \pi(s_t), s_{t+k}] \tag{7.3}$$

Hence, the optimal policy π^* from a class of policies Π is defined as

$$\pi^* = \underset{\pi \in \Pi}{\operatorname{argmax}} \rho^{\pi} \tag{7.4}$$

This result means that all policies attain the maximal value of ρ^{π} to be optimal. Therefore, the result is transient to specify $V^{\pi}(S)$ as a state-value function with the expected future reward relative to ρ^{π} starting from any state under policy π. The result is a relative value to the average reward under the policy.

$$V^{\pi}(s) = \sum_{1<=k<=n} E_{\pi}[r(s_t, \pi(s_t), s_{t+k} - \rho^{\pi} | s_t = s] \tag{7.5}$$

The optimal value of any state s is defined as

$$V^*(s) = \max_{\pi} V^{\pi}(s) \tag{7.6}$$

Similarly, the action-value function is the transient differential value in reward when a state-action pair has taken place. The result is a relative value to the average reward under the policy.

$$\tilde{Q}^{\pi}(s,a) = \sum_{1<=k<\infty} E_{\pi}[r(s_t, \pi(s_t), s_{t+k}) - \rho^{\pi} | s_t = s, a_t = a] \tag{7.7}$$

The optimal Q-value is defined as

$$Q^A(s,a) = \sum_{1<=k<\infty} E_{\pi}[r(s_t, \pi(s_t), s_{t+k}) - \rho^A] \tag{7.8}$$

Hence, the objective of an RL agent is to adopt off-policy control methods to order policies according to the maximized reward ρ^{π} at each time step.

Since the state and action spaces are finite, the state and action set of a finite MDP is a one step dynamic of the learning environment. The reward dynamic is characterized as

$$R_s^a = E[r_{t+1} | s_t = s, a_t = a] = \sum_{s' \in S} P_{ss'}^a R_{ss'}^a \tag{7.9}$$

Given any state and action,s and a, the transition probability is defined as

$$P_{ss'}^a = Pr\{s_{t+1} = S' | s_t = s, a_t = a\} \tag{7.10}$$

In other words, a state signal has the Markov property. It is a Markov state. Since the learning environment owns the Markov property, its one step dynamic enables the agent to predict the next state and expected next reward given the current state and action. Even when the state signal is non-Markov, it is still appropriate to think of the state in reinforcement learning as an approximation to a Markov state. Hence, it is useful to think of the state at each time step as an approximation to a Markov state, although it may not satisfy the Markov property. The assumption of Markov state representations is not unique to reinforcement learning but also to most studies on artificial intelligence. Intuitively, the expected value of the next reward is

$$R^a_{ss'} = E[r_{t+1}|s_t = s, a_t = a, s_{t+1} = s'] \quad (7.11)$$

By iterating this equation, the agent can predict all future states and expected rewards only from the current state. Specifically, the agent needs to maintain $Q(s, a)$ as parameterized functions and tune the parameters to better match the observed returns.

To express the above recursive relationship between the value of a state and the value of its successor state, the Bellman equation for Q^* is defined as

$$Q^*(s, a) = \sum_{s' \in S} P^a_{ss'}[R^a_{ss'} + \max_a Q^*(s', a)] - \rho^* \quad (7.12)$$

It is implicit that the actions a, is taken from the set $A(s)$ and the next state, $s^{'}$, is taken from the set S or from $S^{'}$ in case of an episodic problem. In addition, the result averages over all possibilities, weighting each by its probability of occurring. The result states that the value of the start state must equal the expected return for the best action from that state. Intuitively, the above optimality equation indicates that the value of a state-action pair under an optimal policy must equal the expected return for the best action from that state. Hence, for MDP, the Bellman equation is a system of equations. One for each state-action pair so if there are N states, then there are N equations in N unknown states. If the dynamics of environment $(P^a_{ss'} R^a_{ss'})$ is known, then in principle one can solve this system of nonlinear equations. It forms the basis to compute, approximate, and learn a state-value function.

Having Q^* makes optimal action selection easier. Because the Bellman equation caches the results of all one-step-ahead searches in the action space with Q^*, the agent finds only any action that maximizes $Q^*(s, a)$ without a single step ahead search. This implies that an agent selects an optimal action with no knowledge of the dynamics of a learning environment. However, the cost of the optimal action-value function restricts the applications of the learning in large-state and action spaces.

The fundamental property of the value function is used throughout the entire study of the learning agent for buffer management tuning. This can produce accurate estimation. Moreover, this estimation is represented as a table with a set of tuples which are states or state-action pairs

$$Q(s, a) = Q(s_t, a_t) + \alpha_t \delta_t \quad (7.13)$$

$$\delta_t = r(s_t, \pi(s_t), s_{t+k}) - \rho_t + \max_a(Q(s_{t+1}, a) - Q(s_t, a_t)) \quad (7.14)$$

$$\rho_{t+1} = \rho_t + \beta_t(\gamma(s_t, a_t, s_{t+1}) - \rho_t) \quad (7.15)$$

where ρ_t, β_t are positive step parameters set to $\frac{1}{t}$. The discount rate is $\gamma \in [0, 1)$. The above iterative learning converges to the optimal state-action value with a discount. However, there is no convergent proof in the average reward cases. In addition, the above equations do not fit for large or continuous action and state spaces.

As we have noted, this choice results in the sample average method, which is guaranteed to cover the true action values by central-limit theorems. This work applies function approximation techniques to take samples from a value function and attempts to generalize from them to construct an approximation of the buffer function.

Instead of approximating a function as a table, the action-value function is represented as a parameterized functional form with a k dimensional parameter vector of connection weights. By adjusting weights, any of a wide range of functions can be implemented. This means that function is totally dependent on the input vector, varying from time step to time step only as input varies. Any kind of parameterized value function approximation can be used in the proposed adaptive tuning framework since the only criterion for this compatibility with RL methodology for tuning parameter values is function differentiability with respect to each tunable parameter.

A fuzzy rulebase is a proposed function approximation that transparently maps a k dimension of vector inputs into a scalar output.

Rule i, IF (x_1 is S_1^i) and (x_2 is S_1^i) and ... (x_k is S_1^k) THEN (p^i)

$$y = f(x) = \frac{\sum_{1<=k<=n} p^i w^i(x)}{\sum_{1<=i<M} w^i(x)} \tag{7.16}$$

where M is the number of rule and $w^i(x)$ is the weight of rule.

The product inference is commonly used for computing the weight of each rule

$$w^i(x) = \prod_{1<=j<K} \mu_{S_j^i} x_j \tag{7.17}$$

if the membership function is tuned well.

Buffer management policy decides whether to use one or more buffer blocks to allocate or replace existing data items for algebraic computations. All of these policies make scheduling decisions by selecting buffer configurations that provide the best starting point for buffer manager's future operations in terms of maximizing the long-term utility from all jobs completed in the future. The key component of the proposed adaptive buffer management policy is the possibility of learning the value of cost (long-term expected utility sum) function for each instance of buffer pool. Once such a value function is obtained, any kind of scheduling decisions can be considered.

7.6 Conclusion

Dynamic tracing, adaptive tuning and resource constraints are proven critical characteristics to provide self-organization to next generation buffer management. Future work is considering conducting a further study on the various semantics of contention management within a large-state space.

References

[1] Fernández, E. B., T. Lang, C. Wood. Effect of replacement algorithms on a paged buffer database system. *IBM Journal of Research and Development*, 22(2), 1978.

[2] Stonebraker, M. Operating system support for database management. *Communications of the ACM*, 24(7), 1981.

[3] Belady, L. A. A study of replacement algorithms for virtual storage computers. *IBM Systems Journal*, 5(2):78–102, 1966.

[4] Denning, P. J. The working sets model for program behavior. *ACM Transactions on Database Systems*, 11(5):323–334, 1968.

[5] Reit, A. A study of buffer management policies for data management system. *Technical Summary Report*, 1976.

[6] Kaplan, J. A. Buffer management policies in a database environment. *Masler Report, UC Berkeley*, 1980.

[7] DeWitt, D. and H. Chou. An evaluation of buffer management strategies for relational database systems. In *Proceedings of the 11th International Conference on Very Large Data Bases*, 11:127–141, 1985.

[8] V. R. Konda, and Tsitsiklis, J. N. Actor-critic algorithms. *SIAM Journal on Control and Optimization*, 42(4):1143–1166, 2003.

[9] Vengerov, D., H. Berenji, and N. Bambos. A fuzzy reinforcement learning approach to power control in wireless transmitters. *IEEE Transactions on Systems, Man, and Cybernetics*, Part B, 2005.

Chapter 8

A Quantum Method of Representing Recurring Data Deduplication Policy States

8.1 Introduction

Policies represent interactions between storage activities and environments. Schedules may trigger periodic jobs. A job has both potential energy and kinetic energy. A scheduled job is in the state of zero point energy. A running job has kinetic energy. Hence, policy states can be represented by energy levels. Policies move between the states by canceling jobs or by emitting new jobs. Higher energy states are caused by emitting jobs or by creating new schedules. A deduplication job can be either in state *Idle* or in state *Running*. *Running* and *Idle* are orthogonal states. A job is either running through a reduction appliance for a specific volume or pool or is idle. This is sufficient for the classic storage policy world. Time-based reduction policy represents recurrences of storage activities. For a repeated policy, the policy is in *Idle* and *Running* states simultaneously. A daily deduplication activity may be scheduled to run at 10:30 PM every day. The policy has wave properties. The policy represents a two-dimensional quantum system. Upon failure or completion of the job, the state comes back to *Idle*. The job represents a running schedule associated with the policy

$$policy = \begin{bmatrix} c_0 \\ c_1 \end{bmatrix}$$

where $|c_0|^2 + |c_1|^2 = 1$. $|c_0|^2$ and $|c_1|^2$ are the probability of $Idle$ and $Running$ states. The uncertainty depends on how much time the policy spent in the higher energy state.

$$|\psi> = \sum_{i=1}^{n} x_i |x_i> \tag{8.1}$$

where x_i represents coordinate of pure state $|x_i>$.

The recurring policy has quantum states. Job executions make policy state transitions. The executions represent wave properties of the quantum system.

In the meantime, the policy and related schedules are in all possible states simultaneously. Schedules denote energy states of the policy. Similarly, the jobs represent energy states of the schedules.

$$e_p = \begin{bmatrix} Idle \\ Running \end{bmatrix}$$

The orthogonal basis of policy is *Running* and *Idle*. The same rule is applied to recurrence schedules. Hence, schedule is the canonical basis of policy states.

$$e_s = \begin{bmatrix} Idle \\ Running \end{bmatrix}$$

Jobs are the specific positions of each schedule. A job is the canonical basis of schedule states. The job exists only upon execution of a specific schedule. Hence, it is isomorphic to schedule a *Running* state. The job orthogonal basis is specified below.

$$e_j = \begin{bmatrix} Commit \\ Abort \end{bmatrix}$$

The above studies have interpreted the detailed structure of the excited job executions of policy systems. Observation of levels of job throughput require precise information concerning millions of storage events and associated job states, while all structures may become random. In such a large ensemble, only policy spin (phase) and job parity (Commit or Abort) remain good. The excited job execution requires a policy management at the job level. The policy method will not predict the detailed sequence of job executions in any schedule. But the method represents the general appearance and the degree of irregularity of the level structure that is expected to occur in any policy. The level structure may be hard to understand in detail. Hence, this work focuses on a general method of policy state representation as system states transit. As systems evolve, this work predicts system behavior without exact knowledge of the resembled states.

8.2 Problem Formulation

8.2.1 State representation using momentum basis

A policy system is expanded by a pair of read-write momentums. Specifically, a schedule state for a policy can be described in terms of its read-write eigenbasis, that is, the set $\{\mathbf{R}, \mathbf{W}\}$. $\{u\}$ can be written in any orthogonal base, corresponding to different physical observables. A discrete model of read-write momentum is up to the constant $-i * \hbar$, the rate of changes of the policy state vector from one point to the next. The generalized momentum relation [1] can be represented by the following equation

$$M(\psi) = -i * \hbar * \frac{\psi(s + \delta s) - \psi(s)}{\delta s} \tag{8.2}$$

where $M(\psi) = b * Ops/s$ represents the read-write momentum of a policy system. b is the bandwidth utilization of a read-write channel. Ops/s is the number of read-write operations per second. s represents the state on the integral curve using policy systems. Hence, for a executed job of a specific schedule, the rate of policy state changes is proportional to the read-write momentum. The concrete dynamics are given by the equation, which determines the evolution of a policy system. By solving the equation with some initial conditions, one is able to determine read-write momentum over state changes whenever the rate of the changes is specified.

8.2.2 State representation using orthogonal basis

A directional angle is another observable. A policy state can be written in an orthogonal base corresponding to angle. Hence, a policy system can be expanded by a discrete angle eigenbasis.

(1) *2-D Geometric Representation*: Each policy can be represented as a physical quantity with its magnitude and a direction by two-dimensional geometrical intuition. The magnitude is the state measure of the policy whereas the direction $\theta_i \in [0, 2\pi)$ is the unique identifier of the policy. If the initial point of the policy is set at the origin, a unique vector $V_i = (r, \theta_i)$ represents the policy for storage activities. Hence, the restart or failure of a policy represents an equivalent class of policies with the direction of $\theta_i \in [2\pi, 2k\pi]$.

(2) *Algebraic Representation*: In algebraic interpretation, a policy is represented by a complex number $a + bi \mapsto (a, b)$. The complex number is nothing more than an ordered pair of ordinary real numbers. The components of each policy have several properties. All real numbers excluding 0 form a group with respect to usual multiplication. The addition identity is $(0, 0)$ and the multiplication identity is $(1, 0)$. Every element has its inverse. Hence, a policy group is a field. The policy field contains all solutions for any of its polynomial equations. So, the policy field is algebraically completed. It is guaranteed to derive solutions to ensure policy progresses. The field isomorphism ensures a one to one relationship between a deduplication activity and a policy group.

(3) *3-D Geometric Representation*: The above two-dimensional policy representation can be extended in a three-dimensional geometric way. The canonical representation [2] of a policy vector space has only two real numbers (θ and ϕ)

$$\psi = \cos\theta \; C + e^{i\phi} \sin\theta \; R \tag{8.3}$$

where C represents the state *Idle* and R represents the state *Running*. θ is half the angle that a policy makes with the z axis. ϕ is the angle that a policy makes from the basis x axis along the equator. The standard parameterization of the three-dimensional representation is

$$x = \cos\phi \sin 2\theta \tag{8.4}$$

$$y = \sin 2\theta \sin\phi \tag{8.5}$$

$$z = \cos 2\theta \tag{8.6}$$

The physical interpretation of the above three-dimensional model relies on the two physical parameters. In Equation 8.3, $e^{i\phi}$ is the phase parameter. θ controls the probability of collapsing policy *Idle* to *Running*. A job measurement decomposes a policy as the probability of *Idle* and *Running*.

From parameter z, the probability of a policy terminating at running mode C depends exclusively on θ. The angle θ controls the strength of terminating at C mode or R mode. It indicates the prediction of a job termination. On the contrary, the changes of ϕ without θ do not alter the probability but phase $e^{i\phi}$ changes. This parameter is a phase state that represents periodic policy motions with classic states of C or R.

8.2.3 Policy vector space

Two policy vector spaces of the same dimension over the same field are isomorphic. N tuples are the prototypes of vectors. This means we can restrict our attention to n tuples without loss of generality. The metric of Hilbert space [3] may result not from a physical principle, but rather as a consequence of an optimal statistical inference procedure. With arbitrary distinguishable criteria, the distance between two vectors is propositional to the angle between the two vectors and does not depend on the position of the vectors. In a two-dimensional Hilbert space, researchers [4] compute the distance as

$$W(\theta_1, \theta_2, n) = |\theta_1 - \theta_2|\sqrt{\frac{2n}{\pi e}} \tag{8.7}$$

where θ is the angle of the vector from some reference direction in the plane spanned by the two vectors. n is the number of identical states in a sample space.

Equation 8.7 shows that the number of distinguishable states in the interval of angles $[\alpha_1, \alpha_2]$ depends on the length of the interval and the square root of the number of identical states with a rigorous notion of distinguishibility. It does not depend on the position of the arcs comprising the range of the unit circle.

The result can be generalized for the N-dimensional Hilbert space of states of a system [4]. The number of distinguishable states is

$$W(n, \Omega) = \Omega(cn)^{\frac{N-1}{2}} \tag{8.8}$$

where n is the number of copies of identical states. c is a constant.

That means that the number of distinguishable states depends only on the area Ω of the domain on the sphere from which states can be chosen, but does not depend on the shape and position of the domain. The optimal distribution is uniform over the domain in a polar orthogonal basis.

8.2.4 Statement of problem

Given a running policy system, how can one improve or keep its time averaged performance? To answer this question, we need to answer the following questions.

- How do we measure job states?
- What is the joint distribution of the eigenvalues in a job ensemble?
- Given job states of a specific schedule, how do we compute the schedule state?
- Given schedule states of a specific policy, how do we compute the policy state?
- How do we represent a policy in bits of information?
- How do we determine policy performance by its physical state (probability of *Idle* and *Running*)?

8.3 Review of Literature

8.3.1 Fourier analysis

Continuous relations can be represented by a Taylor series. For periodic phenomena, infinite Fourier series are universal to represent general periodic (both continuous and discontinuous) functions. Fourier's idea was to model a complicated ordinary differential equation (ODE) or partial differential equation (PDE) as a superposition (linear combination) of simple sine and cosine waves, and to write the solution as a superposition of the corresponding eigensolutions. This superposition or linear combination is called the *Fourier series*. Fourier integrals and Fourier transforms extend techniques of Fourier series to non-periodic functions. Discrete Fourier transforms (DFT) and fast Fourier transforms (FFT) work with sampled values rather than with functions

$$\mathbf{U} = [e^{(-2\pi i/N)(nk)}]u \tag{8.9}$$

where n, $k = 0, \ldots, N-1$. When known measurements (sample values) are given, a desired memory throughput state can be computed by an arbitrary initial state. Hence, discrete Fourier analysis relies on large amounts of equally spaced data. Both Fourier and Laplace transforms have a dependency on the time variables.

8.3.2 Vector expansion method

The difference Equation 8.2 can be solved by the eigenvector expansion method. Within vibration phases, the eigenvectors of A can be used as the policy basis but not as any basis for the N tuple.

$$(\boldsymbol{A} - \lambda \mathbf{M})\mathbf{x} = 0 \tag{8.10}$$

The idea is that the vector Ae_j is simply $\lambda_j e_j$ if e_j is an eigenvector of A, whereas it would be a linear combination of all the base vectors if some other basis were used. The eigenvalues are the natural frequencies. The eigenvectors are the mode and configuration of solutions. Hence, each activity location becomes a degree of freedom. If there are n activity locations and n degrees of freedom $x_1(t), \ldots, x_n(t)$, then read-write motions of each activity location consist of a linear combination of n eigenmodes of an $n \times n$ matrix. There will be a solution only if the forcing vector F does not excite that particular eigenmode, or F is orthogonal to e. Therefore, read-write momentum can be further expanded with its natural frequencies and amplitude.

$$x_n(t) = a_n \sin \omega t + r_n \cos \omega t \tag{8.11}$$

However, singular points exist when driving frequencies are equal to natural frequencies or forcing vector F is not orthogonal to e. In addition, the expansion method does not provide a feasible presentation to the aperiodic behaviors and randomness.

8.3.3 Ordinary statistics

A renunciation of exact knowledge is made in statistical mechanics. The ordinary method assumes all states of a very large ensemble to be equally probable [5]. One obtains useful information about overall behavior of a complex system when the observation of the state of the system in all its detail is impossible. However, this type of statistical method is not adequate for discussion of throughput levels since a statement about the fine detail of the level structure cannot be made in terms of an ensemble of states. However, studies on an ensemble of systems have difficulties in calculating the ensemble average of many-body systems with strong interactions. In addition, there is no proof that an ensemble average will correctly describe the behavior of one particular system that is under observation.

8.3.4 Random matrices

A random matrix is a matrix-valued random variable. With multiple cocurrent transactions, physical transactional memory is disordered. The corresponding matrices are randomized. The mathematical properties of matrices with elements are drawn randomly from random matrices to determine the physical properties. The eigenvectors and eigenvalues of random matrices are critical. Quantum chaos is an application of random matrix theory (RMT). These compose chaotic and disordered systems. The mathematical foundations of RMT were established in a series of researches [5].

8.4 Methodology

8.4.1 Measuring job states

A physical policy system can be specified by a double list. The list is composed of a state space and a set of its observables. One of the observables is the job state Ω_j, which is a physical quantity that can be observed in each state of the policy space. Hence, it is a 2×2 hermitian operator. Since observation $\Omega\mathbf{J}$ is not a scalar multiplication, it modifies the job states. Thus, the result does not represent the same physical state. Specifically, it alters the probability of job staying J_{Commit} and J_{Abort}. The expected value of observing the job state observable repeatedly on the same state is a real number.

(1) *Eigenvalue*: For the C^n domain, the trace of a system state holds as: $Trace(A^\dagger, B) =< A, B >$. For a squared operator C, $Trace(C) = \sum_{i=0}^{n-1} C[i,i]$. $Trace(C)$ is the sum of all diagonal elements of the matrix. $Trace(C)$ is the basis of the job state measurement. Hence, with two measurements on job state (λ_1, λ_2), we can define the job operator as

$$y = \begin{bmatrix} \lambda_1 & x_1 \\ x_2 & \lambda_2 \end{bmatrix} \tag{8.12}$$

What is left is to derive the other two elements.

(2) *Eigenvalue Distribution*: Researchers obtained a formula to compute the joint distribution function of the eigenvalues in the job ensemble [5]. The formula states the probability for finding eigenvalues $[exp(i\phi_j)]$ of S with an angle ϕ_j in each of the intervals $[\theta_j, \theta_j + d\theta_j]$, $j = 1, \ldots, N$, is given by $Q_{N\beta}[\theta_1, \ldots, \theta_N]d\theta_1 \ldots \theta_N$

$$Q_{N\beta}(\theta_1, \ldots, \theta_N) = C_{N\beta} \prod_{i<j} |e_i^{i\theta} - e_j^{i\theta}| \tag{8.13}$$

where $\beta = 1$ for the orthogonal, $\beta = 2$ for the unitary, and $\beta = 4$ for the symplectic ensemble.

The most obvious consequence of Equation 8.13 is the repulsion of job levels. The probability of finding an unusually small separation $\triangle = (\theta_i - \theta_j)$ between two levels tends to zero with $\triangle$ like $\triangle^{\beta}$.

8.4.2 Compute schedule states

A deduplication schedule is separable in terms of deduplication jobs. Because a specific job may be entangled with multiple tasks, the schedule state is not a union of related job states. The schedule state is to be thought of as the vector space whose basic states are the pairs of states, one from job J_1 and one from job J_2. Job states coexist before the schedule state can be derived. Hence, the schedule state can be computed as a tensor product of all its related job states.

$$J_1 \otimes J_2, \ldots, \otimes J_N \tag{8.14}$$

Given an element of J_1

$$J_1 = c_0|Commit> + c_1|Abort> \tag{8.15}$$

and an element of J_2

$$J_2 = c_0'|Commit>' + c_1'|Abort>' \tag{8.16}$$

Hence, $J_1 \otimes J_2$ is computed as

$$\begin{aligned} S_i = {} & (c_0 \times c_0')(|Commit> \otimes |Commit>') \\ & + (c_0 \times c_1')(|Commit> \otimes |Abort>') \\ & + (c_1 \times c_1')(|Abort> \otimes |Commit>') \\ & + (c_1 \times c_1')(|Abort> \otimes |Abort>') \end{aligned} \tag{8.17}$$

From tensor associative rule, Equation 8.14 can be computed incrementally with Equation 8.17.

8.4.3 Compute policy states

A deduplication policy is separable in terms of its deduplication schedules. Because a specific schedule may be entangled with multiple jobs, a policy state can be computed as a tensor product of all its related schedule states.

$$S_1 \otimes S_2, \ldots, \otimes S_N \tag{8.18}$$

Similar to Equation 8.17, a policy state can be computed with the association rule.

8.4.4 Information theoretical description

A policy bit (pbit) is a unit of information describing a two-dimensional quantum policy system. A pbit is represented as a 2 × 1 matrix with complex numbers

$$\begin{bmatrix} c_0 \\ c_1 \end{bmatrix}$$

where $|c_0|^2 + |c_1|^2 = 1$

Notice that a classic policy is a special case of pbit. $|c_0|^2$ is interrupted as the probability that after measuring the pbit, the bit will be found in the state *Idle*. $|c_1|^2$ is interrupted as the probability that after measuring the pbit, the bit will be found in the state *Running*. Both *Running* and *Idle* are the canonical basis of C^2. Thus, any pbit can be written as

$$c_0|Running > +c_1|Idle > \tag{8.19}$$

so it describes the physical state as the pbit.

A series of N eigenvalues taken from a job ensemble can carry only a reduced amount of information.

$$I(\beta) = I_0 + S(\beta)[N/ln2] \tag{8.20}$$

This loss of information content is a direct measure of the statistical regularity of the eigenvalue series of the job ensemble.

8.5 Implementation

Policy updates the status at each schedule level and policy level. It sends notifications to Bui when a scheduled job is triggered. As a schedule is triggered and the job is requested, the schedule status is updated. As the requested job is responded with *Commit* or *Abort*, the schedule status is updated. We may need to consider extending the failure scheme in recovery iterations. For progress guarantee, even reduction returns with an *Abort*, policy logs it with *WARN* but still cleans up the session and returns the calling thread. The flow of state updates is demonstrated in Figure 8.1. In addition, the object model of state updates is shown in Figure 8.2.

8.5.1 Structure of policy state

```
‘‘messageId’’ : ‘‘/obtained from activity/’’,
‘‘messageType’’:’’notification’’,
‘‘subsystem’’: ‘‘policy’’,
```

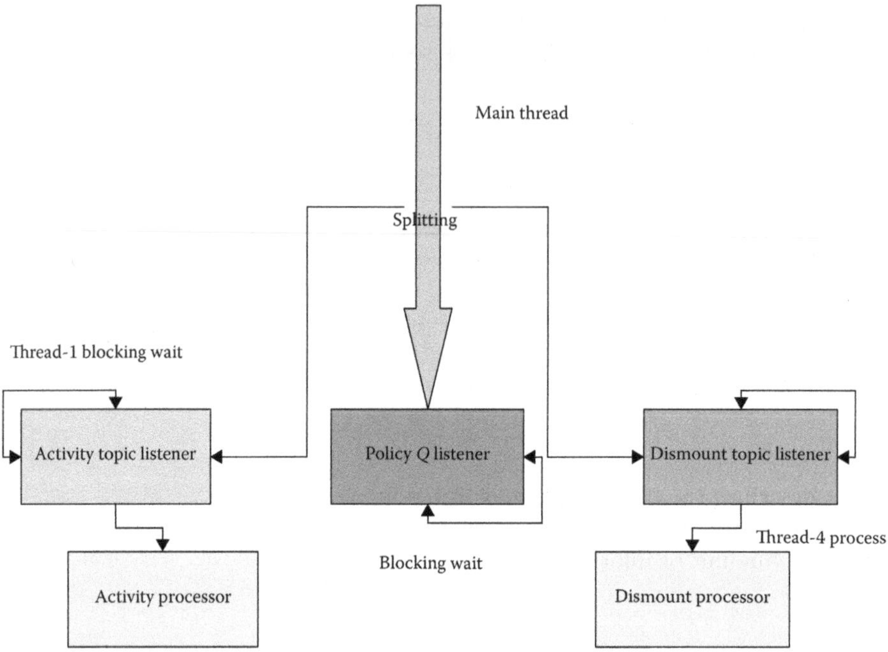

FIGURE 8.1: The flow of policy status update.

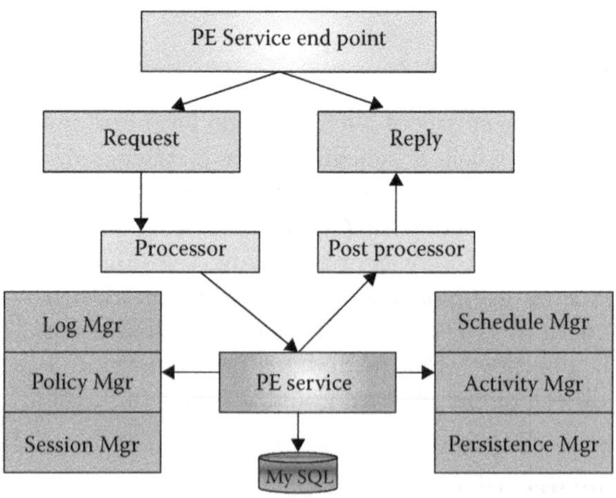

FIGURE 8.2: The flow of data deduplication policy management.

```
''type'': ''/obtained from activity// /reductionPolicy'',
''action'':''status '',
''policy'': [
''id'': ''123'',
''name'': ''my policy'',
''description'': ''my description'',
''createdBy'':''user id'',
''modifiedBy'': ''job id'',
''enable'': ''True | False'', //default to False
''runImmediate'': ''True | False'', //default to False
''targetId'': [1, 5, 987], //array of long. Storage Pool Id ]
''status'':'' Running | Idle'',
''timeSchemes'': [
{''timeSchemeId'':''456'',
''calendarStart'': ''time stamp'',
''calendarEnd'': ''time stamp'',
''eventStart'': ''time stamp'',
''eventEnd'': ''time stamp'',
''recurrence'': ''once | daily | weekly | monthly | yearly''
''frequency'': ''2'',
''eventDuration'':''60'', //Hard stop integer in Minutes.
''recurrenceParameters'':[/keeps it as policy payload definition/] ,
''status'':'' Running | Idle'', // new attribute at schedule level
''enable'': ''True | False'', //default to False
''createdBy'': ''user id'',
''modifiedBy'': ''job ID'',}
]
]
```


8.5.2 Policy state persistence model

```
CREATE TABLE IF NOT EXISTS POLICY_SCHEDULE
(
SCHEDULE_ID INT UNSIGNED NOT NULL AUTO_INCREMENT,
POLICY_ID INT UNSIGNED NOT NULL,
RECURRANCE_TYPE VARCHAR(30) NOT NULL,
FREQUENCY SMALLINT NOT NULL,
RECURRENCE_PARAMETER VARCHAR(100) NOT NULL,
CREATED_BY VARCHAR(50) NOT NULL,
MODIFIED_BY VARCHAR(50) NOT NULL,
LAST_UPDATE TIMESTAMP NOT NULL DEFAULT CURRENT_TIMESTAMP ON
    UPDATE CURRENT_TIMESTAMP,
CREATED_TIME TIMESTAMP NOT NULL,
EVENT_START TIMESTAMP NOT NULL,
EVENT_DURATION INTEGER,
```

```
ENABLED VARCHAR(5) NOT NULL DEFAULT "False",
EVENT_STOP TIMESTAMP,
STATUS VARCHAR(50) NOT NULL DEFAULT "Idle",
UNIQUE INDEX POL_SCHED_IDX_1 (SCHEDULE_ID, POLICY_ID),
PRIMARY KEY (SCHEDULE_ID)
)
ENGINE=INNODB
DEFAULT CHARACTER SET LATIN1;
```

8.6 Conclusion

System interactions and usability are shown in Figure 8.3. Administrators see only the virtualized quantum (at both policy and schedule level) states as *Running* or *Idle*. But the detailed job state measurements are hidden away from user experience.

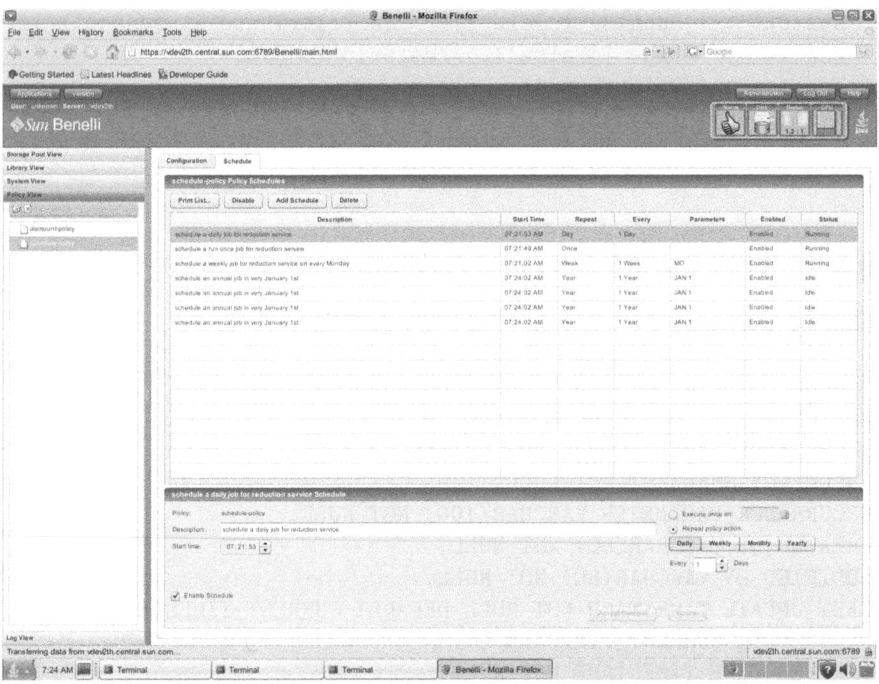

FIGURE 8.3: User experience of policy status update.

References

[1] Schrdinger, E. An undulatory theory of the mechanics of atoms and molecules. *Physics Review*, 28(6):1049–1070, 1926.

[2] Chrus'cin'ski, D. Geometric aspect of quantum mechanics and quantum entanglement. *Journal of Physics Conference Series*, 39:9–16, 2006.

[3] Wooters, W. K. Statistical distance and hilbert space. *Physics Review D*, 23:357–362(1049–1070), 1981.

[4] Levitin, L. B. et al. Information and distance in hilbert space. *Fifth International Conference on QCMC. AIP Conference Proceedings*, 2001.

[5] Dyson, F. J. Statistical theory of the energy levels of complex systems, i, ii,iii. *Journal of Mathematical Physics*, 3(1):140–156, 1962.

Chapter 9

QAM—Quantum Availability Mechanics without Recovery for Storage and Data Management

9.1 Introduction

9.1.1 Nonreversible operations

A classic availability problem is that storage mechanics interacts with a load structure P. Consider a simple structure, the capacity of the storage is denoted as L. As we increase P, data flows as in the usual scenario. However, until a certain volume is reached, storage activities will collapse under that load. The dynamic process of collapse proves the existence of critical point.

$$P = \frac{k^2\pi^2}{L^2} \tag{9.1}$$

where k is an integer. The failure point is not reversible. It results in service discontinuity.

If we superpose infinitely many activities into a phase plane, the elementary singularity of storage trajectories prefers to take center topology. However, there is a center representing a failure point such as the power outage. It is not reversible. Or it maybe a nonelementary singularity trajectory.

Nonsimple relations such as one-to-many relations or many-to-many relations lead to information conflicts. Their reverse functions do not exist. There is no way to determine their inputs. They are nonreversible operations. Hence, failure of in-memory transactions needs to be aborted. So the abort performs the following operation on an arbitrary transaction.

$$\begin{pmatrix} \cos\alpha \\ e^{\theta}e^{i\phi}\sin\alpha \end{pmatrix}$$

Instead of writing information, it erases information and causes energy loss and heat. It is not reversible either. As a result, we cannot abort the abort operations.

Not all measurement operations are reversible. Nonreversible operations result in discontinuity of services.

There is a persistent 9% overshot of the jump as a series of tasks is performing. This Gibbs phenomenon occurs in the Fourier series representation of any function with a jump discontinuity. It does not diminish as the number of tasks increase. This is of considerable importance because it implies that the convergence of Fourier series may be slow in the case of a jump discontinuity.

9.1.2 Reversible operations

Reversible operations represent continuous functions. But a reverse action represents a phase operation or a unitary operation. Classic availability solution represents a composite functional pair $s * r(t)$.

$$s * r(t) = \int_{-\infty}^{\infty} s(\tau) r(t - \tau) d\tau \tag{9.2}$$

where s represents a service function and r represents its recovery function.

Reflection ensures the energy conservative law. The phase operation represents the delay of service activities. The convolution theorem reveals the existence of the delay as $\tau > 0$ since the energy is dissipating through wave mechanics, which have a period $l > 0$. In addition, $t = x/V_{light}$ ensures the delay.

Hence, the physical intuition is to develop operational mechanics (evolvable QA operator) to evolve the storage activities. Here, the evolution replaces reversible operation. Hence, no phase operator and reflection operator are required. In addition, evolution is dynamic and it is a simple one-to-one relation. It becomes a time machine that is computationally convenient to reverse history or evolve into the future. Evolution guarantees continuity.

9.2 Problem Formulation

To eliminate the delay τ, we need to develop an operator to continue service operations.

9.2.1 State representation using canonical basis

For a physical storage system, the state can be written in a canonical base corresponding to $\{|0>, |1>\}$. The observables are policy, schedule, and job.

9.2.2 Separable states

A storage activity can be a three-particle system. Let us introduce a policy state as $|p>$, a schedule state as $|s>$, and a job state as $|j>$. Then policy and job have a directional relation. However, policy and schedule states are separable. Schedule and job are separable. A state of storage activities can be separable as a tensor product of states of the constituent subsystems.

$$|\psi> = c_0|p_0> \otimes c_1|s_0> \otimes c_2|j_0> + c_3|p_1> \otimes c_4|s_0> \otimes c_5|j_1> + c_6|p_1> \otimes c_7|s_1> \otimes c_8|j_1> \tag{9.3}$$

where $|j_0>$, $|s_0>$, and $|p_0>$ represent idle states of policy, job, and schedule. $|j_1>$, $|s_1>$, and $|p_1>$ represent running states. c_k is probability of related states.

Regardless of their actual distance in Hilbert space, a measurement's outcome for a job will always determine the measurement's outcome of policy state. However, policy and schedule are independent. There is no linear relation between job and schedule either.

9.2.3 Statement of problem

Given a steadily running storage system, how can one keep its service continuity? To answer this question, we need to answer the following questions.

- How do we obtain a single operation to replace the composite operation $s * r(t)$?
- How do we reverse an operation from $s(t)$ to $s(t-1)$ without any delay τ?
- How do we ensure availability for a nonreversible function $s(t)$?

9.2.4 Goal statement

Let us give a precise goal statement.

- We need to develop an operator upon a single operation $s(t)$ instead of the composite operation $s * r(t)$.
- We need to develop an operator from $s(t)$ to $s(t-1)$ without any delay τ.
- We need to develop a mechanism for functions whose reverse function does not exist.

9.3 Review of Possible Solutions

There are several ways to resolve the conflicts of message states.

9.3.1 Clustering

Clustering is one of major classic availability methods. It achieves availability by reflecting energy as Equation 9.2. The convolution theorem reveals its disadvantage of the phase operation, which results in $\tau > 0$.

9.3.2 Move or backup

The noncloning theorem [1] and the Pauli principle state that a single state can stay at only a single physical location at a given time. Moving 1 qubit is a translation operation that has a π phase shift involved as

$$|q'> \quad = \mathbf{Z}|q> \quad = \alpha|0> + e^{i\pi}\beta|1> \tag{9.4}$$

where $|q'>$ and $|q>$ represent 1 qubit. α and β represent constant coefficients.

9.3.3 Evolution with wave mechanics

Storage trajectories rely on the periodic recurrence of the events. The phase operation has a period of l. In addition, even with a harmonic load function, there are collapse points and elementary singular points. Service trajectories may transform from harmonic oscillation and subharmonic oscillation to randomness with infinite periods. Storage activities can vary dramatically at bifurcation points. Jump phenomenon cannot be reproduced by simulation and is observed from physical storage systems. Infinitesimal perturbation points remain in the same regions as nonlinear ones. In addition to the above limitations, this method may require reproducing and retransmitting data periodically.

9.3.4 Transactional management

Storage transactions are chaotic by representing a transactional state through its basis expansion. From geometric intuition, a transaction has its algebraic representation and physical interpretation. As discussed in Section 9.1, abort operations have phase operations and they are not reversible.

9.3.5 Data persistence

Data persistence provides a primary diagonalization with policy in memory states. As addressed earlier, policy, schedule, and job are separable observables. For dismount actions, a full distribution of job and policy relations computes the policy states. However, for schedule actions, job, schedule, and policy are entangling. Hence, we do not take $3rd$ form normalization of linear algebra to separate the job types. We keep the entanglement of job and policy in dismount actions versus job and schedule as a scheduling event occurs.

Data persistence does not provide availability of the current job in execution. It is a common disadvantage of persistent-based availability methods.

9.3.6 Cloning

A continuous variable denotes a system presented by a canonically conjugated observables $(\mathbf{x}, \mathbf{x}^{\dagger})$ with continuous spectra. The repelling and attracting actions $\mathbf{A}$ form the continuity of the trajectories as $\mathbf{Ax} = \lambda\mathbf{x}$. Hence, the eigenvalues are λ_1 and λ_2. Due to noncloning theorem [1] and noncommutativity of $[x, x^{\dagger}] = i$, there is an error $E \geq \frac{1}{4}| < [x, x^{\dagger}] > |^2$ during measurement of each observable. Hence, there is no perfect cloning to support the availability. Cloning is a linear combination of read (rotation) and translation (displacement) operations to obtain data duplication. A rotation is specified as

$$\begin{pmatrix} \cos\theta & -\sin\theta \\ \sin\theta & \cos\theta \end{pmatrix}$$

where θ can be considered as the identifier of the observables.

Cloning 1 qubit is a rotation operation that has a π phase shift involved as

$$|q' >= \mathbf{Y}|q >= e^{-i\frac{\pi}{2}}(\beta|0 > +e^{i\pi}\alpha|1 >) \tag{9.5}$$

where $|q' >$ and $|q >$ represent 1 qubit. α and β represent constant coefficients.

9.3.7 Multicast with synchronous computation

Computation is a way to achieve no error availability. Specifically, synchronous computation eliminates the recovery and delay actions of the phase operations.

$$L[f(t)] = L[f(t)] \tag{9.6}$$

where $L = -\frac{1}{w}[\frac{d}{dx}(p\frac{d}{dx}) + q]$ is a differential operator and $L[y] = \lambda y$.

To obtain $f(t)$, it requires vector convergence.

$$\lim_{k\to\infty} \int_{-l}^{l} \left[f(x) - a_0 - \sum_{n=1}^{k} \left(a_n \cos\frac{n\pi x}{l} + b_n \sin\frac{n\pi x}{l} \right) \right]^2 dx = 0 \tag{9.7}$$

9.3.8 Quantum teleportation

Teleportation applies a reconstruct matrix to transport a state to another location. However, it is limited to entangled states.

9.4 Methodology

9.4.1 Throughput trajectory

As illustrated in both Figures 9.1 and 9.2, we can inspect the relation between job displacement and throughout. Substituting with an auxiliary variable, we can reduce the order of the relation. We can further cancel the time variable and obtain throughput trajectories by first-order integration. In the throughput phase plane, trajectories approach singular points asymptotically as $t \to \infty$. This derives theorem 1. Do not study job displacement but study throughput trajectories.

9.4.2 State encoding

All storage states are encoded as policy, schedule, and job states as shown in Figures 9.3 and 9.4. The encoding scheme is done in such a way that no special decoding procedure is required to read states. In addition, the encoded states are transmitted and received as a block of attributes. This is done to reduce the probability of failure.

$$p^N = \sum_{n=1}^{k} C_N^k p^k (1-p)^k \tag{9.8}$$

where k is the number of errors in a N bit block. p^N is the probability that there are errors in the block.

Hence, the failure rate is $O(p)$.

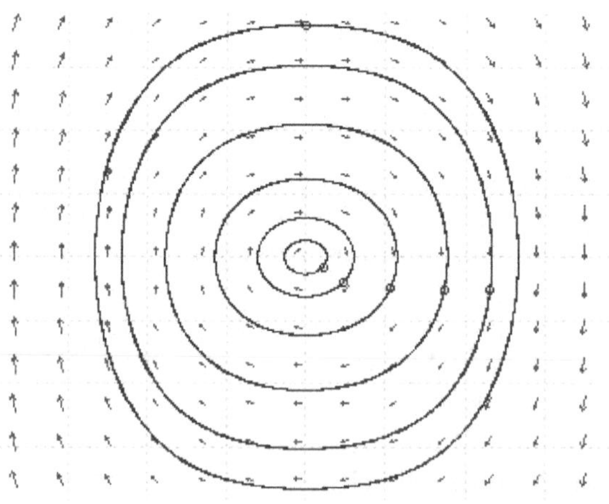

FIGURE 9.1: Elementary storage trajectories.

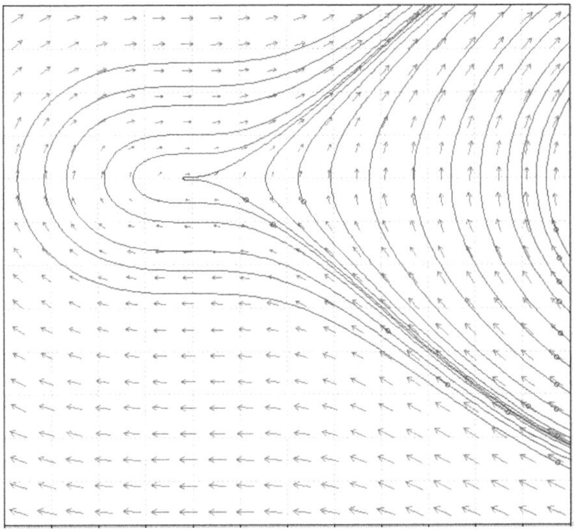

FIGURE 9.2: Nonelementary storage trajectories.

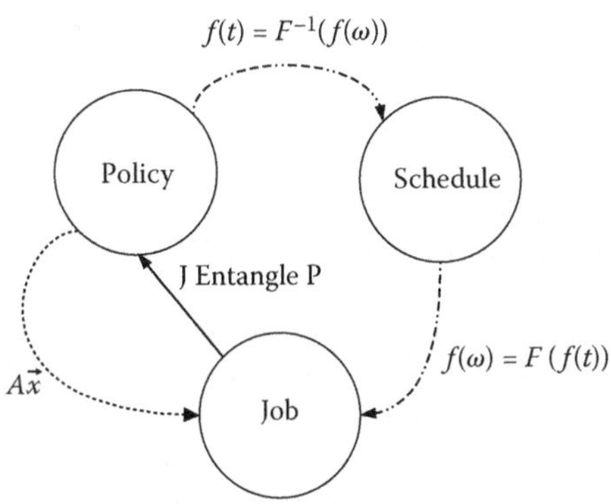

FIGURE 9.3: Policy relations.

9.4.3 Linear blocking

Dismount events are discrete and are specified in the frequency domain. Schedules can be represented in the continuous time domain. The relation transforms from onto to one-to-one relation. It becomes an invertible operation. Hence, availability can be achieved by evolution of reversed computation. It can be done without recovery.

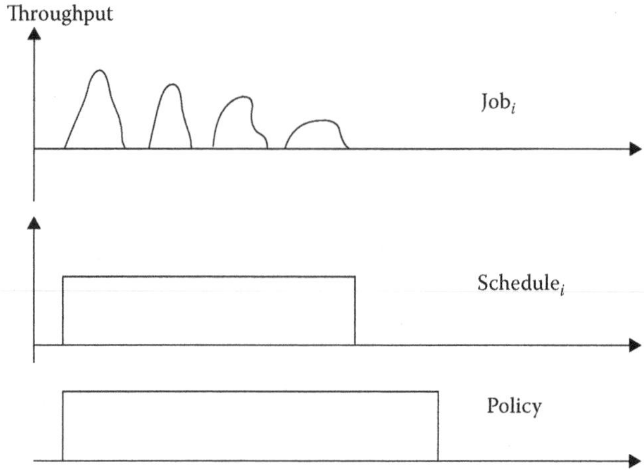

FIGURE 9.4: Physical initution.

9.4.4 Job decomposition and composition

We need to decompose jobs by their inner products of tangent vectors and norm vectors. Doing so, we obtain superimposed job states. We need to compose the jobs from the job superposition upon failures to reverse computation.

9.4.5 Uncertainty principle of availability

The first principle is about vector uncertainty. Storage trajectory and momentum are a pair of physical observables. The higher the accuracy of storage trajectories, the higher the uncertainty of service availability. Both path and momentum are vectors of storage activities. Momentum is related to density or arrival rate of storage activities. In addition, momentum also has a relation with throughput. The higher the momentum, the higher the certainty of service availability. We recommend specifying IP range, port range, and virtual identifiers such as subnet or domain names to reduce accuracy of storage sources and targets for obtaining higher certainty of availability.

The second principle is about scalar uncertainty. Storage service time and activity energy are a pair of physical quantities. The more accurate the time measurement, the higher the uncertainty of service availability. Both service time and energy are scalar observables. Energy is related to density or arrival rate of storage activities. Energy also has a relation with throughput. The higher the energy, the higher the certainty of service availability. We recommend specifying time intervals of service level and quality to reduce accuracy of service time for obtaining higher certainty of availability.

9.4.6 Quantum availability operator

Repeatedly scheduled jobs become a group, which is reversible automatically. A group operator is the basis of availability operations. In addition, to emit energy by restarting jobs, we can increase potential energy by scheduling new jobs or triggering dismount events. Hence, both time domain operators and frequency domain operators play critical roles for storage service continuity. The canonical representation of an activity vector space can be represented as

$$H_{i,j} =< \psi_i|H|\psi_j > \tag{9.9}$$

where ψ represents the state of a storage activity.

9.4.7 State evolution

A message action applies a sequence of identifiers $\{o_1, ..., o_k\}$ into their meta payload.

$$\begin{aligned} A_\sigma|\sigma, \overline{x} >= \overline{x}|\sigma, \overline{x} > \\ \textit{regular message} \end{aligned} \tag{9.10}$$

Please note that the sequence identifier does not alter the original payload scheme. Hence, the sequence identifier becomes another observable of a finite message vector space.

9.4.8 Diagonalization by job observable

According to the spectral theorem for finite-dimensional self-adjoint operators, every self-adjoint operator can be represented by a diagonal matrix whose diagonal entries are the eigenvalues of **U**, and whose eigenvectors form an orthonormal basis.

Physical quantities of jobs **J** can be persisted into a database. They form an eigenbasis for the storage activties. In addition, the persist operation is represented as a diagonal matrix. With diagonalization, activity states can be reconstructed.

```
CREATE VIEW POLICY_SCHEDULE_VIEW AS
    SELECT  POLICY.POLICY_ID,
       POLICY.POLICY_NAME,
       POLICY_DESC,
       POLICY.ENABLED AS POLICY_ENABLED,
       POLICY.RUN_IMMEDIATE,
       POLICY.CREATED_BY AS POLICY_CREATED_BY,
       POLICY.MODIFIED_BY AS POLICY_MODIFIED_BY,
       POLICY.STATUS,
```

```
    POLICY.TYPE,
    POLICY.LAST_UPDATE AS POLICY_LAST_UPDATE,
    POLICY.CREATE_TIME AS POLICY_CREATE_TIME,
    POLICY_SCHEDULE.SCHEDULE_ID,
    POLICY_SCHEDULE.RECURRENCE_TYPE,
    POLICY_SCHEDULE.DESCRIPTION AS POLICY_SCHEDULE_DESCRIPTION,
    POLICY_SCHEDULE.FREQUENCY,
    POLICY_SCHEDULE.RECURRENCE_PARAMETER,
    POLICY_SCHEDULE.STATUS AS POLICY_SCHEDULE_STATUS,
    POLICY_SCHEDULE.CREATED_BY AS POLICY_SCHEDULE_CREATED_BY,
    POLICY_SCHEDULE.MODIFIED_BY AS POLICY_SCHEDULE_MODIFIED_BY,
    POLICY_SCHEDULE.LAST_UPDATE AS POLICY_SCHEDULE_LAST_UPDATE,
    POLICY_SCHEDULE.CREATE_TIME AS POLICY_SCHEDULE_CREATE_TIME,
    POLICY_SCHEDULE.CALENDAR_START,
    POLICY_SCHEDULE.CALENDAR_STOP,
    POLICY_SCHEDULE.EVENT_START,
    POLICY_SCHEDULE.EVENT_STOP,
    POLICY_SCHEDULE.EVENT_DURATION,
    POLICY_SCHEDULE.ENABLED AS POLICY_SCHEDULE_ENABLED,
    TARGET_ID,
    TARGET_TYPE,
    POLICY_TARGET.LAST_UPDATE
FROM POLICY LEFT JOIN POLICY_SCHEDULE ON POLICY.POLICY_ID=
    POLICY_SCHEDULE.POLICY_ID
LEFT JOIN POLICY_TARGET ON POLICY.POLICY_ID=
    POLICY_TARGET.POLICY_ID\p;
```

Reference

[1] Wotters, W. K. and W. H. Zurek. A single quantum cannot be cloned. *Nature*, (299):802–803, 1982.

Chapter 10

A Quantum Method with Unknown Future Tasks to Resolve Storage Message Conflicts

10.1 Introduction

Messaging represents a space curve. Existence of messaging integrals requires spaced and ordered messages as n arcs. Storage activities communicate with a sequence of messages. However, the disordered messaging may occur due to parallel job executions, asynchronous processes, locks, and multiple phased or distributed transactional contexts. These activities may create unexpected sequences of messages.

For action $\mathbf{A}$ upon system $\mathbf{x}$ or a system relation as $\mathbf{x}' = \mathbf{Ax}$, the solution is to identify a linear transformation $x = Q\widetilde{x}$. The linear substitution ensures its invertible operation to transform a set of sequential operations into a diagonal structure. The problem can be solved by $x = \mathbf{Q^T A Q}\widetilde{x}$. The sequence of structure is critical for storage activities to operate properly.

10.2 Problem Formulation

A sequence of a finite set of messages can be encoded with their message as $\mathbf{M} = [m_1, ..., m_k]^T$, where m_i represents the *ith* message during the sequence of interactions.

10.2.1 Message representation

The canonical representation [1] of a message vector space has only two real numbers (θ and ϕ).

$$\rho = \cos\theta \ \mathrm{C} + e^{i\phi} \sin\theta \ \mathrm{R} \tag{10.1}$$

where C represents the state of order and R represents the state of disorder. θ is half the angle that an activity makes with the z axis. ϕ is the angle that an activity makes from the basis x axis along the equator.

In Equation 10.1, $e^{i\phi}$ is the phase parameter. θ controls the probability of collapsing a message sequence. The state representation decomposes a message as the probability of order and disorder. From parameter z, the probability of a message terminating at disordered mode R depends exclusively on θ. The angle θ controls the strength of terminating at C mode or R mode. It indicates the prediction of a message termination. The changes of ϕ without θ do not alter the probability but phase $e^{i\phi}$ changes. This parameter is a phase state, which represents periodic message motions with classic states of C or R. Equation 10.1 proves that the message conflict problem occurs due to randomness of system behaviors and motions of activities.

10.2.2 State representation using orthogonal basis

For a physical storage system, the state can be written in an orthogonal base corresponding to the sequence of the messages as $\mathbf{M}$. The observable is the order of the current messages $\mathbf{O} = [o_1, ..., o_k]^T$. As the measurement is a linear operator to map $\mathbf{M}$ to $\mathbf{O}$, the disordered messages represent a message state conflict during job executions and activity interactions

$$\mathbf{\Omega M} = \mathbf{O} \tag{10.2}$$

where $\mathbf{\Omega}$ is the measurement operator to detect the conflict.

Hence, the conflict problem requires detection of disordered messages. Equation 10.2 proves the existence of the operator to probe the conflict.

10.2.3 Message conflict relation

A message conflict represents an operator that maps a disordered message state and observable relation. Since there is a sorting operation to resequence the disordered messages, the conflict relation is invertible. This conflict operator $\mathbf{U}$ is a unitary operator. The unitary operator has an invertible operator $\mathbf{U}^\dagger$ that is a sorting operator.

$$\begin{aligned} \mathbf{UM} &= \mathbf{M}' \\ \mathbf{U}^\dagger\mathbf{UM} &= \mathbf{M} \end{aligned} \tag{10.3}$$

Equation 10.3 proves the existence of the resequencing operation for recovering the message states from disordered ones. The conflict problem is derived as a problem of resequencing of the disordered messages.

10.2.4 Statement of problem

Given a steadily running storage system, how can one keep its order of messages? To answer this question, we need to answer the following questions.

- How do we identify the message state conflicts?
- How do we name a sequence for a set of disordered messages?
- How do we assert the order of messages?
- Given a sequence of messages, how do we compute the new sequence based upon asserted messages?
- Given the resequenced messages, how do we send out the messages in the new sequence?

10.3 Review of Possible Solutions

There are several ways to resolve the conflicts of message states.

10.3.1 Message queue

A traditional message queue provides an ordering mechanism. However, there are several limitations to this approach. First, only message publishers are embedded with the logic of the sequence of the messages. But the messages may be sent in parallel or the messages may reach a destination with a delay. Even if senders know the order, they cannot ensure that message listeners receive the messages in the correct order. Second, the queue may not be the ready destination setting up for message receivers. Third, a single queue transforms parallel messaging into sequential processing that decreases messaging throughput. Hence, if the messages are sent out in unexpected order, receiver messages are in conflict states.

10.3.2 Transactional management

Storage activities may be chaotic by representing a state through its message expansion. From geometric intuition, a transaction has its algebraic representation and physical interpretation. A transactional procedure introduces phase operations to activity relations. However, the transition has an availability problem. In addition, abort operations have phase operations and they are not reversible.

10.3.3 Protocol management

A disordered message may be discarded. The message can be retransmitted through a messaging protocol. However, it requires a predefined scheme of acknowledgement. The interactions may effect states of activities. The scheme have phase operations and they are not reversible.

10.3.4 Message persistence

Message persistence provides a primary diagonalization with activities in memory states. Message persistence does not provide availability of the current job in execution. It is a common disadvantage of persistent-based methods.

10.3.5 Arbitrary delay of messages

The phase parameter introduces an arbitrary delay to message interactions. The delay or spin of δ may avoid a temporal resolution of disordering for a specific message. However, due to the randomness of job activities, there are no reliable heuristics to adjust the physical delay parameter to each individual message at a particular time. Arbitrary delay of messaging may result in delay of job executions. In addition, an improper threshold will result in throughput degradation.

10.3.6 Encoding order of messages

One possible solution is to encode the sequence within the messages. So the message becomes self descriptive to show receiver's the order of the messages. However, this method requires receivers to buffer all the messages in advance, and then sort the messages during post processing. This method introduces overhead at the receiver end and may not be proper for long run jobs. Hence, the receivers may not be the optimal endpoint for resequencing.

10.3.7 In memory nuffering and sorting

Another possible solution is to buffer the disordered messages and sort them by a proper sequence at sender endpoints. This method takes advantage of classic memory structures and sorts the finite dimensional vector in memory. However, this method relies on a blocking mechanism to wait for the completion of the sequence of messages before the sorting algorithm can start. There are two limitations to the approach. First, the numbers of messages to complete the activities is unknown ahead of time. Hence, the method may require the mark of completeness of the messages. Second, the space complexity of message buffer is unknown. For a typical governed environment, a scheduling policy manages more than $3K$ jobs per second. The method could result in more than $10K$ messages on the control path at a specific time. Without completeness and space requirements, in memory buffering and sorting are not adequate for long-run jobs and high-throughput activities.

10.3.8 Diagonalization

For action A upon system state x, the solution could be simplified as A is diagonal since the equations are uncoupled. To solve the equations, Gauss elimination and Laplace transform can be applied. However, diagonalization is more flexible since any invertible action Q can be applied to transform action A into a uncoupled action $Q^{-1}AQ$.

10.3.9 Resequencing messages by eigenbasis

Since senders know the proper orders of messages, message senders may ensure the sequence before publishing messages. Without static buffering, this work proposes to enforce the sequence and reordering at the endpoints of message senders. The detailed method is presented in the following sections.

10.4 Methodology

10.4.1 Measuring message states

A physical storage system can be specified by a double list. The list is composed of a state space (messages) and a set of its observables. One of the observables is the message identifier, which is a physical quantity that can be observed in each state of the message space. Hence, they are $n \times n$ hermitian operators.

10.4.2 Asserting message orders

At the sender end points, senders assert a sequence of identifiers $\{o_1, ..., o_k\}$ into a message meta payload.

$$\begin{aligned} &sequence_{id} : k \\ &regularmessage \end{aligned} \tag{10.4}$$

Please note that the sequence identifier does not alter the original payload scheme but modifies a sender's internal message object attribute. Hence, the sequence identifier becomes another observable of the finite message vector space.

10.4.3 Diagonalization by message persistence

According to Spectral Theorem [2] for finite-dimensional self-adjoint operators, every self-adjoint operator can be represented by a diagonal matrix whose diagonal entries are the eigenvalues of **U**, and whose eigenvectors form an orthonormal basis.

Asserted message states **M** can be persisted into a database. The normalized messages represent the orthonormal basis. With database persistence, each message is decoupled from others. They form an eigenbasis for the asserted messages. In addition, the persist operation is represented as a diagonal matrix. With diagonalization, message persistence eliminates in-memory buffering with block-based elimination via data partitioning and paging algorithms.

```
CREATE TABLE IF NOT EXISTS STORAGE_MESSAGE
(
MESSAGE_ID INT UNSIGNED NOT NULL AUTO_INCREMENT,
SEQUENCE_ID INT UNSIGNED NOT NULL,
SESSION_ID INT UNSIGNED NOT NULL,
MESSAGE VARCHAR(256) NOT NULL,
CREATED_BY VARCHAR(50) NOT NULL,
MODIFIED_BY VARCHAR(50) NOT NULL,
LAST_UPDATE TIMESTAMP NOT NULL DEFAULT CURRENT_TIMESTAMP ON
    UPDATE CURRENT_TIMESTAMP,
CREATED_TIME TIMESTAMP NOT NULL,
UNIQUE INDEX MSG_SEQ_1 (SEQUENCE_ID),
PRIMARY KEY (MESSAGE_ID)
)
ENGINE=INNODB
DEFAULT CHARACTER SET LATIN1;
```

10.4.4 Quantum messages and resequencing

The most significant benefit of message persistence is obtaining a quantum state for storage messages.

$$|m>=\begin{bmatrix} c_0 \\ \ldots \\ c_n \end{bmatrix} \tag{10.5}$$

The persisted messages represent the coexistence of a quantum state of storage messages. The resequencing illustrated by Equation 10.3 can be done easily using a database query operator.

```
SELECT MESSAGE FROM STORAGE_MESSAGE GROUP BY SESSION_ID ORDER
   BY SEQUENCE_ID
```

10.4.5 Concurrency of message sending

We can use a concurrency object to represent the result of an asynchronous computation, only sending out messages after resequencing.

We construct a CallableMsg object and pass it to the submit method of the executor. The submit method will place it as a task in the queue, and it will be executed.

```
ThreadPoolExecutor executor = new ThreadPoolExecutor(xxxxxxxxx,
   buffer);
CallableMsg callableMsg=new CallableMsg();
FutureTask sorter = new FutureTask(callableMsg);
executor.execute(sorter);
try {
   send(sorter.get());
   // sequence assertion
   // message persistence
   // query messages
   // send messages
}
catch (InterruptedException e) {}
```

We sort messages without in-memory buffers for all messages. The CallableMsg class asserts the sequence-id at the sender end. The sorter detects the conflicts by the sequence-id and resequences them in order by the sequence-id. Finally, the sender sends the resequenced messages sequentially.

10.4.6 Information of messages

To measure the average information from a storage target, entropy is applied

$$H_{\max}(M) = -\sum_{i=1}^{N} p_i \log_2 p_i \qquad (10.6)$$

where p_i is the frequency of finding a message from a finite number of messages N. The frequency can be represented as $p_i = N_i/N$.

If all messages are equiprobable with a uniform distribution, the entropy can be computed as $H_{\max}(M) = \log_2 N$. This is the average size of information required to resolve message conflicts. The worst case of message complexity superimposed entire allowed message states. The well coded messages approach the maximum entropy shown in Equation 10.6. A higher entropy corresponds to a fuller use of the message spectrum, which creates more uncertainty among the different messages. We suggest sending a chunk of messages in a group to obtain revertible operations without frequent message retransmission.

The information of messages received by a listener is computed as mutual information

$$H(listener) = H(output) - H(output|input) \qquad (10.7)$$

where $H(output)$ represents uncertainty of the output source. $H(output|input)$ is the absolute measure of the noise of message communications.

As we can see in Equation 10.7, received messages are related to input message probability distribution. Hence, an input distribution must exist to maximize information acquired by the listener. If we represent the minimal size of a message as L_M, we obtain a relation $H_{max}(input) <= L_M < H_{max}(input) + 1$. This result means there exists a message M to represent the source entropy $H(input)$.

The uncertainty of received messages loses unique correspondence between input and output messages. The expected number of message conflicts $E[Conflicts]$ is computed as

$$E[conflicts] = 1 - \sum_{i=1}^{N} p(output_i, input_i) \tag{10.8}$$

where $p(output, input)$ is the probability of regular message communications.

For a nonbinary and asymmetric messaging channel with a set of message producers $\{x_1, \ldots, x_k\}$ and a set of message listeners $\{y_1, \ldots, y_k\}$, the transition matrix is

$$\begin{bmatrix} \varepsilon_1 & \ldots & \varepsilon_k \\ \ldots & \ldots & \ldots \\ \varepsilon_k & \ldots & \varepsilon_{kk} \end{bmatrix}$$

where ε represents an error rate associated with a message channel.

If we send messages at information rate R that is less than capacity, there are nR payload bits generated for n bits of messages. The probability of sending a coded message $input_i$ is $p(input_i) = 2^{n[R-H(input)]}$. For a sequence of output messages *output* corresponding to the input message *input*, there exist $2^{nH(input|output)}$ origins *input*. Hence, the probability of messages without conflicts is $\{1 - 2^{n[R-H(input)]}\}^{2^{nH(input|output)}}$. Since the second term approaches zero as $n \to \infty$, we can conclude that any storage activities can be transmitted through messaging mechanics. If the length of input messages becomes large, we can achieve zero conflicts. However, a larger input message causes higher uncertainty of message processing such as coding, sequencing, and efficient use of bits for message transmission.

According to the Shannon–Hartley theorem [3], for continuous storage activities, optimal Gaussian pdf maximizes source message entropy $H_{max}(M) = \log\sqrt{2\pi e\sigma^2}$, where σ is the variance of the source pdf. Therefore, the storage message capacity is computed as

$$C = H(input; output) = \frac{\log_2\left(1 + \dfrac{\sigma^2_{input}}{\sigma^2_{output} - \sigma^2_{path}}\right)}{2} \tag{10.9}$$

where σ^2_{path} is the variance of message pathway.

10.5 Conclusion

The maximum number of messages without conflicts is 2^{nC}, where C corresponds to the rate of encoded storage messages and n corresponds to the dimensional space of input messages. The rate is illustrated in Equation 10.9. It means encoding schemes exist for storage message transmission with arbitrary low error if the bit rate of messages is less than the above capacity. However, if the bit rate of messages is larger than the capacity, storage messages conflicts will occur. Within optical storage networks, nonlinear messaging is power dependent. The nonlinear parameter does not affect the major conclusions of the above analysis on linear messaging. We may need to consider error correction coding (ECC) in real-life systems or make the optical storage systems operate as linear messaging systems do.

References

[1] Chrus'cin'ski, D. Geometric aspect of quantum mechanics and quantum entanglement. *Journal of Physics Conference Series*, 39:9–16, 2006.

[2] Halmos, P. What does the spectral theorem say? *American Mathematical Monthly*, 70(3):241–247, 1963.

[3] Istratov, A. A. and O. F. Vyvenko. Exponential analysis in physical phenomena. *Review of Scientific Instruments*, 70(2):1233–1257, 1999.

10.5 Conclusion

[illegible]

Chapter 11

A Quantum Automatic Controlled Method for Storage Test Coverage

11.1 Problem Statement

A test coverage is measured for Tikea UUI implementation based upon a 1.3.x code base. Table 11.1 shows the test coverage configuration, where line coverage means the percent of lines executed by a test.

Branch coverage means the percent of branches executed by a test. Complexity means average McCabe's cyclomatic code complexity for all methods. The configuration illustrates the number of different code paths in a method. The complexity increases by 1 for each if statement, while loop, and so on.

As shown in Table 11.1, a state of test coverage can be modeled by a three-dimensional space $[line - coverage, branch - coverage, path - coverage]$ as

$$|coverage> = \sum_{i=1}^{k} \alpha_i |line - coverage> + \beta_i |branch - coverage> + \gamma_i |path - coverage> \quad (11.1)$$

where α, β, and γ are the frequency amplitude of the coverage.

The dimension of UUI coverage state could go to $3408 \times 1358 \times 18.546 = 8.5 \times 10^7$. The dimensionality of coverage shows that the energy required for improving test coverage of UUI implementation grows exponentially. We need an efficient way to test UUI implementation with acceptable coverage. In addition, UUI implementation is just a small subset in the Tikea code base. Hence, it is significant to discover a solution to improve UUI test coverage efficiently.

TABLE 11.1: Tikea UUI coverage configuration.

Package	Classes	Line Coverage	Branch Coverage	Complexity
com.sun.vle. messaging.uui.command	14	0/904	0/346	2.844
com.sun.vle. messaging.uui.xml	4	0/163	0/61	3
com.sun.vle. messaging.uui.response	18	0/837	0/414	3.768
com.sun.vle. messaging.uui.http	7	0/362	0/140	4.324
com.sun.vle. messaging.uui	15	19/1142	4/397	4.61

11.2 Wave of Programs

The length of each line of code and the complexity of program constructs represent uncertainty of test coverage. A program is a wave. The length represents wave length. Complexity of the program constructs represents complex probability amplitude of test coverage required.

Among program constructs, the objects are particles and they are superposed relations. Classes are composite systems. The composed systems are tensored objects. Attributes of objects are measurement operators. Object relations are entangled. Function calls are transitions. Attribute getters and setters are measurement operators. Threads form channels. Hence, a program represents a quantum system of messages. A program represents a wave of uncertain test coverage and test preparation. Frequency represents moment. Wavelength represents power or energy of tests. We can test leaves. Other codes are entangled. We can test any one of them. However, tests generate noises. They are not invertible. Hence, test failures cannot be recovered (Figure 11.1).

11.2.1 Alternative solutions

11.2.1.1 Code mining

Functional implementation can be superimposed by a set of interfaces. Function composition derives association relations with weight. Code mining does row transformation. Code mining has no set patterns to follow. It depends on ingenuity and each implementation varies. In addition, superposition can

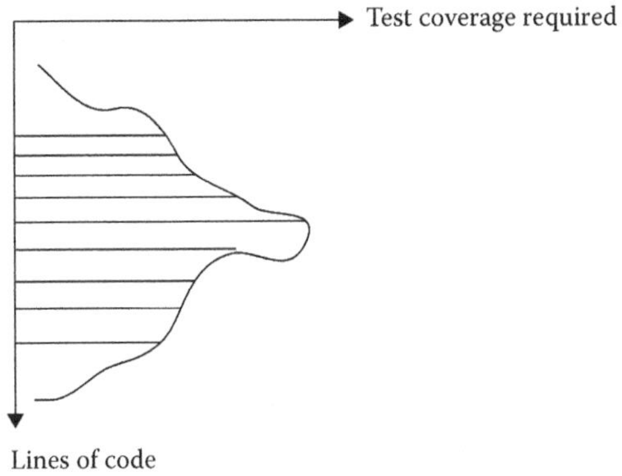

FIGURE 11.1: Program wave.

be created between a pair of methods at a time. Code mining is vector analysis. Code mining does diagonalization. The weight represents coefficients of transformation. The weight matrix forms eigenvalues. Complex relations can be represented by logic. Test uncertainty can be represented by weights. They are scalars. However, code mining depends on ontology for function composition. Only leaf nodes can be generalized to their parents and root nodes cannot be generalized. This means kernel space cannot be further generalized. In addition, the composition introduces uncertainty. In addition, code mining requires source program support in practice. Interface-based tests ensure momentum certainty of test coverage. However, interface-based tests increase the uncertainty of displacement of test executions.

11.2.2 Program configuration

Observables are results of dot products of the rule field. They form the configuration space. Eigenspace can be used to determine the configuration space. A code space can be projected into a configuration space. However, it requires prior known program vectors and the coefficients of class systems.

11.2.3 Unit tests

Unit tests provide certainty of test displacement. However, unit tests introduce momentum uncertainty of test coverage.

11.2.4 Aspect based test

Code entanglement exists within a short time period during executions. Time and space wave into objects. Aspect-based tests require specification of wave rules and prior knowledge of the code base to improve coverage. Test cases are projective measurement operators. They are testing eigenstates of a system.

11.3 Methodology

For simplicity, we can view a target system (UUI) as being a physical system with which one can associate a state expressed onto some pure state basis and a set of linear operators. We need to know what can be physically measured in such a system, and how it can be measured. Only pure states can be physically measured. Hence, for n lines of code, there exist finite possible measurements $\{M_m\}$.

11.3.1 Test coverage pattern

The test environment can be represented by states of tests. The known environment can be represented by pure states, whereas an unknown environment can be represented by superposed states. Hence, test coverage can be represented by superposed test cases against known or unknown states.

$$|M >= \sum_i a_i M_i \tag{11.2}$$

where M_i represents different tests. A simple test coverage is a set of tests under a known environment. A more complex test coverage could be a set of tests with superposed states. A clean and independent test environment is proposed to prepare system states for the test. Hence, we propose a pure state pattern and mixed state pattern for tests in known and unknown environments.

11.3.2 Complete test pattern

For the above measurement outcomes, the probability of measuring m is defined as

$$p(m) =< \psi|M_m^\dagger M_m|\psi > \tag{11.3}$$

where $\sum_{m=1}^{n} p(m) = 1$ and m represent a measurement. Elements of set $M_m^\dagger$ and M_m form a pair of measurement input and measurement output.

To obtain test coverage, we need to define a set of measurement operators as $\sum_m M_m^\dagger M_m = I$. The operators project test coverage onto each test case, which means we need to execute a complete set of test cases. Hence, test coverage requires a complete relation, which represents a measurement operator. The cost of achieving completeness is a phase operation. Synchronous tests should wait for responses and asynchronous tests require consumption of requests. We propose a synchronous request/response pattern and an asynchronous publishing and consumption pattern to obtain completeness.

11.3.3 Sequential test pattern

Successive measurement from different measurement operators K_1 and K_2 forms a serial operation. A single measurement operator can be expressed with a set of sequential operators.

$$M_{1,2,\ldots,m} = K_1 K_2, \ldots, K_m \tag{11.4}$$

Hence, we should develop a set of measurement operators for each test case. We propose a sequential test pattern to simplify a complex test measurement for large systems.

11.3.4 Phase elimination pattern

Two states with different phases generate the same measurement properties and outcome.

$$\gamma = e^{i\delta}|\gamma| \tag{11.5}$$

Hence, phase has no corresponding measurement operator in functional tests. We will leave phase eigenstates and phase measurement operators in performance analysis only.

In addition, test measurement reduces information to associated eigenvalues. There is no absolute certainty that expected test outcomes will occur. Sometimes, even when the expected outcome occurs, it is not certain that we can reason the causes of the effects. This means we should evaluate only successes as tests succeed and evaluate failure as tests fail. The results are invariant. We can reuse them in tests. However, failure evaluation during successes results in annihilation and becomes irreversible loss of information. We can not reuse the states. The test cases halt in processes. Hence, the advance information we need to know is pure states (all primitive data types, including string data types). However, if input states are mixed states such as object references or pointers, there could be equal chances of success or failure, so there is no need to measure the mixed states. What we need to know is that mixed states are passed in for the tests. In general, wrong operators result in annihilation and cannot be reused. We also derive another conclusion that test cases should be developed with pure states passed in as parameters. We propose a test pattern to place measurement at the end of test executions unless intermediate measurements are required.

11.3.5 Projective test pattern

An eligible set of test cases represents a set of n eigenstates of an observable even if the number n of pure states is not specified. A test case is a projector defined for the observable. We need to develop unit test cases to measure leaf nodes, including classes, methods, and attributes. A unit test case P_{UUI} forms a projective measurement operator for increasing UUI test coverage.

$$P_{UUI} = \sum_{m=1}^{n} \lambda_m |\lambda_m >< \lambda_m| \tag{11.6}$$

where λ is real.

Since $P_{UUI}^2 = P_{UUI}$, we need to execute a test only once for improving functional test coverage. The uniqueness of the projector P_{UUI} proves that we need to develop a single test case for a program. Duplicated test cases should be generalized.

$$p(\lambda_m) = |x_m|^2 \tag{11.7}$$

where x_m is one of orthogonal states.

Hence, frequency of execution a line of code is the probability of executing a measurement operator.

$$|\psi' >= |\lambda_m > \tag{11.8}$$

Hence, all post test states are eigenstates of tests, which do not have to be orthogonal states.

Since measurement values are real, measurement becomes observable A.

$$< A >=< \psi|A|\psi > \tag{11.9}$$

where $|\psi >$ represents a state of test coverage.

Hence, a test case is a programmable A. The element of A is the expected value of the observable measurement. Due to asymmetric A, eigenvalues may be degenerated. We can interpret the results of measurement as information reduction into basis values, respectively.

11.3.6 Joint state pattern

A unit test represents a joint state measurement operator E_{im}. For a projective test case $M_m = |m >< m|$

$$E_{im}|\psi_1, \ldots, \psi_n > \equiv |\psi_1, \ldots, \psi_{i-1}, m, \psi_{i+1}, \ldots, \psi_n > \tag{11.10}$$

where phase operator $e^{i\delta} = x_m^i / |x_m^i|$ is ignored.

Hence, we can leave phase operations for performance analysis. Test states are tensored with system states. At any given point, the system state collapses into its test state. This means we can evaluate bugs or system states from joint test states. Linearity and distributivity of joint state measurement operators ensure we can develop multiple unit test cases and execute them sequentially. In addition, joint state measurement operations are commutative. Hence, there is no order of unit test cases. We propose the joint state test pattern to develop test cases.

11.3.7 Measurement apparatus pattern

All getters are observable operators of an object of a quantum system. Hence, getters are projective measurement operators associated with real physical quantities. For objects with entangled states, Bell state measurement can be applied with a basis transformation in addition to a pair of getters. The proposed measurement apparatus pattern provides a control to end users. This pattern is recommended for specifying at the end stage of tests. We should not use it for intermediate tests unless it is necessary.

11.3.8 Tensored test pattern

We consider unit tests as higher-order $n - qubit$ measurement. This method is a general measurement without domain knowledge. As $n - state$ measurement, this method can be represented as

$$E_{im}|q> \equiv |x_1, \ldots, x_{i-1}, m, x_{i+1}, \ldots, x_n> \tag{11.11}$$

where x_i is one of the basis.

So the state of test coverage is the state of a test case executed in sequence. We propose a tensor constructor pattern to initialize tensor states. The phase operation is ignored. We can extend the test tool to test multiple thread programs, which perform tests on mixed states. For states without sequences, such as server sockets, we need an entangled measurement tool. We propose a tensored pattern for large system tests.

11.3.9 Entanglement construction pattern

A mixed state may not be able to generate by tensors. Entangled states cannot be factorized with a sequence. There is no way to measure what the states of the first, second, or n qubits are. Entangled states can be constructed from tensored states but require test gates. A test of server socket construction is a typical entangled Bell state measurement. A API call changes the basis from a system state to a well prepared (tested) development library state. Upon return of the API call, a $CNOT$ operator (representing translation and rotation) serves as a blocking port binding on the specified host.

This derives a mathematical structure for test coverage below.

- Modules, packages, and classes form an orthonormal functional basis.
- A object can be represented by a qubit with superposed n pure states.

- Methods are tensored within a class.
- A line of code is composed of n tensored qubits.
- A line of code is tensored within a method.
- Object constructors create entanglement.
- Thread execution is superposed.
- Getters are measurement apparatus.

Hence, we propose a tangling constructor pattern to initialize entangled states. Delegation, composition, and adaptation are the proposed tangled patterns to construct library calls and dependencies for initializing bell states. An infinite loop composes translation and rotation of test states. Energy is reflected and returns objects as stripped electrons. Energy may be absorbed with a return of void. Dependencies create a long-lived entanglement. Adaptation creates an entangled relation for a short time. Significant properties of entanglement states show that there is a 50% chance of projecting into any of the pure states, which are positive measurement operations. Only a single measurement determines results of entangled tests. In addition, with initial states known in advance, we only need to make one measurement for a test. This concludes paired test patterns for entanglement.

11.3.10 Entanglement measurement pattern

With entangled states known in advance, Bell basis forms an orthonormal basis and the corresponding mixed states. We propose an entanglement measurement pattern in practice. It is a reversed composition of the entanglement construction pattern proposed in the above section. An entangled state should be either blocked and wait, or translated into different eigenstates. Since entanglement involves changes of basis, we need to track back into the test basis. We can add measurement apparatus as a pair of outputs of entanglement measurement. For a generic test pattern, we add a control pattern into the above entanglement pattern. The choices of controls are I, Z, X, iY to perform translation, swapping, and phase shift to the input states. Apparently, the entanglement measurement reduces 200% complexity of information rate during tests. The reduction is critical for distributed or remote tests to pass in mixed states and obtain pure states. To pass in mixed states among different tests or remote objects, we use teleportation. For simplicity, we propose a mediator pattern for bell basis measurement.

11.3.11 A sample of entanglement measurement

The properties of Bell states indicate that Bell states need to be constructed from a constructor entangled with API library calls. A 1 to n

relation represents n pairs of entangled calls. In addition, Bell states form an orthonormal basis for any $2 - qubit$ and their superposed states. This means an application software program can be represented by joint states of tensor products or entangled Bell states. From basis representation, it is clear that Bell states have a 50% chance of successful projection into pure states. For simplicity, we can initialize a constructor in a state of β_{00}. There are two successive measurements required to test the server socket creation. First, operator E_{11} is applied to measure the server socket returned from the API library. Second, operator E_{21} tests host and port binding associated with the specified server socket object from its projective measurement. Since the second measurement of the server socket sends a ping command to the library, information of a server socket in the first measurement conditions the measurement in the second test. Hence, they are entangled. To obtain a complete relation, we design a ping request/response with eliminated phase operations.

11.3.12 Diagonalization and superposition pattern

Program source code represents a basis for test coverage. Transposition of the code base forms a set of column vectors. The column vectors are a set of eigenvectors. They are configuration spaces of the test coverage. The probabilities of the test executions are associated eigenvalues. The basis for test coverage is statistical. To solve the nonlinear test problem, we need to diagonalize tests for coverage of measurement without a change of basis. Hence, we need to develop sequential test cases for translation and iterative tests for rotation. For concurrent programs, we need to develop multiple threaded test cases for superposition. In an n-dimensional space, diagonalization has n^2 elements. The orthogonality relations place constraints as

$$s = \frac{1}{2}n(n-1) \tag{11.12}$$

Hence, for a two-dimensional local system, we need one parameter. For a high-dimensional distributed system, we need s parameter as input for the tests.

11.3.13 Request response based measurement pattern

The output of a test is a dagger operation of the input of the test. Similarly, the request of a test is a dagger operation of response of the test. They form a complete relation. Hence, the conjugated pair preserve test state measurement results.

$$< \psi'_{uui} | \psi'_{uui} >= (< \psi'_{uui} | U^{\dagger}_{output})(U_{input} | \psi_{uui} >) =< \psi_{uui} | \psi_{uui} > \tag{11.13}$$

where $\sum_{x \in V^n} |\psi_{input} >< \psi_{output}| = I$ means the complete sum of all projection operators over the test cases of V^n request and response achieves a completeness relation.

We can design symmetric tests so that the test operator becomes hermitian. The eigenvalues will not be degenerated. All test cases should be orthogonal or independent. In addition, eigenvalues will be observable. But any linear operator has at least one eigenvalue and eigenvector. We must develop at least one test case for any given code base. Different test cases can be executed with different probabilities. The sum of all independent test cases obtains completeness. The complete set of test cases defines the test eigenspace.

A failure test case results in a failure return code or error response. Responses do not change the measurement outcomes. It seems we may not need to record or leave any log entry during tests. However, log entries or traces degenerate energy caused by test failure or noises.

11.3.14 Automatic controlled test pattern

For tests requiring resources at remote sites, we propose a resource sharing test pattern. The above entanglement pattern is applied to provide resource sharing. To transport test data, we provide the flexibility for locally generated data. In addition, we need to append translating, phase shifting, and swapping functions to the test site. One property of this test pattern is that we need to give two additional classical bits. In general, there are two input channels for both the remote end and the local test site. For simplicity, we prepare a known entanglement state for the tests. The automatic control function is used for the required two bits. If we prepare a system state other than β_{00}, we need an index or a cache structure to transform measured bits into correct control bits to generate the expected bits for testing. Since the remote end needs to notify the local test for the successes of measurement, a simple acknowledgement returns the result on the remote end. The significant advantages of automatic controlled tests are tensored states. For $N-qubit$ at once (ensemble of states), we recommend developing a third-party mediator design pattern to simplify entanglement measurement. To resolve the potential conflicts of processing entanglement measurement, we propose a queuing pattern to sequentially process distributed test results.

11.3.15 How many test cases

Given N lines of code, the number of information required to identify a bug is $I = \log_2 N$. There are m independent test cases. Information given from a single test can be evaluated as $I_m = \log_2 m$. Hence, the number of test execution required is I/I_m.

Probability distribution of test cases execution can be represented as a density matrix ρ. Hence, the information gains from test cases can be expressed as

$$H = -\mathrm{tr}(\rho \log \rho) \tag{11.14}$$

Hence, number of information bits required for representing outcome of test coverage is H. We suggest creating test groups to reduce number of tests required for discovering bugs.

11.4 Conclusion

Physical quantities are frequency with wavelength and energy with time. They are momentum and energy uncertainty. We do not define fixed test time and scheduled tests. Random tests ensure speed of test scanning. Tests jump with no fixed test cases to run. Tests jump for momentum uncertainty.

Chapter 12

Protection Mechanics with a Quantum Operator for Anomaly Attacks

12.1 Introduction

Detection of anomalous attacks is a distinguished research question [1]. Anomaly detection refers to the problem of discovering unknown attacks that do not conform to normal behavior. This problem has received considerable discussion in the literature. Many detection researchers focus on application domains. Others study general methods.

The Cauchy–Kovalevskaya theorem indicates a general solution to the anomaly detection problem [2]. However, the solution may not exist in closed forms. Even with continuity, solutions may be hard to find. System behavior can change dramatically at bifurcation points. Jump phenomenon cannot be reproduced by simulation and observed from physical attacked systems. However, the Hartman-Grobman theorem tells us that the singularity types of the nonlinear system and its linearized version are identical. Infinitesimal perturbation points stay in the same regions as nonlinear ones. Linear independence of solutions and general solutions including all specific solutions can be determined by the Wronskian function [2].

The previous studies have succeeded in interpreting the detailed structure of the anomaly attacks of complex systems [1, 3]. Observation of different attack types requires precise information concerning millions of data sets, while all structures may become random. In states of such a large attack ensemble, only system spin (phase) and parity (normal or Attack) remain faithful. The excited data require a method of detection of attack types. The detection method will not predict the detailed sequence of attacks, but the method will describe the appearance and the degree of irregularity of the attack structure. The appearance and irregularity may occur in any attack, which is too complicated to be understood in detail. Hence, this chapter focuses on a general method of anomaly detection as states transit without domain heuristics. This chapter predicts system behavior without exact knowledge of resembled states as systems evolve.

This chapter computes the basis of normal data flow and attacks. The independent subset could be large attacks. Attacks may be entangled. They tend to occur together in a system. One attack may influence other attacks. More subtle methods than the concept of orthogonality are needed. This chapter proposes a novel detection on the basis of physical intuition derived from quantum mechanics.

12.2 Problem Statement and Objectives

This section gives a precise formulation of the problem.

12.2.1 Problem formulation

Clustering methods can explore anomaly attacks [1]. Classic partitional-clustering techniques separate attacks on the basis of data, geometric or probabilistic, characteristics. There are unsupervised learning methods of clusters derived from physical intuition. Some researchers [4] intend to associate data points with Potts spins and a model of statistical mechanics. There are researchers [5–8] who study clusters with quantum-based methods. Inspired from Horn's work, we formulate the attack clustering problem with physical intuition derived from quantum mechanics.

12.2.1.1 State representation using orthonormal basis

Among partitional-clustering, parametric methods assume some knowledge of attack structures. Since anomaly detection has a prior knowledge about the attack structures, it is more common to use nonparametric methods. In physical mathematics, kernel is a nonparametric approach to transform a function from one domain to another. For the detection with a boundary, a spectral representation can be transformed as Equation 12.1.

$$\widehat{\psi}(\omega) = \int_{-\infty}^{\infty} \psi(x) e^{-i\omega x} dx \tag{12.1}$$

The nature of the representation of a continuous function 12.1 can be considered as a superposition of sinusoidal oscillations of all possible frequencies. The representation becomes the density function measuring the intensity of attacks in ω domain.

$$\psi(x) = \sum_{n=-\infty}^{\infty} c_n e^{in\pi x/l} \quad \text{where } c_n = \frac{1}{2l}\int_{-l}^{l} f(x) e^{-in\pi x/l} dx \tag{12.2}$$

From a finite N data points in a Euclidean space with dimension d, kernel density estimation generates an attack probability distribution with a Gaussian kernel. A data point becomes an expected value of the position operator of a Gaussian wave-function (Equation 12.3). It determines the location of the peak of the probability. Every point has a Gaussian representation. Even without any assumption of the probability distribution, we still can map the means of the Gaussians to data points. Since a Gaussian has a single mean, Gaussians are an orthonormal basis. The superposed state of all data points is also a Gaussian. Hence, the state of an attack can be formulated as the sum of the Gaussians.

$$\psi(\mathbf{x}) = \sum_i e^{-(\mathbf{x}-\mathbf{x}_i)^2/2\sigma^2} \tag{12.3}$$

where $\mathbf{x}_i$ represent N data points as vectors in an abstract Hilbert space. The vectors form an orthonormal set. ψ is an eigenstate state space. σ denotes the standard deviation and σ^2 represents the variance of the distribution. As we discussed earlier, we consider each data point as the mean of its Gaussian. Hence, distribution here is only for computational convenience but not a statistical assumption.

12.2.1.2 Ground state of Schrodinger Hamiltonian

Classic nonparametric clustering methods consider Equation 12.3 as a probability distribution. The maxima determines the location of attack structures (cluster centers). Hence, to discover more attacks, the sensitivity of σ becomes arbitrary. This chapter focuses on a Schrodinger equation [7] as the basic framework of the Hilbert space to study attacks

$$i\frac{\partial\psi(\mathbf{x},t)}{\partial t} = \mathbf{H}\psi(\mathbf{x},t) = \left(-\frac{\nabla^2}{2m} + V(\mathbf{x})\right)\psi(\mathbf{x},t) = E_0\psi(\mathbf{x},t) \tag{12.4}$$

where $\mathbf{H}$ is the Hamiltonian operator with positive eigenvalues to ensure attacks with diffused temporal evolutions. V represents potential energy.

Equation 12.4 represents of the eigenvalue problem. $\psi(\mathbf{x},t)$ is eigenvector. $\psi(x,t)$ is an eigenstate. Eigenvalues $\mathbf{E}$ are possible eigenvalues of $\mathbf{H}$. With eigenfunction $\psi(\mathbf{x},t)$ derived from known data points, one can determine potential function $\mathbf{V}$. Hence, the proposed quantum detection associates a data point with a state in Hilbert space. The lowest eigenstate represents the ground state of the Hamiltonian.

12.2.1.3 Evolution of Schrodinger Potential

With a few design parameters such as σ, Schordinger Hamiltonian formulism (Equation 12.4) helps learning attacks by analyzing temporal evolution of wave functions representing actual data points. It forms fluid association of attacks instead of classic static clustering. The potential function $\mathbf{V}$ attracts attack distribution to its minima. The Laplacian operator $\nabla^2 = \nabla \cdot \nabla$ represents divergence of gradient of attacks. It repels to the minima and spreads the wave effects. As researchers reported [6], V has relevant minima as a local maxima occurs. V concentrates on a local minimum even without a local maximum.

$$V(\mathbf{x}) = E - \frac{d}{2} + \frac{1}{2\sigma^2\psi}\sum_i(\mathbf{x}-\mathbf{x}_i)^2 e^{-(\mathbf{x}-\mathbf{x}_i)^2/2\sigma^2} \tag{12.5}$$

Instead of interpreting probabilistic of ψ, this chapter studies probabilistic amplitude. This chapter defines a problem of discovering the minima of the associated potential.

12.2.1.4 Attack composition

Attacks occur as a superposition as discussed in the preceding section. As attack coherence disappears, the attacks can be associated with each other. This chapter represents the composite attacks by a density operator as $\rho_\psi = |\psi >< \psi|$. The composite attacks, which cannot be factorized, are entangled attacks. As researchers studied [9], an attack entanglement partition Ω implies attacks can be divided into equivalent classes on the basis of the entanglement relation. The harmony of an entangled attack partition Ω is

$$\mathbf{H}(\Omega) = \sum_{U\in\Omega} w(U)h(U) \tag{12.6}$$

where U is an equivalence class. $h(U) = \sum_{C_i\in U} S(\rho^i)^2$. $w(U)$ is a weight of U.

The transition of attack entanglement is

$$P(\Omega_1 \Rightarrow \Omega_2) = f(\Delta\mathbf{H}) = \frac{1}{1+e^{(\Delta\mathbf{H}/T)}} \tag{12.7}$$

where $\Delta\mathbf{H} = \mathbf{H}(\Omega_1) - \mathbf{H}(\Omega_2)$.

According to researchers [10], the influences between two attacks can be represented mathematically by the mutual information between attack i, j

$$I_{i,j} = \sum_{\psi_i,\psi_j} p(\psi_i,\psi_j) ln\left[\frac{p(\psi_i,\psi_j)}{p(\psi_i)p(\psi_j)}\right] \tag{12.8}$$

where $p(\psi_i,\psi_j)$ represents joint probability distribution. $p(\psi_i)$ denotes independent probability distribution.

12.2.2 Statement of problem

Given N data points, how can one detect anomaly attacks?

- What is the proper geometric representation that can be used as an attack metric intrinsic to data?

- What are the mechanics of attack process?

- What is the space of attacks?
- What are the observables acting upon data points associated with minima of local potential?
- What are the expected values of the observables?
- How can one quantify the attack trajectories?
- How can one assess the proposed method empirically?
- What will be the data set used for the tests?
- How can one select an initial subset for attack evolution?

The first and second problems relate to attack structures. The third, fourth, and fifth problems have connections with experiments.

12.2.3 Goal statement

Let us provide an explicit goal statement.

- With a qualitative and virtual analytic method, this chapter defines a metric determined by matrix projection and factorization.
- Without solving differential equations, this chapter defines and evaluates mechanics analytically with
  - A symmetric $N \times N$ matrix to represent attack space
  - A reduced H to represent the attack operator
  - Time-dependent states to quantify attack trajectories trajectories
  - Expected values of the states
- This chapter forms a series of theorems on attack space, attack convergence, attack basis, and detection.
- This chapter defines a process of SVD for data reduction.
- This chapter defines an experiment procedure and a publicly accepted data set for the tests.
- This chapter defines selection criteria to obtain an initial data set for evolving attacks.

The first, second, and the third goals relate to attack structures. The fourth and fifth goals have connections with experiments.

12.3 State-of-the-Art and Existing Methodologies

12.3.1 Ab initio methods

Ab initio methods are useful in chemistry, physics, and material science. Ab initio methods solve Schrodinger equations analytically. The methods study properties of materials only by computation instead of experiments and tests. Researchers [10] use ab initio electronic structure calculations to predict crystal structure. This analysis provides exact evaluation in density-functional theory formalism to generalize gradient approximation. The computation uses the Perdew-Wang parameterization of the exchange correlation energy. Specifically, there are two independent quantities required for calculations: charge density and wave functions. Charge density initializes the Hamiltonian. The wave functions are optimized iteratively to the exact wave functions of the initialized Hamiltonian. The optimized wave functions derive a new charge density. The new charge density can be mixed with the old input-charge density to create a final density for the next iteration. Equation 12.9 represents the core residual vector

$$|R_n >= (\mathbf{H} - E)|\phi_n > \qquad \text{where } E = \frac{< \phi_n|\mathbf{H}|\phi_n >}{< \phi_n|\phi_n >} \tag{12.9}$$

where E is a free energy. ϕ is a wave function. **H** denotes Hamiltonian.

One of the tools available is the Vienna ab initio Simulation Package, which implements the projector augmented-wave method. This computer program gives accurate analysis of the instantaneous ground state at each dynamic operation using an iterative matrix diagonalization scheme and Pulay mixing.

Ab initio methods limit analysis of properties of known materials. They rely on experiments to predict structures. Researchers [10] intend to integrate the ab initio methods with data mining techniques. Data mining provides mechanic-independent, mathematical correlation, and mutual information from experimental data. The results predict structure-structure correspondence and evaluate structure influence. Hence, the above energy method may apply to investigating attributes of known attacks but not anomaly detection. Public literature does not reveal direct application of ab initio methods in computer science. The proposed analysis on structure-structure correlation and element-structure influence inspires this effort to investigate anomaly attacks from physical intuition.

12.3.2 Quantum clustering

Anomaly detection uses classic clustering methods [1]. Clustering algorithms depend upon geometric or probabilistic characteristics. Traditional unsupervised clustering methods define new attacks by proximity of data pieces. Researchers propose a quantum clustering method from physical intuition [5–7, 11]. With experimental data, a scale-space probabilistic function presents the lowest eigenstate of the Schrodinger equation. Hence, cluster centers become the minima of the potential function derived. This method is an analytic operation. Data analysis evaluates in two-dimensional space in the research report. The quantum-clustering methods motivate this chapter.

12.3.3 Random matrices

A random matrix is a matrix-valued random variable. With multiple concurrent attacks, the physical systems may have sequence conflicts. The corresponding matrices become random. For random matrices, the eigenvectors and eigenvalues are critical. Quantum chaos is an application of random-matrix theory (RMT). The theory of random matrix starts from a series of researches [12]. Random matrices can be applied to evaluate system evolution and attack partitioning.

An ensemble of attacks represents the behavior of intrusion when the system changes. Gaussian ensemble is the most convenient one in practice. However, Gaussian ensemble cannot define a uniform probability distribution on an infinite range. Orthogonal ensemble is a valid one to apply under different circumstances, but researchers [12] reported that orthogonal ensemble is always appropriate for even-spin systems with time-reversal invariance and a system invariant under space rotation. Orthogonal ensemble is the space of symmetric unitary matrices. An attack is symmetric with respect to time. An attacked system has characteristics of space rotation, but for odd-spin systems, orthogonal ensemble does not apply. A much simpler ensemble is unitary ensemble. Unitary ensemble applies only to systems without invariance under time reversal. Unitary ensemble is the space of a Hamiltonian that may be not restricted to be symmetric or self-dual. A general ensemble proposed by Dyson is a symplectic ensemble that applies to both spin systems. The symplectic group can be expressed in terms of quaternion

$$[r_1] = \begin{bmatrix} 0 & -i \\ -i & 0 \end{bmatrix} \quad [r_2] = \begin{bmatrix} 0 & -1 \\ 1 & 0 \end{bmatrix} \quad [r_3] = \begin{bmatrix} -i & 0 \\ 0 & i \end{bmatrix} \tag{12.10}$$

As shown, symplectic ensemble is the space of self-dual unitary quaternion matrices. The symplectic ensemble represents the notion of uniforming a priori probability in the space. The dimension of the general ensemble space is $[2N^2 - N]$, where N is the dimension of the symplectic group. This chapter leverages the above results and utilizes a Gaussian ensemble for attack state representation due to its convenience in practice.

12.3.4 Statistical mechanics

Renunciation of exact knowledge occurs in statistical mechanics. The ordinary method assumes states of a very large ensemble have equal probability [12].

One obtains system information when the observation of the detailed state of the system is impossible. On the basis of physical properties, researchers [4] propose to associate data points with Potts spins to formulate a model of statistical mechanics. The Hamiltonian of the Potts model is defined as

$$\mathbf{H}[\{s\}] = -\sum_{<i,j>} J_{ij}\delta_{s_i,s_j} \quad \text{where } J_{ij} = J_{ji} = \frac{1}{\widehat{K}}e^{-\frac{||x_i - x_j||}{2a^2}} \tag{12.11}$$

where $< i, j >$ represents a neighboring pairs. J is a positive monotonically decreased function of the distance. δ_{s_i,s_j} is the spin correlation. $\widehat{K}$ is the average number of neighbors per site. a is average distance.

Without an assumption of any structure of the underlying distribution of the data, a Potts spin corresponds to each data point. The average spin-spin correlation function $< \delta_{s_i,s_j} >$ decides if the spins belong to the same cluster. The Monte Carlo method evaluates spin-spin correlations to partition the data points into clusters. This study has no a priori knowledge about the anomaly structure. It is natural to use quantum-based nonparametric methods. This chapter uses local amplitudes to form clusters by utilizing local structures of the data. However, with wave effects in Equation 12.4, this chapter represents attack states with Gaussian wave-function instead of the spin model.

12.3.5 Lattice models

As opposed to continuous-space or space-time, lattice models [13] can be applied. This is another clustering method on the basis of physical intuition. It associates a physical system to data points and uses spin-spin correlation or mutual information as the similarity index. In addition, it is a nonparametric method. This chapter utilizes quantum wave effects instead of the spin model.

12.3.6 Fuzzy-evolutionary clustering algorithm

Among classic clustering algorithms, the fuzzy c-means (FCM) algorithm is well known [14]. The FCM algorithm minimizes the intracluster variance as k-means. The algorithm may trap into a local minimum depending on the initial weights. To provide a global solution, researchers [8] propose a quantum-inspired genetic algorithm to optimize the fuzzy-clustering algorithm. The proposed algorithm uses a probabilistic representation of superposition of a qubit. A $2 \times n$ matrix can be used to encode a string of qubits by aggregating each individual qubit. This achieves compactness by reducing a $n \times 1$ vector $[s_i, s_2, \ldots, s_n]^T$ as a $2 \times n$ matrix as

$$\begin{bmatrix} \alpha_1 & \alpha_2 & \ldots & \alpha_n \\ \beta_1 & \beta_2 & \ldots & \beta_n \end{bmatrix} \tag{12.12}$$

where $|\alpha|^2$ represents the probability of the qubit being state 0. $|\beta|^2$ represents the probability of the qubit being state 1.

Hence, an encoded m-qubit matrix can represent 2^m states. The state mutation operator and crossover operator can be represented as a rotation operator and All-inference-Crossover for recombination. The fitness can be evaluated by the minima of manifold distances. The quantum-inspired clustering algorithm introduces evolution into computation instead of rigid clusters. However, the genetic algorithm provides no insight to the dynamics of the state transitions. There is no way to evaluate time-based animation and playback to assess attack evolution. Hence, this chapter proposes to investigate attacks in a dynamic framework with temporal characteristics.

12.4 Barriers, Issues, and Open Problems

To cluster attacks, there are difficulties for anomaly detection.

12.4.1 Data coherence

If we cannot obtain a metric to reason data geometry from the label points, many nonparametric techniques lead to poor results [15]. Geometry may be difficult to learn, due to disparate structures of anomaly attacks. In addition, an ordinary Euclidean distance cannot reflect the global coherence of clustering problem [8]. Manifold distance can be used to get the shortest path between two points

$$D(x_i, x_j) = min \sum_{k=1}^{|p|-1} L(p_k, p_{k+1}); L(x_i, x_j) = \rho^{dist(x_i,x_j)} - 1 \qquad (12.13)$$

where $D(x_i, x_j)$ is the Manifold distance. $L(x_i, x_j)$ denotes the length between two data points. $dist(x_i, x_j)$ is the ordinary Euclidean distance between two data points. ρ is greater than one.

Manifold distance reduces high-dimension evaluation into simple spaces. However, it lacks dynamics. Diffusion distances among points can be used to replace Euclidean ones [15]. In data classification, geometric diffusion computes upon the existence of all data points. It can identify arbitrarily shaped clusters with partially labeled data. If the potential evolves, the diffusion distance will change. A straight calculation upon dynamic distances is

$$D_{i,j}(t) = || < \mathbf{x}_i(t) > - < \mathbf{x}_j(t) > || \qquad (12.14)$$

Researchers [7] reveal semiperfect clustering may cause diffusion distance to become zero. However, there are temporal steps of data points during declassification or class labeling. Hence, the dynamic matrix $\mathbf{D}(t)$ may provide insight for the proximities and attack substructures. This chapter studies the distance from dynamic evolution to evaluate performance of quantum-based clustering as data geometry cannot be well presented.

12.4.2 Errors of simultaneous measurement

Errors in data measurement, and errors to declassification, cause data points close to others even if they are different attacks. However, a simultaneous observation of the observables leads to an error due to noncommutativity of the operations. According to Heisenberg's uncertainty principle [16], simultaneous measurement of any two observable results in errors that are dependent on energy. The error can be computed as

$$Error >= \frac{1}{4}| < \Omega_1, \Omega_2 > |^2 \tag{12.15}$$

where $< \Omega_1, \Omega_2 >$ is the commutator of two simultaneous measurements of two observables.

This relation demonstrates that there is a lower bound of measurement error as the noncommutativity exists. For one attack, the commutativity of normal flow and the attack holds. Hence, there is no order for identification measurement. However, for multiple attacks, detection probes may not be commutative. Hence, an attack group under different attacks is not albelian. This chapter evaluates the error effects during preliminary tests.

12.4.3 Analyzing attacks with large data sets

The problem of high dimension and a large number of data points continues to be one of the fundamental problems in attack analysis. Principle component analysis (PCA) and dimensional analysis (DA) require intensive computation as digitizing large matrices. The singular value decomposition can be a factorization tool for real or complex matrices. It maps data into N-tuple but not the states represented in Hilbert space. Hence, classic instance reduction may not apply directly for studying quantum-based attack analysis. However, quantum mechanical time evolution is a linear process. The linear independency ensures that the additional states can be expressed as a selected subset with the evolution operator. The accuracy does not matter as dynamics generate the steps to evolve into different clusters. Hence, this chapter proposes a quantum evolution process to label attacks of large data sets. However, this chapter still needs to examine the criteria to select an initial subset whose Gaussians are a set of linear independent states.

12.4.4 Learning properties of known attacks

Anomaly attack studies are discussing clustering of unknown attack types but do not talk about learning properties of an unknown attack. There are attribute reduction techniques in classic clustering literature. However, they cannot be applied to Hilbert space computation. Researchers [7] propose modified SVD-based (singular value decomposition) entropy of data set $\mathbf{S}^{n\times m}$. Given entropy of $\mathbf{S}$, the contribution of the ith attribute can computed as

$$CE_i = E(S_{n\times m}) - E(S_{n\times(m-1)}) \tag{12.16}$$

where r is the rank of S. $E = -\frac{1}{\log r}\sum_{j=1}^{r} v_j \log v_j$.

If $CE_i <= 0$, the features can be filtered. This chapter uses entropy analysis to determine the attribute used for attack analysis.

12.4.5 Error detection of entangled attacks

For entangled attacks, it is essential to determine whether an attack state ρ is an entangled or independent state. This is especially true for different attack schemes. A given attack state may be contained in the convex envelope of product states. The entangled state cannot be decomposed as a tensor product of two distinguishable states. Researchers suggested [17, 18] a number of separability criteria. The most recent report [19] proposed covariance matrix criterion (CMC) for separability. If the correspondence below holds, it is a separable state; otherwise it is an entangled state

$$2\sum_{i=1}^{d_A^2} |C_{i,i}| <= [1 - \mathrm{tr}(\rho_A^2)] + [1 - \mathrm{tr}(\rho_B^2)] \tag{12.17}$$

where A and B are two subsystems with dimensions d_A and d_B, respectively. $C_{i,j} =< A_i \oplus B_j > - < A_i >< B_j >$

If the observable can be chosen in such a way that C is diagonal, CMC can be computed from trace $\mathrm{tr}(\rho^2)$. Evaluation of CMC shows none of the detection methods succeeded even in low dimensional spaces, such as 3×3 and 2×4 systems. Hence, the error detection of state entanglement for multiple attacks will decrease the performance of detection. For entanglement distribution, there is a research report [20] to utilize classic feedback to provide reverse coherent information to improve performance. This could be applied to discover attack substructures across entangled attacks.

12.5 Methodology

Attacks represent a high-order nonconstant-coefficient differential function space. Because of the error function $erf(x) = \frac{2}{\sqrt{\pi}}\int_0^x e^{-\xi^2} d\xi$, the functions cannot be solved in analytical closed form. In exceptional cases, there are orthogonal attacks. They can be reduced by independent variable substitution of $x = e^t$. The function space admits at least one solution in the form x^λ.

However, attacks are influential and entangled with other attacks. We can obtain the solution by inspection of attack trajectories and metrics. In addition, we can discover attacks by reduction of order (dimension). For substructures, we need to factor out independent attacks. They are all exceptional cases. We apply a transformation to represent nonconstant-coefficient differential attacks in Section 12.2. For attack function space, we diagonalize attack actions to identify eigenvalues and eigenfunctions of attacks. The single free parameter λ is an analogy to our parameter σ or m. Hence, we design and develop an experiment to define the parameter field.

Although we are interested in detecting attacks at initial phases, early attacks may behave as normal flows. Hence, we also encounter boundary conditions until attack phenomena reveal their impacts to normal data flows. This indicates attacks may not have unique functions. In fact, we may have no solution basis, unique solution basis, or a nonunique solution basis.

12.5.1 Attack trajectory

With only first integral and compact representation, the infinite-many of attack trajectories can be superposed by an attack phase plane. Upon detection, a single attack phase collapses into a finite many attack trajectories. To analyze the trajectories of attacks, we derive Equation 12.18 with variable substitution.

$$\frac{1}{2\sigma}y^2 - (V - E_0)\psi^2 = C \tag{12.18}$$

$(V-E_0)\psi^2$ is a hard string function with nonlinearity. Even though V is not a constant coefficient, we still can substitute it by several different scalar values to study the trajectories as a set of constant-coefficient equations. Hence, the structures could be mixed with these structures with constant coefficients. So the key attack structures can be represented with a saddle shape. C represents the total energy (kinetic energy and potential energy). σ represents the kinetic energy to repel away attack centers. V is a potential function attracted to attack centers. The result of qualitative analysis is illustrated in Figure 12.1.

A single integral curve represents a quantum state superposed by a wave function. A larger kinetic energy and smaller potential energy create a single attack center. A large potential energy creates distortions. Higher energy level represents higher dimension of eigenvectors. Eigenfunctions are further away the center of a central attack. Each attack curve has a paired local minimum and a single local maximum. Local minima are not close to local maximum. The curve is constructed close to the attack center. Hence, it requires detection methods that are sensitive to attacks with many local minima of substructures. Hence, classic clustering methods have limitations to detect substructures. Even the evolution-based genetic algorithm depends on finite many random trials. Quantum-based methods are energy driven by design parameter σ and m to discover the local minimum of substructures.

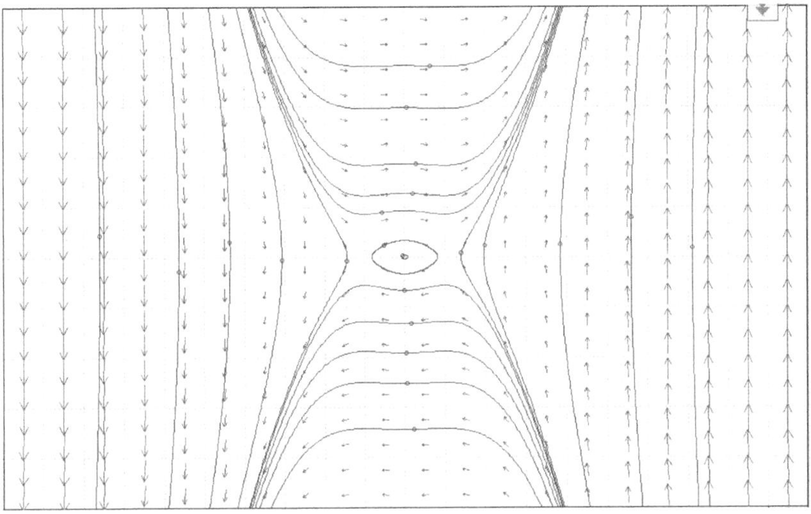

FIGURE 12.1: Attack trajectories.

A qualitative or topological sense can be derived from the saddle shaped attack trajectories. The first significant geometric intuition is the ring existing in the center of the saddle. It indicates that if attacks occur during the early stages as normal data flows are established, attacks will behave similarly to normal data flows. At this time, the data coherence problem becomes serious and hard to detect since classic clustering methods will not be effective to detect the attacks. Quantum-based methods can detect the local minimum of the substructures based upon the ground energy states.

Another intuition is striking in how three local phenomena set up the global data flows. Every attack trajectory that is not within the center corresponds to a nonperiodic motion. Hence, most of the attacks appear as nonperiodic functions but some initial attacks appear as normal data flows and have closed orbits. Hence, attack detection needs to handle uncertainty. It is the limitation of classic logic-based detection methods and geometric-based clustering methods. Even though it is a trajectory presentation with a single constant, the phase changes illustrate key structures of attack space. The superposed state representation and the proposed quantum-based method are able to identify attacks with randomness.

An attack field could be initiated from a point source to form star attacks in Figure 12.2. Similarly, the field could create defensive attacks to protect a spherical region to broadcast attacks as shown in Figure 12.4. In addition, dipole attacks illustrated in Figure 12.3 could be shaped as a magnetic field. Theses attacks have limited influences to the targets. The attack flux and divergence will decrease by $1/r^2$, where r is the distance from the center of attack sources. They are finite attacks. Infinite attacks could be formed by

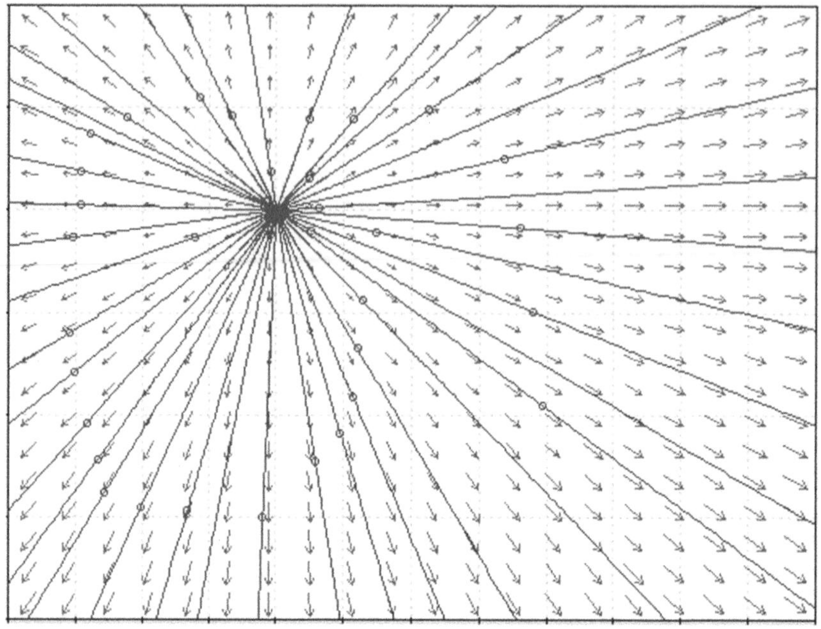

FIGURE 12.2: Star attack trajectories.

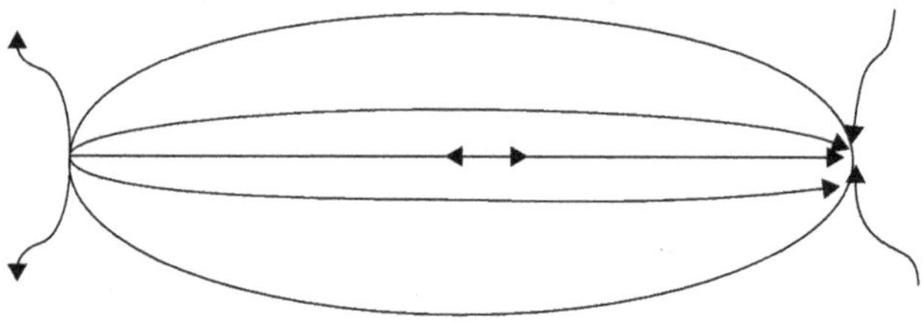

FIGURE 12.3: Dipole attack trajectories.

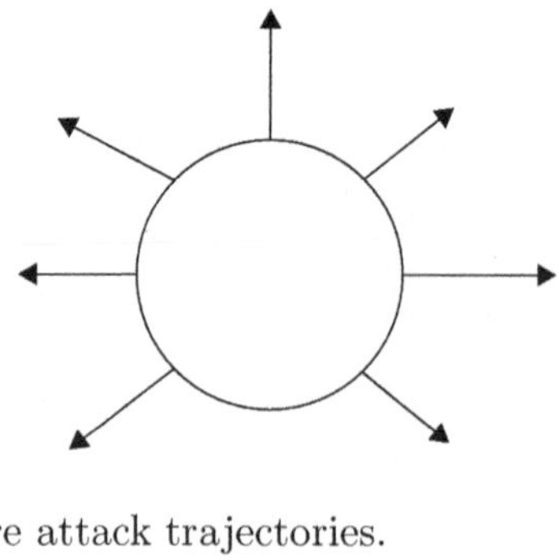

FIGURE 12.4: Sphere attack trajectories.

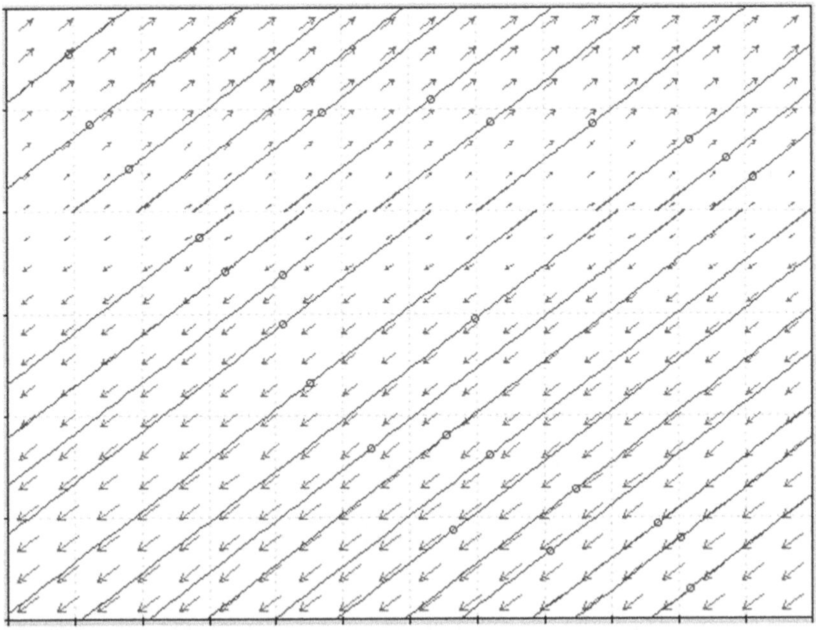

FIGURE 12.5: Parallel attack trajectories.

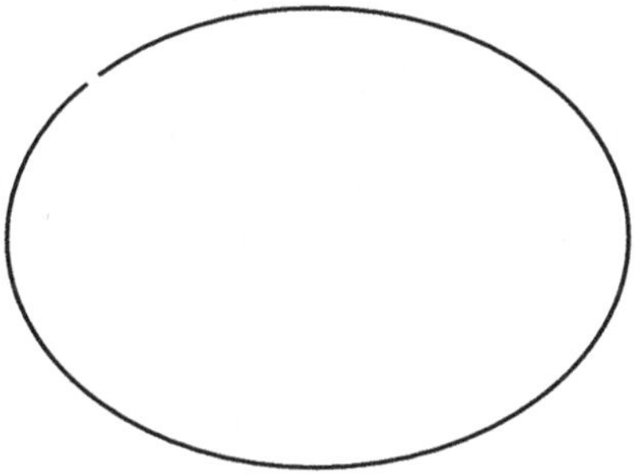

FIGURE 12.6: Superposed steady attack trajectories.

paralleled attacks. They are nonelementary trajectories of an attack plane. In addition to the attack plane in Figure 12.5, orthogonal attacks form a line of attacks. They are infinite attacks.

Considering second order linear equations and their classification, we can study the trajectories as a Laplace equation ($B^2 - AC = 0$) where B is the coefficient of ψ_{xy}, C is the coefficient of ψ_{tt}, and A is the coefficient of ψ_{xx}. As attack trajectories transit to steady states, the superposed trajectory forms an elliptic orbit (see Figure 12.6) in a global view. It indicates that a basis of four

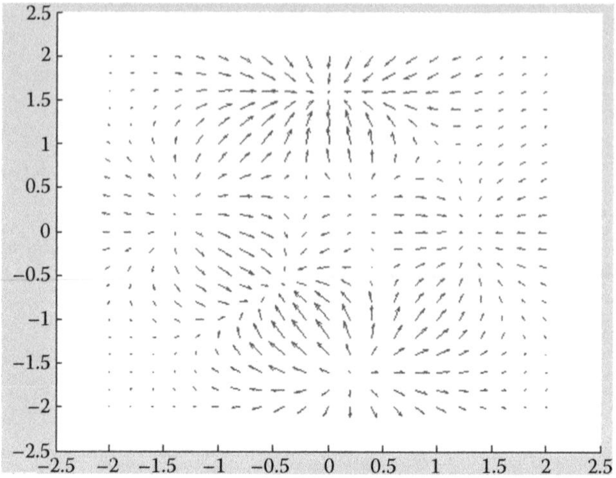

FIGURE 12.7: Superposed steady attack contour.

classes of attacks can be detected as steady attacks formed. The associated contour plot is shown in Figure 12.7.

12.5.2 Collapse points of attack structures

The above topological sense of the attack structures gives inception of the shape of attack structures. We need to have an insight into the dynamics of the attack processes. It is important to predict the critical point to analyze attacks before they collapse the normal data flows. We can derive the collapse point for Equation 12.4 as

$$\lambda = \frac{(k\pi)^2 V}{mL^2} \tag{12.19}$$

where V is the weight function and L is the boundary condition $[0, L]$.

12.5.3 An attack metric

In anomaly detection, data space is high dimensional. This research uses PCA to define a projection and a metric to investigate attacks. The principal components (PCs) are eigenvectors of the correlation matrix of data $C_{ij} =< x_i x_j >$. One can use a whitening approach [7] to obtain a scale-free presentation with $\sigma = 1$ in Equation 12.3. This method normalizes the eigenvector projection by dividing the square roots of their eigenvalues. To eliminate the "curse of dimensionality," this research only evaluates potential at the locations of data points. We start with three-dimensional data composed of the first three PCs. With incrementally increased PCs, we can further study the significance of the minima and separation of the clusters.

For PCA analysis, singular value decomposition can expressed as

$$\mathbf{M} = \sum_{i}^{k} \mathbf{U}_i \sigma_i \mathbf{V}_i^T \tag{12.20}$$

where $\mathbf{M}$ is a $m \times n$ matrix. $\mathbf{V}$ represents $n \times 1$ input vectors and $\mathbf{U}$ denotes $m \times 1$ output vectors. σ represents eigenvalues to prove the significance of attribute vectors.

This means we can reduce transform a matrix of $m \times n$ elements into a polynomial of multiplication with $k \times (m + n)$ numbers. Figure 12.8 shows a strong structure with components $1, 2, 3$, which represent significance of features $1, 2, 3$ to detect attacks.

12.5.4 Theorems of quantum detection

Data evolves during the discovery processes. A trajectory of a data point is an eigenfunction of attacks and detection. Parameters such as σ and m are eigenvalues of detection. The trajectory of each data point can be represented a N dimensional piecewise continuous eigenfunction space. Its boundary condition is $[t_{start}, t_{end}]$. t_{start} is the starting point of detection. t_{end} represents the end of the detection. There are several theorems providing proofs on feasibility of the proposed quantum detection method.

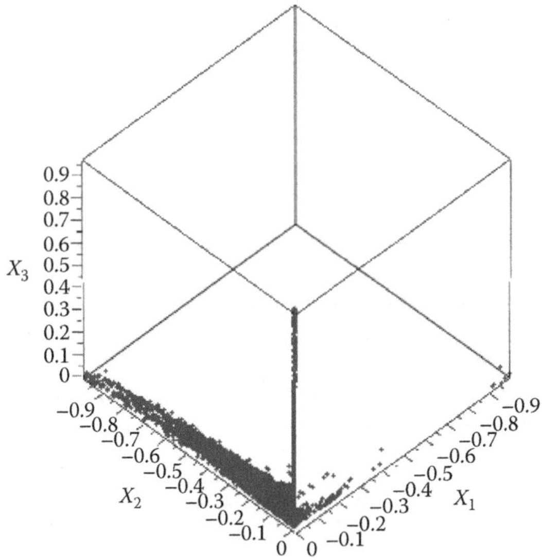

FIGURE 12.8: Three-dimensional representation of X_1, X_2, and X_3.

Attack field theorem *Data points form an attack function space. The attack space is a vector field in which the vectors are functions.*

Proof *Consider the attack function space $A[t_{start}, t_{end}]$ of all piecewise continuous functions defined in $[t_{start}, t_{end}]$. Let $\boldsymbol{f} = \psi_1, \boldsymbol{g} = \psi_2$ be any two functions representing attack trajectories of the two points in $A[t_{start}, t_{end}]$. We define equations below*

$$\mathbf{f} + \mathbf{g} = \psi_1 + \psi_2, \quad \alpha\mathbf{f} = \alpha\psi_1 \tag{12.21}$$

where α is any scalar.

Since $\boldsymbol{f}$ and $\boldsymbol{g}$ are piecewise continuous on $[t_{start}, t_{end}]$, $A[t_{start}, t_{end}]$ is closed under detection vector addition. Similarly, $\alpha\boldsymbol{f}$ is continuous on $[t_{start}, t_{end}]$, so $A[t_{start}, t_{end}]$ is closed under scalar multiplication. Furthermore, there is a zero vector $\boldsymbol{0}$. The function is identical to zero so $\boldsymbol{f} + \boldsymbol{0} = \boldsymbol{f}$. There is also negative inverse of $-\boldsymbol{f} = -\psi$ so that we have $\boldsymbol{f} + (-\boldsymbol{f}) = \boldsymbol{0}$. Hence, the attack function space $A[t_{start}, t_{end}]$ is a vector space. Since $\nabla^2\psi$ is continuous, it is a C^2 vector field.

Basis theorem of attack function space *The orthonormal set $\{\widehat{\mathbf{e}}_1, ..., \widehat{\mathbf{e}}_N\}$ forms an N dimensional eigenfunction set as the basis of attack vector space. The basis consists of classes of attack structures. The nonorthogonal basis spans substructures of an attack.*

Proof *If we normalize $\boldsymbol{f}$ in a inner product vector space A with natural norm $||\boldsymbol{f}||$, and $\{\widehat{\mathbf{e}}_1, ..., \widehat{\mathbf{e}}_N\}$, then the best approximation of attack function $\boldsymbol{f}$ within span $\{\widehat{\mathbf{e}}_1, ..., \widehat{\mathbf{e}}_N\}$ is given by the orthogonal projection of $\boldsymbol{f}$ onto space $\{\widehat{\mathbf{e}}_1, ..., \widehat{\mathbf{e}}_N\}$.*

Hence, the detection function identifies the basis $\{\widehat{\mathbf{e}}_1, ..., \widehat{\mathbf{e}}_N\}$ to represent attack vector space.

$$\mathbf{f} \approx < \mathbf{f}, \widehat{\mathbf{e}}_1 > \widehat{\mathbf{e}}_1 + \cdots + < \mathbf{f}, \widehat{\mathbf{e}}_N > \widehat{\mathbf{e}}_N = \sum_{n=1}^{N} < \mathbf{f}, \widehat{\mathbf{e}}_n > \widehat{\mathbf{e}}_n \tag{12.22}$$

The basis is attack classes discovered during detection processes.

Attack convergence theorem *An attack point is converged locally to a trajectory of detection. N attack points are converged in a vector space.*

Proof *The period of detection is $l = t_{end} - t_{start}$. We represent a data point trajectory $FS\psi$ by the Fourier series*

$$\psi(x) = a_0 + \sum_{n=1}^{\infty} \left(a_n \cos \frac{n\pi x}{l} + b_n \sin \frac{n\pi x}{l} \right) \tag{12.23}$$

where $a_0 = \frac{1}{2l}\int_{-l}^{l} \psi(x)dx$, $a_n = \frac{1}{l}\int_{-l}^{l} \psi(x)\cos\frac{n\pi x}{l}dx$, $b_n = \frac{1}{l}\int_{-l}^{l} \psi(x) \times \sin\frac{n\pi x}{l}dx, n = 1, 2, \ldots$.

According to Fourier convergence theorem, the series of data trajectories of the data points converge to a trajectory eigenfunction ψ at every point of the trajectory at which ψ is continuous. In addition, the representation converges to the mean value $\frac{\psi(x+)+\psi(-x)}{2}$ at every point of the trajectory at which ψ is discontinuous. At a specific single fixed value of x, convergence is specified by

$$\lim_{k\to\infty}\left[\psi(x) - a_0 - \sum_{n=1}^{\infty}\left(a_n \cos\frac{n\pi x}{l} + b_n \sin\frac{n\pi x}{l}\right)\right]^2 dx = 0 \qquad (12.24)$$

This is local attack convergence in the pointwise sense. For N data point vector spaces, the trajectories are represented by the eigenfunction space. We have

$$\lim_{k\to\infty}\int_{-l}^{l}\left[\psi(x) - a_0 - \sum_{n=1}^{\infty}\left(a_n \cos\frac{n\pi x}{l} + b_n \sin\frac{n\pi x}{l}\right)\right]^2 dx = 0 \qquad (12.25)$$

It is global attack convergence. The squared error integrated over the entire interval tends to zero as $k \to \infty$.

Detection operator theorem *Given a multiattack space $(m \times n)$, the expected detection operator has an action space of $k \times m$ with single design parameter σ. There is the $p = m - r$ parameter family of discovered attacks where r is the rank of the action space.*

Proof *First, we need to prove that detection is an operator. Given N data points, we represent them as $N \times N$ function space V. After detection, we obtain $N \times N$ function space W. Hence, detection is a transformation or mapping from V to W, where W is the range of definition of detection function $F : V \to W$. Since both V and W represent the original N data points, they both have $N \times N$ dimensions. V maps onto W. This concludes that detection is a transformation operator. However, other N data points V', V' may map to W as long as they represent the same attack types. This means that the inverse image of W is not a unique space of V. Hence, it is not a simple one-to-one relation. Therefore, detection is not invertible.*

Second, only linear representation of attack space eliminates errors since $F(\alpha_1\psi_1 + \cdots + \alpha_n\psi_n) = \alpha_1 F(\psi_1) + \cdots + \alpha_n F(\psi_n)$. If $F(x) = A\psi, F(\alpha_1\psi_1 + \cdots + \alpha_n\psi_n) = A(\alpha_1\psi_1 + \cdots + \alpha_n\psi_n) = \alpha_1 F(\psi_1) + \cdots + \alpha_n F(\psi_n)$ for all ψ_i in attack space and for all scalar α_i. In addition, if we expand ψ by its basis, we have $\psi = \sum_{j=1}^{n}\psi_j i_j$ and $y = \sum_{k=1}^{m} y_k j_k$. Then, $F(\psi) = \sum_{k=1}^{m} y_k j_k$. Hence, $y_k = \sum_{j=1}^{n} a_{kj}\psi_j$. This means $y = A\psi$. So we can conclude that to make the transformation linear requires detection to be a matrix transformation.

Next, since detection action does not have to be symmetric or diagonalized, k can be any integer number. For actions upon an attack space, the detection operator is $k \times m$ to multiply the state space $m \times n$. Given rank r of action space, the operator contains one large $r \times r$ submatrix with no vanishing *determinant. Using finite row elementary operations, we can obtain the symmetric submatrix by computing its rank r. The nonzero rows are linear independent. Hence, they form the basis of the attack space. If $r < m$, $m - r$ parameters are required to express higher dimensional attacks, which are not included in the submatrix since they are not linear, independent with the r submatrix. The r dimensional attacks are linear independent. They need to be represented by these parameters to gain complete relations with linear independent attacks. These relations represent the substructures of attacks and influence of attacks. Hence, the eigenspace is $m - r$. If $r = m$, a single attack separation is discovered. The eigenvector is $n \times 1$. The eigenspace can be an attack function space. The eigenvalues provide different modes of attacks, and eigenvectors represent the shape and structure of attacks. The substructure relations can be illustrated by the parameter association with the submatrix.*

For a general nonhomogeneous attack space, eigenvalue problem concepts can be applied to solve the single parameter equation $\psi = \sigma\psi + c$. $\mathbf{D}$ represents detection actions and σ can be used to model the single design parameter. c denotes external forces. If we substitute $\psi = \sum_{j=1}^{n} \alpha_j e_j$ and $c = \sum_{j=1}^{n} \beta_j e_j$ in the above equation, we obtain the relation below.

$$\sum_{i=1}^{n} (\lambda_i - \sigma)\alpha_i e_i = \sum_{i=1}^{n} \beta_i e_i \tag{12.26}$$

Since we are to discover independent attacks and e_i represents the basis of attacks, we obtain Equation 12.27

$$(\lambda_i - \sigma)\alpha_i = c_i \tag{12.27}$$

where $i \in [1, n]$.

If the design parameter is $\sigma \neq \lambda_i$, we obtain $\alpha_i = \beta_i/(\lambda_i - \sigma)$. The unique attack discovery will be

$$\psi = \sum_{i=1}^{n} \frac{\beta_j}{\lambda_i - \sigma} e_i \tag{12.28}$$

If the design parameter is $\sigma = \lambda_1$, λ_1 is an eigenvalue of multiplicity 1. If $\beta_i \neq 0$, there is no way to detect the attacks. If $\beta = 0$, α_i is arbitrary. Detection becomes one-parameter family discovery.

$$\psi = \alpha_1 e_1 + \sum_{i=2}^{n} \frac{\beta_j}{\lambda_i - \sigma} e_i \tag{12.29}$$

An attack space with single λ represents a single attack class. Normal data flow is not required to discover attacks. Since $\beta_i = (c \cdot e_i)/(e_i \cdot e_i)$, we cannot discover attacks unless applications or normal data flows do not excite that particular eigenmode of attacks. This means applications should not be orthogonal to the attack basis e_1. This applies to any single attack *environment. If the applications are orthogonal, we may need to consider modifying the attack mechanics. Due to attack convergence theorem, it is feasible to represent attack space with appropriate mechanics.*

If the design parameter $\sigma = \lambda_i$, λ_i is an eigenvalue of multiplicity p, it becomes p family problem. If $\beta \neq 0$, there is no way to detect attacks. If $\beta = 0$, the detection finds p-parameter family of attacks.

$$\psi = \sum_{i=1}^{p} \alpha_i e_i + \sum_{i=p+1}^{n} \frac{\beta_j}{\lambda_i - \sigma} e_i \tag{12.30}$$

where α_i is an arbitrary constant. $\sum_{i=p+1}^{n} \beta_j/(\lambda_i - \sigma e_i)$ represents discovery of particular attacks.

If λ_i in an attack space has multiplicity p, we have a multiple attack environment. It requires detection exciting all attack eigenmodes so that attacks can be discovered. This theorem proves that we may need to consider detection offline. Prevention methods can be deployed for online methods. In addition, polarization methods provide filtering schemes for online methods.

12.5.5 Quantum detection algorithm

Given N data points, we associate them with N attack states $|\psi_i >$. The states are N Gaussians and each Gaussian has a center on each data point. The proposed algorithm is described as

```
Procedure Quantum Detection;
/* It detects data points based upon quantum clustering. */
BEGIN
   FOR each time step t DO
      BEGIN
         Initialize-Matrix N[m,n]
         Compute-Density N[i,j]
         Compute-H H[i,j]
         Construct-Reduced-H
         Compute-Dynamic-Solution
         Compute-Expected-Position-Operator
         If computation converges to cluster centers;
            BREAK
      END
END
```

The above iterations will stop as attacks of points are constructed. The proposed detection algorithm reduces the complexity of potential evaluation to the order of N^2. It is independent of attack dimensionality. This is achieved by given analytic Gaussians.

First, we initialize a matrix.

```
Procedure Initialize-Matrix;
/* Initialize a MxN matrix with a given array of data */
BEGIN
   FOR each array of sample data d[i] DO
      BEGIN
         FOR each row of M r[i] DO
           BEGIN
             r[i] = d[i]
           END
         END
      END
END
```

Second, we need to compute the density matrix and remove all nonsignificant elements.

```
Procedure Compute-Density;
/* It computes a density matrix to include all orthogonal sets */
BEGIN
   EXP(-(x-y)^2/4*sigma^4)
   IF there is a zero vector since they are not orthogonal;
   THEN remove it
   IF the eigenvalue associated with the eigenvector < 10^5;
   THEN remove it;
END
```

Then, we compute the reduced H by its orthogonality

```
Procedure Compute-Reduced-H;
/* It computes reduced H */
BEGIN
   FOR each row of H[j] DO
   BEGIN
      FOR each column of H[k] DO
      BEGIN
         H[j,k] = Compute-H[j,k]
      END
   END
END
```

Next, we do diagonalization.

```
Procedure Compute-H;
/* It computes diagonal H[i,j] */
BEGIN
   Select N[i,j], N[m,n] from Computed Density
   Initialize-Matrix eigenvalue
```

```
   Multiply-Matrix the above matrix, N[j,k]
   Multiply-Matrix the above matrix, N[m,n]
END
```

Finally, we evaluate the expected value of position operators.

```
Procedure Compute-Expected-Position-Operator;
/* Compute a expected value of the position operator */
BEGIN
   Select N[i,j] from Computed Density
   Compute-Guassian x
   Multiply-Matrix x, N[i,j]
   Multiply-Dagger of the N[i,j]
   Multiply-Matrix the above matrix, dagger of N[i,j]
END
```

12.5.6 Attack entanglement

For detected large attacks, their substructures need to be studied. However, entanglement detection reports errors even with low-dimensional systems [19]. With the PCA approach, there are nonsignificant minima close to deep ones. These local cluster centers are candidates for entangled substructures. This research utilizes dynamic clustering to eliminate error effects to produce stable information for learning entangled attacks.

12.5.7 Data preparation

A large, published, data repository hosting intrusion data set is selected to evaluate these proposed methods for several reasons: (1) It is a subset of a standard data set and is a revision of the 1998 DARPA intrusion-detection evaluation data set that originated from the MIT Lincon Labs [21]. (2) It is a data set proven by researchers [17, 22–25] and has been used for the third International Knowledge Discovery and Data Mining Tools competition and the fifth International Conference on Knowledge Discovery and Data Mining. (3) It is an intrusion prediction-specific data set and was used to build a network of intrusion-predictive models to detect intrusions or attacks. (4) It includes the simulation of broad intrusions into a military network environment. (5) This data set has been preprocessed.

In this data set, features characterizing network traffic behavior can be extracted to produce each record. The values of data records contain two categories. One category contains the symbolic values and another contains the real numbers. The data size is 45 MB. It contains 95278 normal data points and 38 attack types including sqlattack, xterm, snmpguess, snmpgetattack, loadmodule, mailbomb, apache2, xsnoop, pod, httptunnel, xlock, rootkit, udpstorm, mscan, processtable, ipsweep, land, nmap, multihop, smurf, named, teardrop, neptune, buffer_overflow, satan, sendmail, perl, worm, phf, ps, saint, ftp_write, portsweep, normal, guess_passwd, back, imap, and warezmaster.

12.5.8 Data and attribute selection

Large data set analysis of attacks is not practical. The no-periodicity and randomness of attack trajectories indicates the validity of random instance reduction. To obtain the reduction, this research produces random subsamples with 10,000 data points as a subset. The Gaussians are a set of principal linearly independent states for the detection problem. They can span a complete data set. However, empirical results are required to evaluate the effectiveness of the instance reduction. Since there is no a prior knowledge of the data set for anomaly attacks, the reservoir sampling algorithm can be used to generate the samples.

In this research, to obtain attribute space, we use the SVD method in Equation 12.16. This research performs PCA and transforms the original feature space into a more compact space. PCA is an orthogonal linear transformation. It calculates the eigenvalue decomposition of a data correlation matrix. PCA transforms a data set into a new coordinate system. The greatest variance by any projection of the data lies on the first coordinate, first PC. The second greatest variance lies on the second coordinate, and so on. PCA is the optimal transformation of given data in least-square terms.

12.6 Examples in Details

12.6.1 Data preprocessing

The first step is to preprocess data sets. Among the $KDDCup99$ samples, we select the corrected data set for clustering analysis. The data set has a 45 MB file size. There are 311,029 data points with 42 columns in the data set. The samples can have five classes of separation including normal data.

We use these data samples to design and develop a data feeder which transforms the published data sets into a space-separated format for analysis. Each parameter in the data set can be formulated like a data feature. The value of each parameter is the corresponding percept of the variable. Hence, there are 42 attributes in the relations of the resulting corrected file. It can be used for attribute selection to compute the subset of feature extraction for further detection. The attribute selection can be applied to the classifier level to achieve compatible results.

There are several modifications to the data set.

- We design a data feeder to compute the frequency of each symbolic value and replace it with its expected value. After this modification, the data set becomes a numerical data set.
- We convert the comma-separated data file into a space-separated data file with a new line return character at the end of each data point for computational convenience.
- We remove the class labels for data input.

12.6.2 Determine cluster center

The second step is algorithmic computation. To discover the cluster center, we need to obtain the attack metric. As we discussed in Section 12.5, with a three dimensional model with no more than 41 PCs, all potential minima can be located. With the best-geometric representation, quantum detection algorithm can be applied. If any large-attack instance is discovered, its substructure should be further analyzed. The design parameters σ and m should be applied to detect entangled attacks and substructures.

12.7 Experimental Results

12.7.1 Overall data representation

The sample data points can be represented in a vector space. The vectors can be projected into a three-dimensional space where we select only the first three dimensions. All points can be plotted in black.

KDDCup99 is a relatively well-structured data set. The collected attack trajectories are the subset of the trajectories as we analyzed in Section 12.5. Since the trajectory may take center or focus type motion paths in other dimensions, it could have ring or uncorrelated structures. Hence, to some extent, the data coherence problem is still an issue as we discussed earlier. This can be proved by analysis of attack metrics. To discover the entangled attacks, we still need to identify all local minimum of all substructures as shown in Figure 12.9.

12.7.2 Attack metric

The SVD analysis is shown in Figure 12.10. Given in 41-dimensional space, the attack projection reveals orthogonal spans along the first, second, and third PCs (eigenvectors) of the correlation matrix of the data. They represent

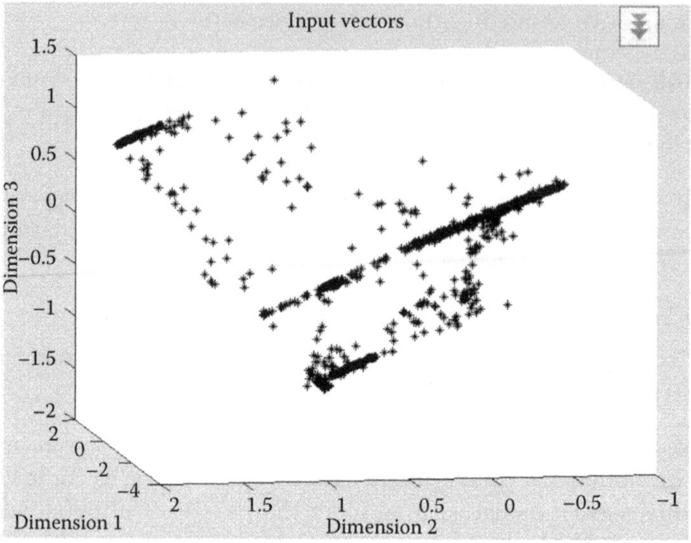

FIGURE 12.9: KDDCup99 Three-dimensional representation.

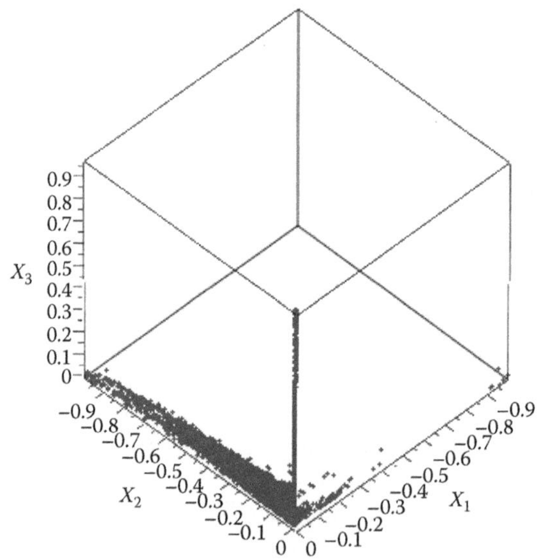

FIGURE 12.10: SVD result-1.

eigenfunctions and eigenvalues. There are two attack bases with X_2, X_3. Figure 12.10 shows attacks attracted by X_2 and X_3. The scalars multiply with the basis to convey the growth of potential energy in the attack trajectories. The degraded kinetic energy causes attraction of attack trajectories. The outcome of the repelling becomes the outlier of $< X_1, X_2 >$, which indicates the repelled attack types. The gain of kinetic energy subtracted from its potential energy shows that there is the incidence of local minimum, which implies different levels of attack energy. It indicates that we need to develop new dimensions of the attack metric. In general, the asymmetric data represent the outcome of attack forces. Figure 12.10 illustrates that there are at least three classes of attacks in the data set.

The significant finding is that there is no clear gravity attack center in these dimensions. The scalar attacks are unstable proper nodes. They are unstable attacks. They can be controlled by justifying or canceling the scalars. However, the spatial attacks are unstable proper nodes. They are unstable attacks and cannot be controlled. The large attacks separated with small attacks require a filtering or balancing prevention scheme and a distributed prevention scheme. These attacks show a strong gradient. Since $\nabla \times \nabla \psi = 0$, there is no rotation after the gradient of attacks. Hence, the span of attacks causes the major impact of these scaled attacks even when they are not random. Prevention schemes are critical. The most effective strategy is to stop these attacks at earlier phases. Since a large data flow may represent a normal data flow, a central detection scheme is also important.

We extend projection with the fourth, fifth, and sixth PCs (eigenvectors) of the correlation matrix of the data. We discover both association and separation of attacks. The association shows evidence of substructures of attacks and influences among different attacks. In Figure 12.11, attack trajectories translate and rotate into X_4, X_5, X_6. The equilibrium can be obtained by canceling potential and kinetic energy. The attack structures are not orthogonal. The translation and rotation diagonalize the evolution of attacks. The phenomena proves that the attacks are reversible. They can be virtually analyzed by animation. The eigenfunctions and eigenvalues can be computed by the diagonalization. The asymmetric and distorted structures indicate the repelling from attack collisions. The structures may be the result of a large attack colliding with several small attacks at higher energy levels. They represent strong influences at different energy levels. The spatial outlier represents corruption of some small attacks. The strong association of attacks remains as a unity of attacks. The more inclosed substructures of attacks may be created by unification of small attacks at similar energy levels or a large attack at a lower energy level. This shows the gravity of attractions to different attacks. In general, the asymmetric data represent attack collisions. Rotation and translation of attacks is the outcome of attacks.

One significant finding is that there is an attraction center in the attack structures. In addition, there are the wind-in focus structures represented as ring structures in X_4, X_5, X_6. They are stable attacks, which will get weak by themselves. However, spatial attacks are unstable proper nodes. They are unstable attacks with lower energy. They are hard to prevent. The attraction forms non-elementary attacks representing higher energy. Hence, classic clustering methods may not be effective to identify these attacks. The

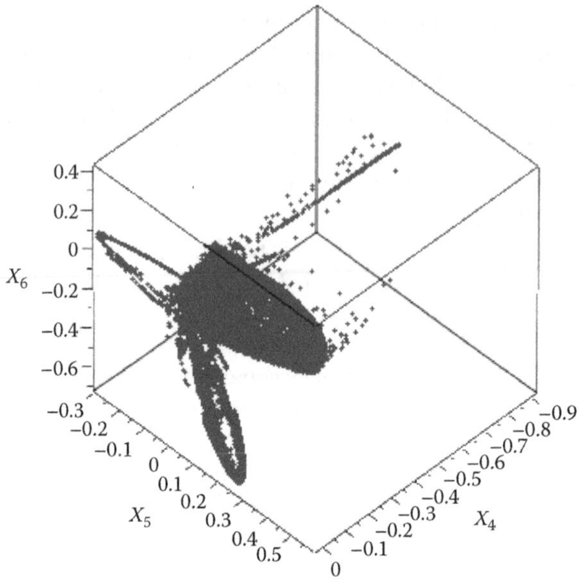

FIGURE 12.11: SVD result-2.

proposed quantum-based method will be critical to discover the attacks and their substructures by finding the local minimum.

These attacks are hard to prevent and control in general. The large-small or small-small attacks require both local and distributed prevention schemes. Since $\nabla \times \nabla\psi = 0$, there is no rotation after gradient of attacks. Hence, expansion of attacks causes the major impact of these random attacks. The attack collision and strong attraction are dynamically formed, which indicates random initial attack points. Therefore, a prevention scheme may not be the most effective method for these attacks. However, the strong attraction shows prevention schemes will be effective there. Distributed prevention schemes need to be considered for expansion of attack edges since the gradient of these attacks causes impacts there. Detection methods may not be effective to these random attacks. There are two spin offs representing rotation of attacks. Since $\nabla \cdot \nabla \times \psi = 0$, there is no divergence after rotation of attacks. Hence, the two attack rings cannot expand further. They are periodic attacks. We can deploy local detection methods to identify these attacks.

We project attacks into the seventh, eighth, and ninth PCs (eigenvectors) of the correlation matrix of the data. In Figure 12.12, we discover a strong rotation center of two principal attacks. The collapsed symmetric denotes a strong attack metric. It reveals the gravity center of attacks. Each attack embeds with rotated substructures. The substructures are also attracted by the attack center. The strong rotation is the outcome of balancing energy levels. It indicates attack collision among small attacks or large attacks with

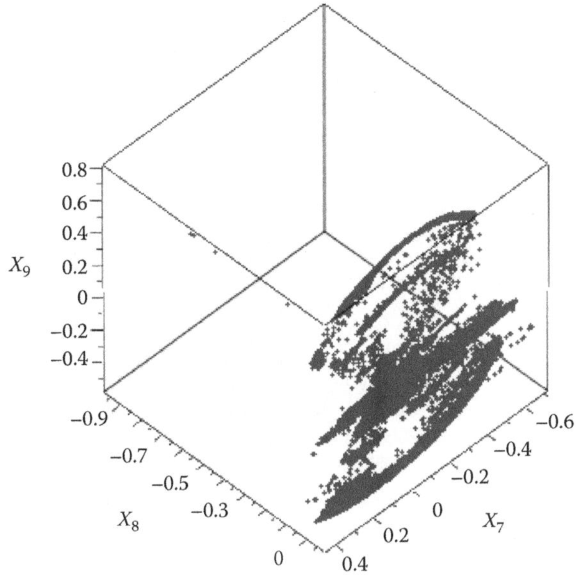

FIGURE 12.12: SVD result-3-1.

similar energy levels. They collapse into different attacks, which have low energy levels. This demonstrates a center metric with the wind-in focus. They are stable attacks. The influences of attacks concentrate on a target among the neighbors of the gravity centers. They limit the center of the attacks. Since $\nabla \times \nabla\psi = 0$, there is no divergence after curl. The attacks will not further distribute after rotations. The rotation forms periodic attacks. There are better chances for detection schemes to identify the attacks. Most influential attacks are not at the center of gravity. Hence, local detection instead of distributed prevention schemes will be more effective. Since there is a gravity center of attacks, it is possible to detect the attack center at the earlier phase to stop the evolution of attacks effectively.

If we zoom in on one of the previous major attacks (Figure 12.13) to examine its substructures, we find that the internal structures represent nonelementary dynamics. What we find indicates the collision of attacks. They are not stable attacks. There is a rich set of substructures encompassing different attack centers. The gravity cancels collision forces and forms unstable focuses. They are unstable attacks. The attack has a serious impact to normal data flows. It requires both an application or system local prevention scheme for different substructures. There is no significant intuition of rotation hidden in the substructures. The randomness of substructures indicates that detection scheme may not be effective measure to subattacks. Local prevention schemes may need to be considered for the subattacks.

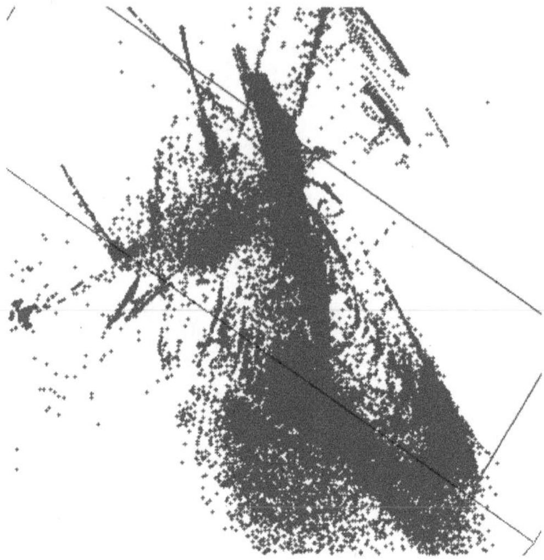

FIGURE 12.13: SVD result-3-2.

As we project attacks into $< X_{13}, X_{14}, X_{15} >$ as shown in Figure 12.14, we find that there is a strong gravity center of attacks. The spatial data indicates a collision exists among different substructures before this attack metric is formed. The attraction generates a nonelementary fluid of attacks, which can be the result of large-small attack collisions. The colliding force generates different attacks represented by spatial attacks. They are wind-out improper nodes. They are unstable attacks. The large-small attacks have more than one central target. They require both distributed and central prevention schemes. Even though there is no indication of the initial starting point of attacks, the strong attraction center does convey that the severe impacted area needs to be identified first since the attraction center will be dynamically formed. In addition, since $\nabla \times \nabla\psi = 0$, there will be no rotation after the gradient of attacks. Hence, the random expansion of attacks causes the greatest impact of attacks. These are nonperiodic attacks. Detection methods may be effective only as the center is formed. However, the center may represent normal flows. Hence, we need more frequent data sampling or distributed online prevention schemes to control expansion of these random attacks.

As we project attacks into $< X_{16}, X_{17}, X_{18} >$, we find that there is a strong collision of attacks in Figure 12.15. The spatial data indicates a collision exists among different substructures before this attack metric is formed. The attraction generates a nonelementary fluid of attacks. It can be the result of small-small attack collisions. The colliding force generates different attacks represented by spatial attacks. They are wind-out improper nodes. They are unstable attacks. The small-small attacks have no fixed targets. Since $\nabla \times \nabla\psi = 0$, there will be no rotation after the gradient of attacks.

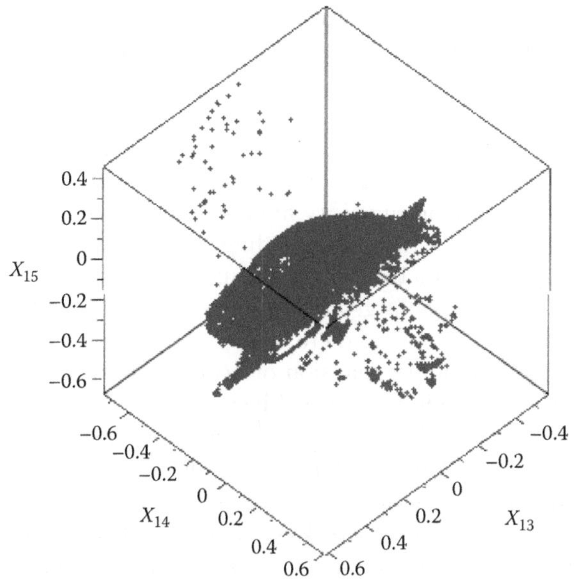

FIGURE 12.14: SVD result-4.

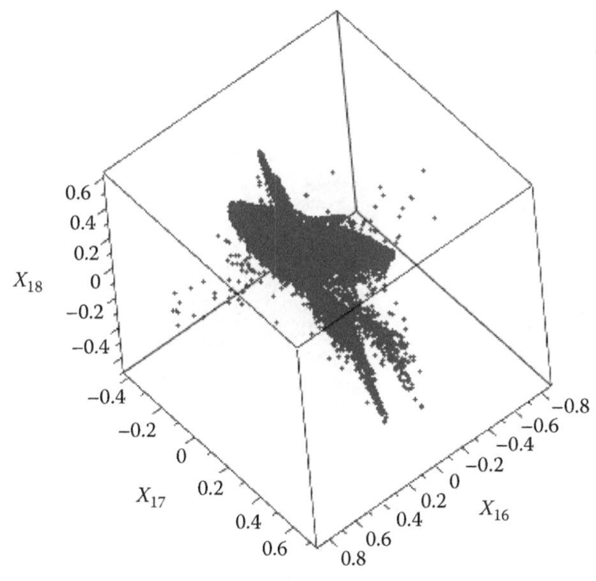

FIGURE 12.15: SVD result-5.

Hence, the random expansion of attacks causes the greatest impact of attacks. These are random attacks. Since the attack structures could be a collision of strong normal flows and attacks at lower energy levels, we need a distributed prevention scheme to limit the attacks.

As we project attacks into $< X_{19}, X_{20}, X_{21} >$, we find that there is a strong collision of attacks in Figure 12.16. The spatial data indicates a collision exists among different substructures before this attack metric is formed. The attraction generates a nonelementary fluid of attacks, which can be the result of large-large attack collisions. The colliding force generates different attacks represented by spatial attacks. They are wind-out improper nodes. They are unstable attacks. The large-large attacks can expose randomly. They have no fixed targets. Since $\nabla \times \nabla \psi = 0$, there will be no rotation after the gradient of attacks. Hence, the random expansion of attacks causes the greatest impact of attacks. These are random attacks. Since the attack structures could be a collision of strong normal flows and attacks at lower energy levels, we need a distributed prevention scheme to limit the attacks.

There is a significant finding as we project attacks into $< X_{22}, X_{23}, X_{24} >$. Figure 12.17 represents a cloud attack. We find that there is a strong evolution of attacks. The gravity center has evolved with many substructures before this attack metric is formed. The attraction generates a nonelementary fluid of attacks, which can be the result of a large number of small-small attack collisions. The colliding force rotates different attacks represented by spatial attacks. Hence, cloud attacks have a gravity center with strong periodic

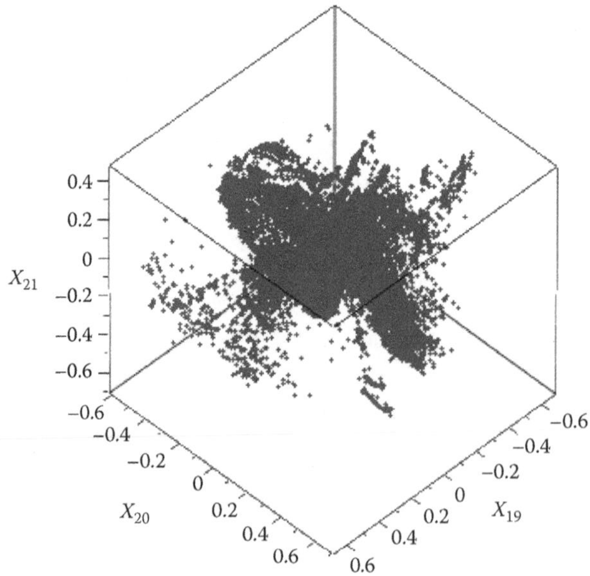

FIGURE 12.16: SVD result-6.

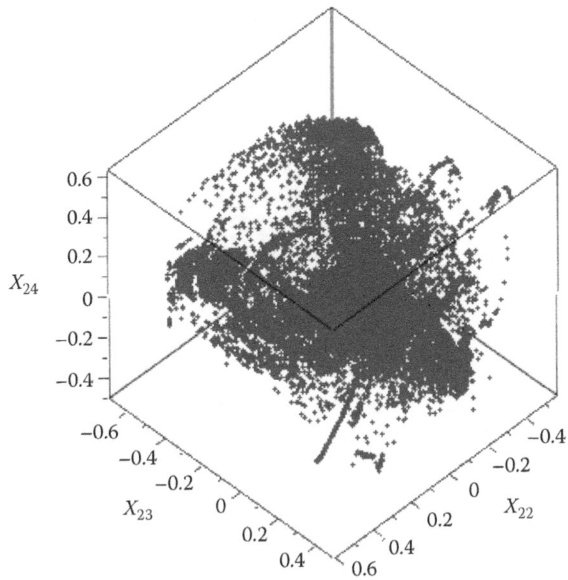

FIGURE 12.17: SVD result-7.

rotation. They are easy to detect from their patterns. The cloud attacks can evolve their targets dynamically. Since $\nabla \cdot \nabla \times \psi = 0$, there will be no divergence after rotation of attacks. Hence, the periodic translation of attacks causes the greatest impact of attacks but the norms of translated attacks will not increase. These are periodic attacks. Detection schemes are effective to identify the attacks. We need to consider combining central detection schemes with distributed ones to these attacks because of translation of attacks. Cloud attacks should be prevented at the early stage. They can be systemically evolved. This attack model is hard to detect.

As we project attacks into $< X_{25}, X_{26}, X_{27} >$, we find that there is a strong gravity of attacks in Figure 12.18. The spatial data indicates a collision exists among a small number of attacks at low-energy levels with large attacks at high-energy levels. The attraction generates a non-elementary fluid of attacks, which can be the result of large-small attack collisions. The colliding force generates different attacks represented by spatial attacks. They are wind-out proper nodes. They are unstable attacks that translate to different targets. The small-large attacks require a central prevention scheme around the attack center. Since $\nabla \times \nabla\psi = 0$, there will be no rotation after gradient of attacks. Hence they are random attacks. We need to consider a central prevention scheme for these attacks. However, the attraction center may represent normal data flows. A distributed detection scheme may also need to be considered for the random attacks.

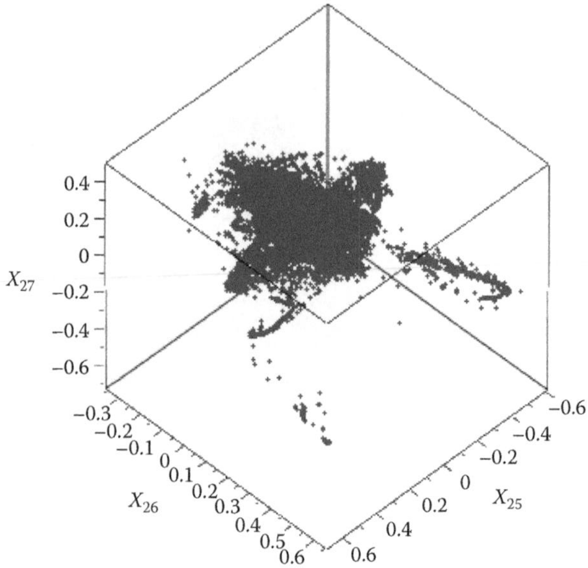

FIGURE 12.18: SVD result-8.

As we project attacks into $< X_{28}, X_{29}, X_{30} >$, we find that there is a strong gravity of attacks in Figure 12.19. The spatial data indicates a collision exists among a small number of attacks at low-energy levels with large attacks at high-energy levels. The attraction generates a nonelementary fluid of attacks, which can be the result of large-small attack collisions. The colliding force generates different attacks represented by spatial attacks. They are wind-out improper nodes. They are unstable attacks to translate to other targets. Since $\nabla \times \nabla\psi = 0$, there will be no rotation after the gradient of attacks. Hence they are random attacks. We need to consider a central prevention scheme for these attacks. However, the attraction center may represent normal data flows. A distributed detection scheme may also need to be considered for the random attacks.

As we project attacks into $< X_{31}, X_{32}, X_{33} >$, we find that there is a strong attraction of attacks in Figure 12.20. The attraction generates a center of attacks. They are wind-out proper nodes. They are unstable attacks. The center attacks require both a central prevention scheme. As it is illustrated in Figure 12.20, these attacks should be prevented during the early phase. The attacks have centralized targets. We may consider a central firewall to prevent the wind-out proper attacks from spreading to their neighbors. Since $\nabla \times \nabla\psi = 0$, there will be no rotation after the gradient of attacks. Hence they are random attacks. We need to consider a central prevention scheme for these attacks. However, the attraction center may represent normal data

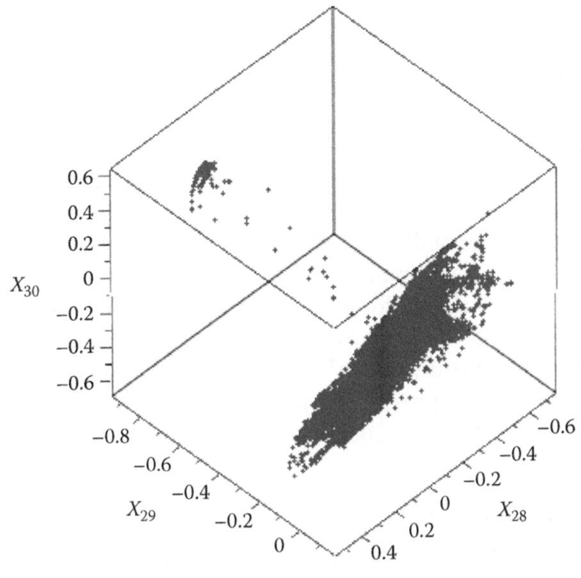

FIGURE 12.19: SVD result-9.

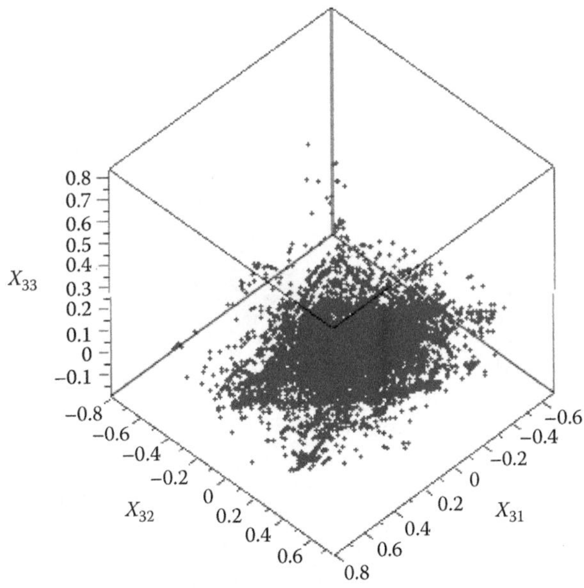

FIGURE 12.20: SVD result-10.

flows. A distributed detection scheme may also need to be considered for the random attacks.

As we project attacks into $< X_{34}, X_{35}, X_{36} >$, we find that there is a complete collision of attacks in Figure 12.21. The collapsed data indicate a collision of attacks with low-energy levels. The activity generates a nonelementary fluid of attacks, which can be the effect of small-small attack collisions. The colliding force generates different attacks structures. They are wind-out improper nodes. They are unstable attack structures. The gravity cancels the collision force to reach equilibrium of potential energy and kinetic energy. The generated structures have similar mass distribution as their gravity center. There are no central targets for these attacks. Since $\nabla \times \nabla\psi = 0$, there will be no rotation after gradient of attacks. Hence they are random attacks. We need to consider a central prevention scheme for these attacks. However, the attraction center may represent normal data flows. A distributed detection scheme may also need to be considered for the random attacks.

12.7.3 Data reduction

A ranking algorithm and PCA are combined for dimensional reduction. Twenty one transformed attributes are selected on the basis of ranking of their eigenvalues as $[8.49728, 4.10527, 3.90639, 2.91242, 1.75189, 1.4161, 1.39554, 1.27079, 1.09575, 1.0287, 1.01221, 1.00437, 0.9984, 0.98842, 0.95443, 0.93555, 0.93146, 0.88048, 0.83856, 0.67198, 0.53947]^T$.

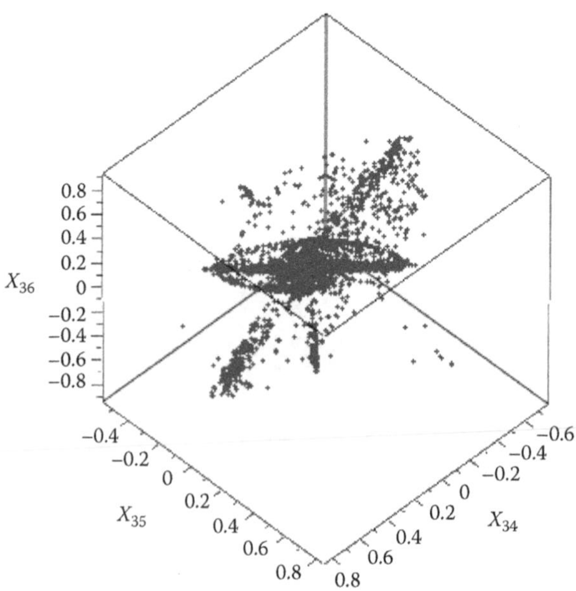

FIGURE 12.21: SVD result-11.

12.8 Comparison of Detection Methods, Algorithms, and Results

12.8.1 Representation scheme

If we order data by detection, color points represent different clusters in the discovery. Each one of the points can be represented as a x-coordinate equal to the location of the cluster in the data matrices, and a y-coordinate indicating the tag reported by the detection. We plot only the first three dimensions of attack space, due to the visibility of data representation. Perfect separation can be represented as homogenous rectangles in its spectrum report. The purity and spectrum will also be analyzed to understand robustness of detection processes.

12.8.2 Experimental analysis

For a reduced experimental data set, we have an attack space ($10{,}000 \times 22$). Hence, the expected detection action is $m \times 10{,}000$. Since detection action does not have to be symmetric, m can be any integer number. According to the attack operator theorem, attack eigenspace for this experiment is $10{,}000 - r$ given rank r. The eigenvector is a form of 22×1. There are multiple parameter settings for σ to test all possible substructures and influences of attacks. The relation can be represented as

$$\psi = \sum_{i=1}^{p} \alpha_i e_i + \sum_{i=p+1}^{10{,}000} \frac{\beta_j}{\lambda_i - \sigma} e_i \tag{12.31}$$

where e_i represents the ith eigenvector. p is the multiplicity of a λ value (see Equation 12.30).

For λ_i with multiplicity 1, the relation becomes

$$\psi = \alpha_1 e_1 + \sum_{i=2}^{10{,}000} \frac{\beta_j}{\lambda_i - \sigma} e_i \tag{12.32}$$

where e_i represents the ith eigenvector (see Equation 12.29).

σ is the only design parameter. Since it is a multiattack environment, detection requires exciting all attack eigenmodes to identify all attacks. Hence, we need to adjust different settings of σ for these independent tests. We test the detection method with different σ settings to obtain a modal associated structure of attacks. The relations can be plotted in three-dimensional detection results and detection spectrum diagrams.

12.8.3 Comparison of quantum detection with different fields

The proposed quantum detection method ($\sigma = 0.9$) discovers four basic types. The detection result is illustrated in Figure 12.22. It is a plot of the first three dimensions of cluster results. If we consider a data point in a class as a detection event, we think of natural representation of detection as a superposition of oscillations of all possible frequencies. The spectral representation of detection is illustrated in Figure 12.23.

With a reduced attack space 10,000 × 22, Figure 12.22 shows that there are four classes of attacks discovered. They represent a four-dimensional eigenspace (span $\{k_1, k_2, k_3, k_4\}$) where k_i denotes the basis of a class of attacks. The corresponding eigenvalues are $\lambda_1, ..., \lambda_4$ associated with $\sigma = 0.9$.

The spectrum in Figure 12.23 shows the modes of four classes of attacks represented in four ranges of frequency of attacks. Four rows of linear independent vectors represent the attack function space. The spectrum is consistent with the result of asymmetric rank analysis. Within the class of attacks with label 1, the attacks seem more homogeneous. The class represents the high mode of attacks. Conversely, class 3 of attacks represents the low mode of attacks. The overall fit is the mixed modes of attacks. The eigenvalues determine the modes of attacks, possibly $\Omega = \sqrt{\lambda}$. The eigenvectors give the structures or configuration of attacks. Since not every dimension of eigenspace in the spectrum conveys a single frequency of attacks, there is a range of frequencies in each dimension. λ has the multiplicity of $p > 1$ in eigenspace. According to detection theorems, the four discovered attack classes can be

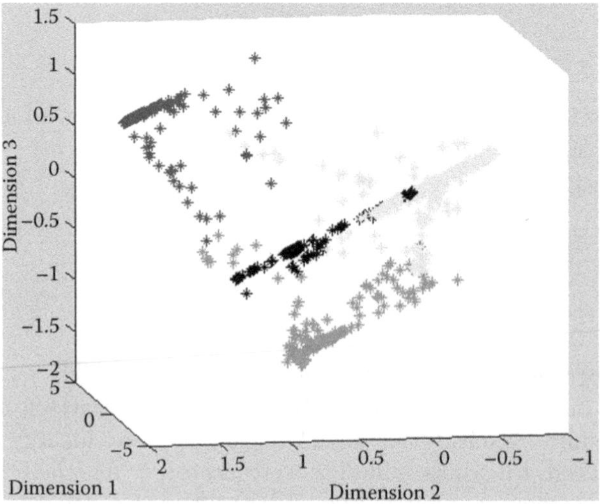

FIGURE 12.22: Quantum detection $\sigma = 0.9$.

FIGURE 12.23: Quantum detection spectrum $\sigma = 0.9$.

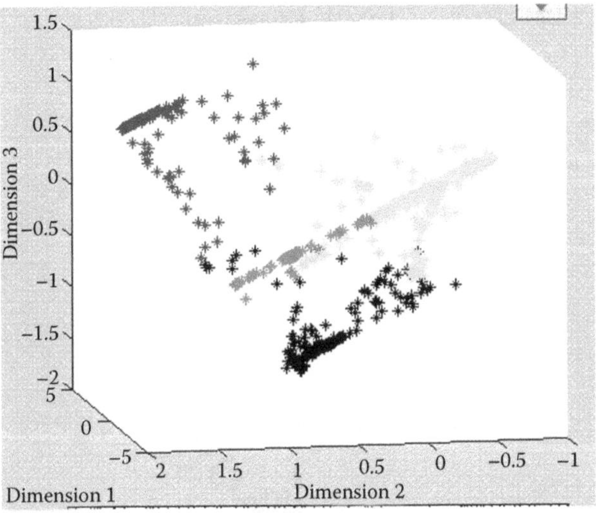

FIGURE 12.24: Quantum detection $\sigma = 0.8$.

represented in

$$\psi = \sum_{k=1}^{4} \gamma k_i \tag{12.33}$$

where γ is a parameter for vector expansion. k_i can be expanded with multiplicity of λ as $k_i = \sum_{i=1}^{p} \alpha_i e_i + \sum_{i=p+1}^{10000} \frac{\beta_j}{\lambda_i - \sigma} e_i$ (see Equation 12.30).

The identified classes of attacks also present four degrees of freedom in attack space. There are unexposed substructures in this test, which indicates that we need to adjust σ to excite other eigenmodes of the tested attack space.

To discover other eigenmodes of attack space, we set the parameter as $\sigma = 0.8$. It discovers four basic types as $\sigma = 0.8$. There is no additional dependent relation identified in the attack space. The detection result is illustrated in Figure 12.24. The spectral representation of detection is illustrated in Figure 12.25. Please note that the same classes of attacks are plotted in different colors as they are shown in Figure 12.22.

Quantum detection with $\sigma = 0.75$ has the same results as previous tests (Figures 12.26 and 12.27).

FIGURE 12.25: Quantum detection spectrum $\sigma = 0.8$.

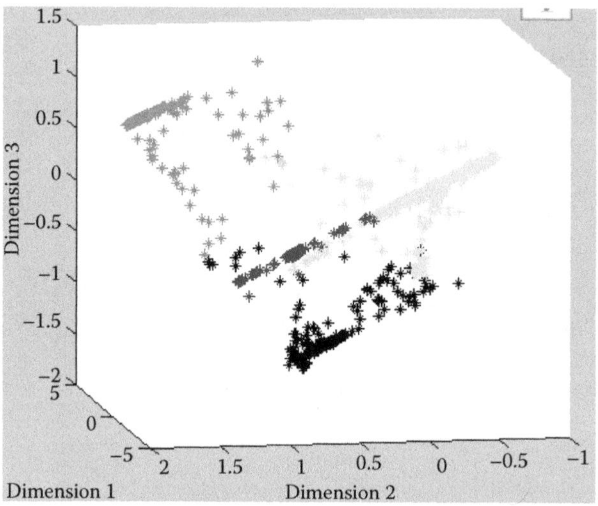

FIGURE 12.26: Quantum detection $\sigma = 0.75$.

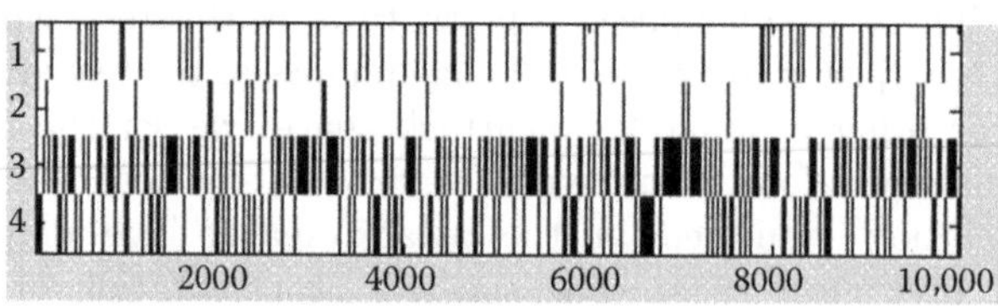

FIGURE 12.27: Quantum detection spectrum $\sigma = 0.75$.

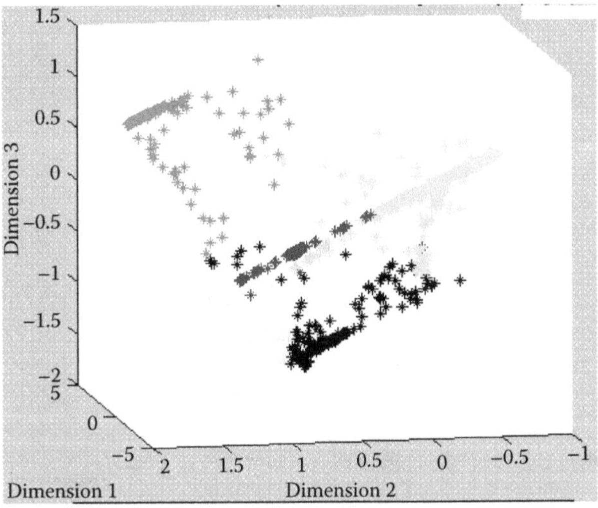

FIGURE 12.28: Quantum detection $\sigma = 0.7$.

FIGURE 12.29: Quantum detection $\sigma = 0.7$.

Quantum detection with $\sigma = 0.7$ identifies the same results (Figures 12.28 and 12.29).

Quantum detection with $\sigma = 0.68$ identifies more local minima. There are five classes of attacks detected in Figure 12.30, which shows sensitivity of the design parameter σ. The spectrum is shown in Figure 12.31.

$$\psi = \sum_{k=1}^{5} \gamma k_i \tag{12.34}$$

where γ is a parameter for vector expansion. k_i can be expanded with multiplicity of λ as $k_i = \sum_{i=1}^{p} \alpha_i e_i + \sum_{i=p+1}^{10000} \frac{\beta_j}{\lambda_i - \sigma} e_i$ (see Equation 12.30).

Quantum detection with $\sigma = 0.67$ identifies more local minima. There are six more classes of attacks detected in Figure 12.32. The spectrum is illustrated in Figure 12.33.

Quantum detection with $\sigma = 0.65$ identifies more local minima. There are eight classes of attacks detected in Figure 12.34. The spectrum is shown in Figure 12.35.

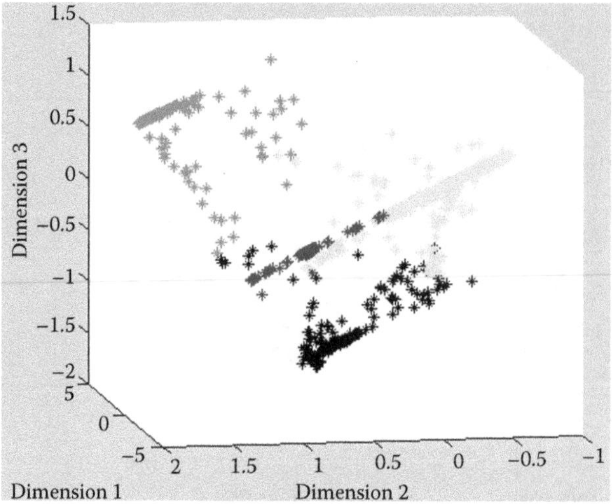

FIGURE 12.30: Quantum detection $\sigma = 0.68$.

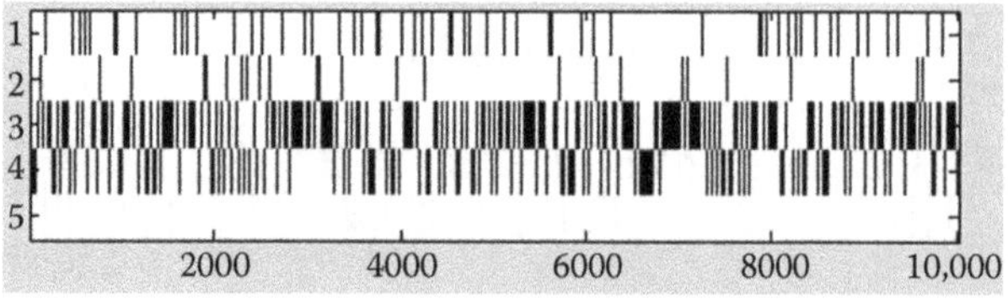

FIGURE 12.31: Quantum detection spectrum $\sigma = 0.68$.

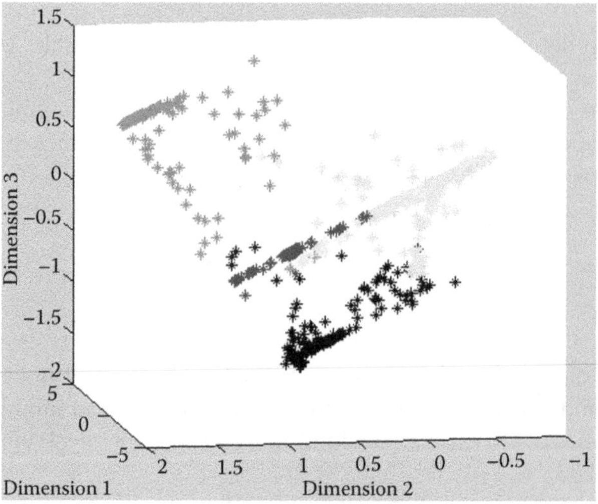

FIGURE 12.32: Quantum detection $\sigma = 0.67$.

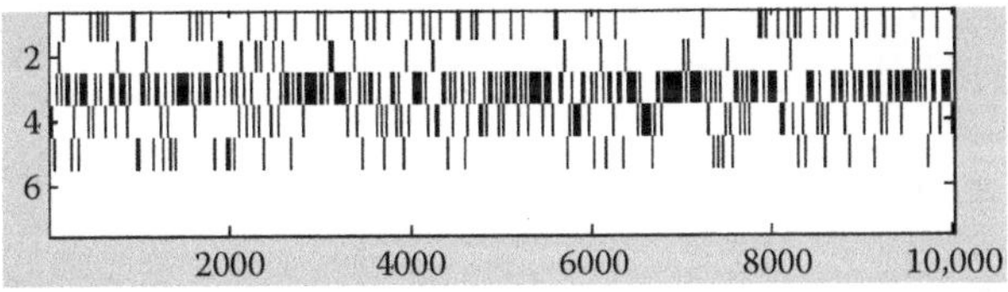

FIGURE 12.33: Quantum detection spectrum $\sigma = 0.67$.

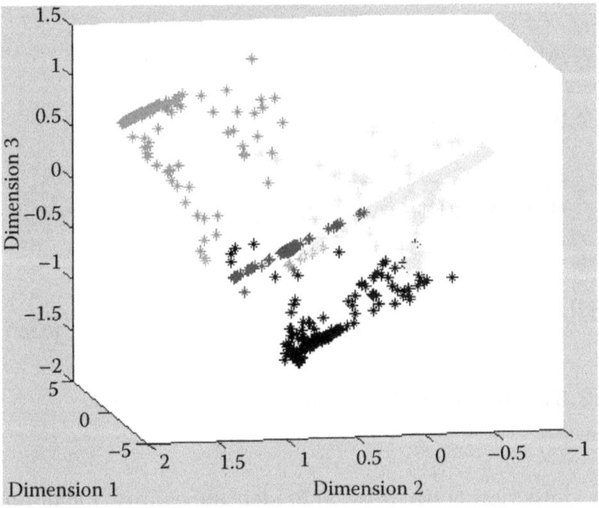

FIGURE 12.34: Quantum Detection $\sigma = 0.65$

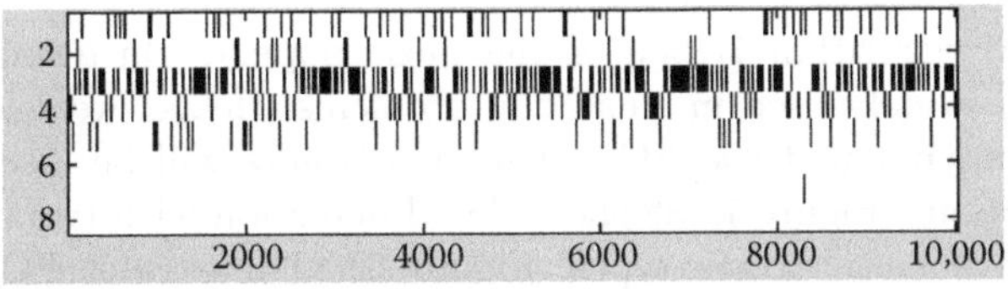

FIGURE 12.35: Quantum detection spectrum $\sigma = 0.65$.

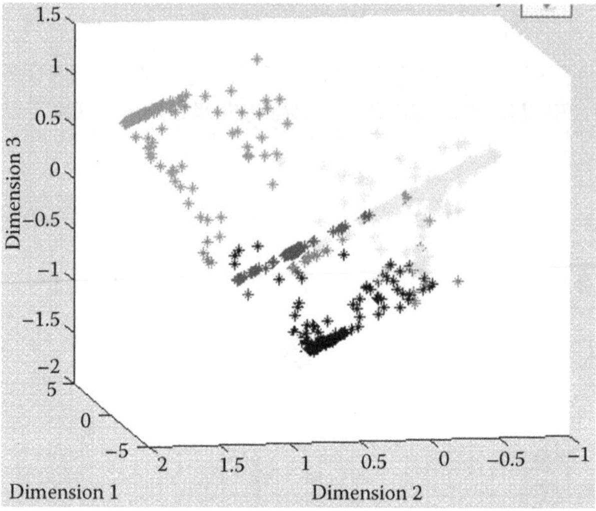

FIGURE 12.36: Quantum detection $\sigma = 0.5$.

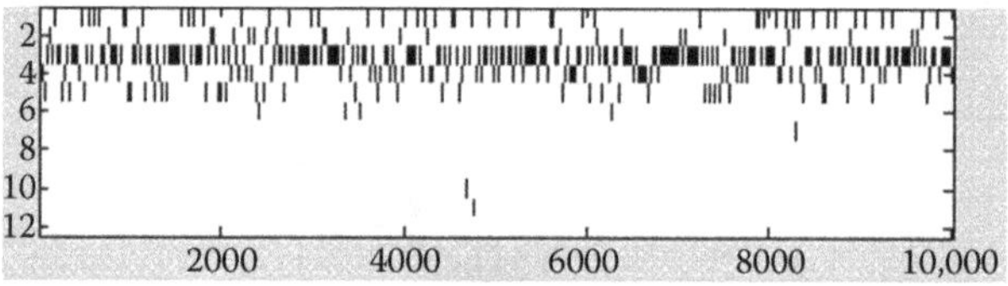

FIGURE 12.37: Quantum detection spectrum $\sigma = 0.5$.

Quantum detection with $\sigma = 0.5$ identifies more local minima. There are 12 classes of attacks detected in Figure 12.36. The spectrum is shown in Figure 12.37.

12.8.4 Comparison of fuzzy C mean detection with different targets

The FCM algorithm is one of the most popular clustering algorithms and has been widely used in clustering problems. Hence, we select FCM for detection comparison study. FCM detection results will be discussed in the following sections. Figure 12.38 shows FCM detection with two initial classes identifying five basic attack types. Figure 12.39 illustrates FCM detection with three initial classes identifying five basic attack types. Figure 12.40 demonstrates FCM detection with four initial classes identifying five basic attack types. Figure 12.41 denotes FCM detection with five initial classes identifying five basic attack types.

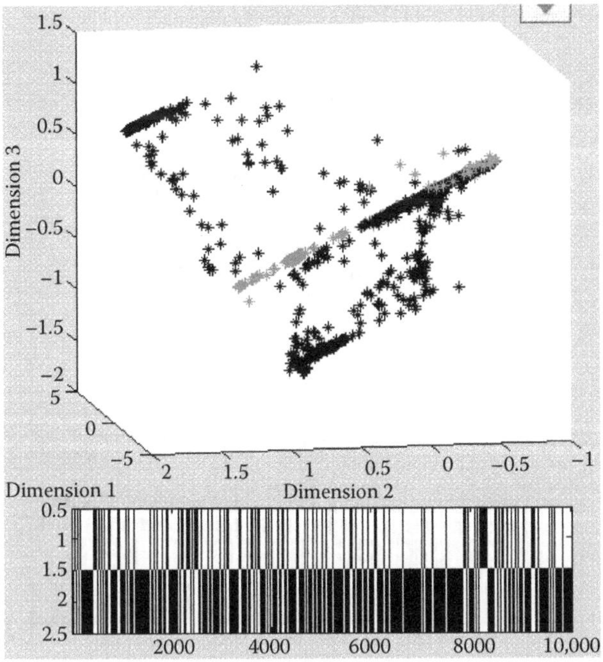

FIGURE 12.38: Fuzzy-C-Mean detection with initial 2 classes.

12.8.5 Comparison of quantum detection and fuzzy C mean

Compared with FCM detection, the proposed quantum-based method shows strength in detecting multiple substructures. More eigenmodes are excited. More attack structures are detected. Another significant advantage of the quantum-based method is that it requires no a prior knowledge of cluster structures and the only design parameter is σ. The advantages of the quantum-based detection method are the result of discovering local minimums instead of the global maximum. In addition, wave representation and matrix mechanics provide analytic evaluation instead of numeric approximation. Finally, the consistent reports on purity and efficiency during the entire test cycle show the robustness of the quantum method and FCM detection method. For the detection operator $D[\psi] = f$, f is a prescribed function of the independent variables. Since detection is a linear operator, the experiment results support the linearity property 12.35.

$$D[\alpha_1\psi_1 + \cdots + \alpha_k\psi_k] = \alpha_1 D[\psi_1] + \cdots + \alpha_k D[\psi_k] \tag{12.35}$$

The relation helps us to reach the robust solution $\psi = \sum_i^\infty C_i\psi_i + \psi_p$. The solution is a series of individual tests by superposition. The robustness comes from k arbitrary constants ensuring ψ meets the different boundary conditions.

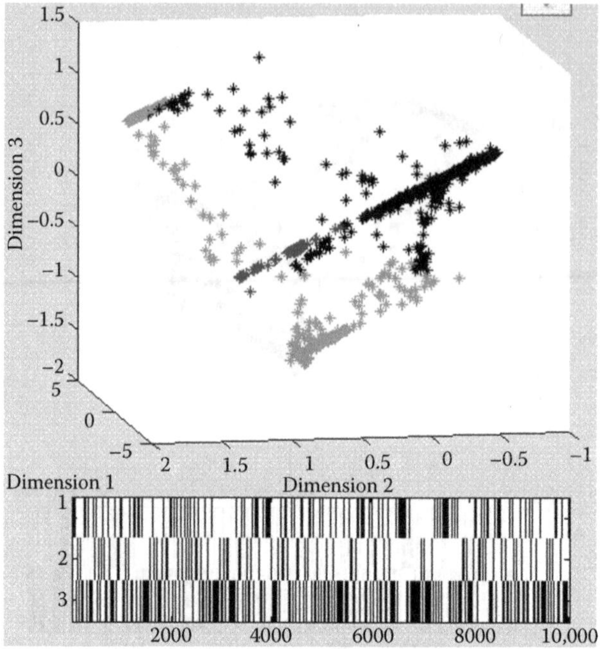

FIGURE 12.39: Fuzzy-C-Mean detection with initial three classes.

The consistent purity report is plotted in Figure 12.42, which shows the proposed detection scheme is robust to span entire experiment processes.

12.9 Conclusions and Future Work

12.9.1 Advantages of the proposed method

The proposed method has some noteworthy advantages against those in literature. I list six of them below:

12.9.1.1 From physical intuition versus data geometric and probabilistic; analytical accuracy versus numeric approximation

Traditional clustering detection relies on geometric interpretation of data distances. Those methods have poor results as data coherence disappears, or there are difficulties in representing data in high-dimensional geometric. Specifically, for attack structures (cluster center, cluster shapes, and cluster

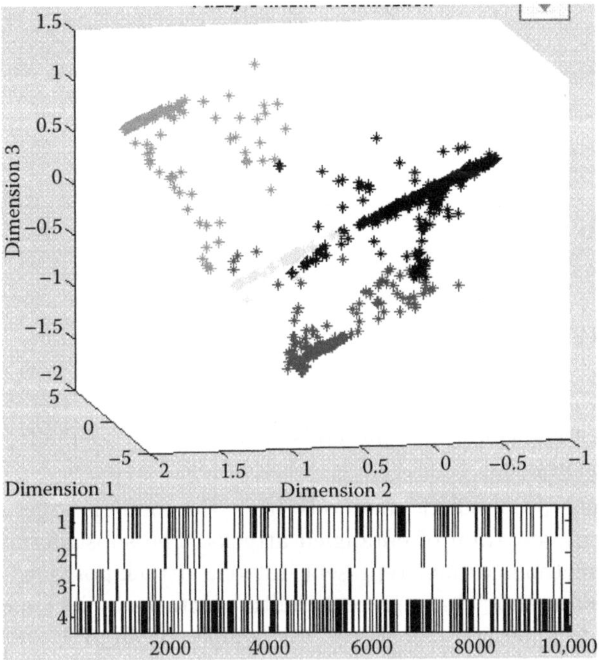

FIGURE 12.40: Fuzzy-C-Mean detection with initial four classes.

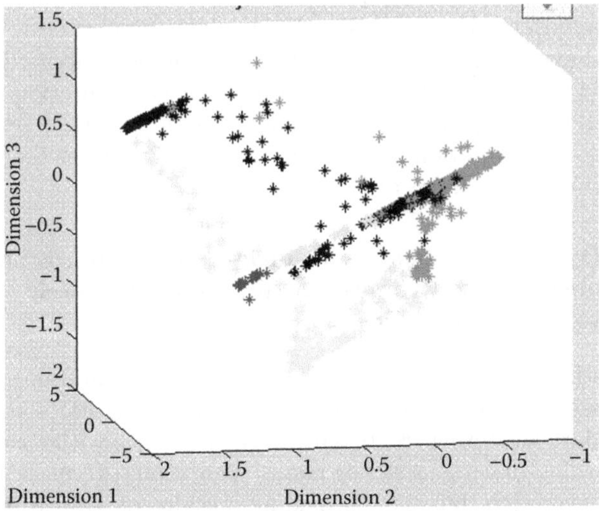

FIGURE 12.41: Fuzzy-C-Mean detection with initial five classes.

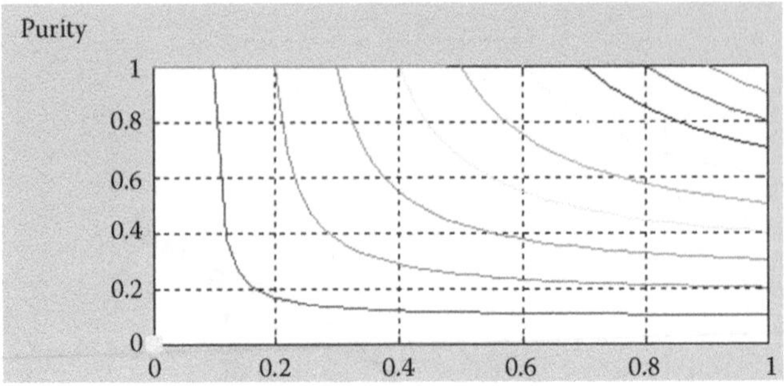

FIGURE 12.42: Purity and efficiency with attack detection.

boundaries), these traditional methods have less-good results from traditional distance measurement.

Traditional probabilistic methods have the similar issues. Even more, there is a representation of entangled attacks. The substructures are vague. Traditional methods cannot represent different attack positions concurrently. The proposed method can represent multiple attacks by its superposed form. In addition, this method can reduce the complexity from 2^N to $2N$.

Instead of rigid-geometric and probabilistic inference, this method uses a quantum energy equation to attain its potential. This transforms from traditional clustering of maximum points computation into minimal computation of energy evolution against three-dimensional PC. The three-dimensional model feeds into the quantum equation to provide accurate clustering instead of approximated one. Hence, this method solves the clustering attacks with an analytical expression but not an established numeric approximation. This method provides the analytical solution to reduce computation time without errors. Even the proposed method may contain errors starting with an initial subset. The evolution achieves accuracy and removes the errors, which traditional clustering cannot do.

12.9.1.2 Dynamics versus rigid, insight versus black box, unsupervised versus learning nonparametric versus parametric

This method introduces dynamics (wave representation) representing states. It has fluid evolution but not traditional-static data clustering. Traditional data clustering treats data as rigid clusters without consideration of time. Learning-based genetic, or neuro, algorithms are black box methods considering evolution but not providing insight of transitions. Learning requires training. Hence, this method can provide animation and play back to understand details of attacks. It is particularly beneficial for multiple attack schemes and random attack cases. The method does not require training or simulations. This is a non-parametric method, it requires no a prior knowledge of attacks. It requires no training.

12.9.1.3 Dimensionality reduction for large attacks

Instead of giving explicit-state formulation, this method represents states by its Gaussians waves. This is particularly critical for anomaly detection since data have high dimensions and large space. This method forms a Gaussian basis so that this method transforms the dimensionality complexity into locations of data points that bind to ($N2$) only.

12.9.1.4 New method of instance reduction and feature selection

This method proposed linear independent waves that guarantee to be spanned to a complete data set with a small initial subset with instance reduction. Traditional methods rely on arbitrary 10 fold training and worry about over-fitting. This method proposes SVD and manifold to resolve global but not local information for attribute selection. This fits into Hilbert space to ensure completeness and convergence. The traditional methods deal with real domains and cannot do this.

12.9.1.5 Generates from originals versus large data collections

With wave basis formulation, we can generate original data instead of just relying on large data sets or data collection. This provides a reliable method to study the stability of the attack detections. Traditional methods rely on public data sets and large data collection cycles. This proposed method is better in studying the substructure of complex attacks, entangled attacks, and simultaneous attacks.

12.9.2 Attack prevention scheme

We plan to derive the attack prevention scheme using entanglement. The method attempts to inject polarized-entangled data channel [18] to detect the anomaly attacks at real time.

References

[1] Chandola, V., A. Banerjee, and V. Kumar. Anomaly detection: A survey. *ACM Computing Survey*, 41, 2009.

[2] Pinchover, Y. and J. Rubinstein. *An Introduction to Partial Differential Equations.* Cambridge University Press, Cambridge, 2005.

[3] Xu, R. and D. Wunsch. Survey of clustering algorithms. *IEEE Transactions on Neural Networks*, 16, 2005.

[4] Blatt, M., S. Wiseman, and E. Domany. Superparamagnetic clustering of data. *Physics Review*, 76:3251–3254, 1996.

[5] Horn, D. and A. Gottlieb. The method of quantum clustering. In *Proceedings of the Neural Information Processing Systems*, 769–776, 2001.

[6] Horn, D. and A. Gottlieb. Algorithm for data clustering in pattern recognition problems based on quantum mechanics. *Physics Review*, 88(018702), 2002.

[7] Weinstein, M. and D. Horn. Dynamic quantum clustering: a method for visual exploration of structures in data. *Physics:Data Analysis, Statistics and Probability. arXiv:0908.2644v1*, 2009.

[8] Li. Y. Quantum-inspired evolutionary clustering algorithm based on manifold distance. In *ACM/SIGEVO Summit on Genetic and Evolutionary Computation*, 2009.

[9] Shuai, D., Q. Shuai, and Y. Dong. A novel quantum particle approach to self-organizing clustering. In *2006 International Conference on Service Systems andService Management*, 1:98–103, 2006.

[10] Fischer, C. C., et al. Predicting crystal structure by merging data mining with quantum mechanics. *Nature Materials*, 5:641–646, 2006.

[11] Aimeur, E., G. Brassard, and S. Gambs. Quantum clustering algorithms. In *Proceedings of the 24th International Conference on Machine Learning. Corvallis. OR*, 2007.

[12] Dyson, F. J. Statistical theory of the energy levels of complex systems, i, ii,iii. *Journal of Mathematical Physics*, 3, 1962.

[13] Angelini, L. et al. Clustering data by inhomogeneous chaotic map lattices. *Physics Review*, 85:554557, 2000.

[14] Bezdek, J. C. *Pattern Recognition with Fuzzy Objective Function Algorithms*. Plenum Pub Corp., New York, 1981.

[15] Coifman, R. R. Geometric diffusions as a tool for harmonic analysis and structure definition of data. In *Proceedings of the National Academy of Sciences*, 102(21), 2005.

[16] Sitaram, A. Uncertainty principle, mathematical. In *Encyclopaedia of Mathematics*, H. Michiel. (ed.). Kluwer Academic Publishers, 2001.

[17] Tsai, Z. Y. and J. J. P.Weigert. An automatically tuning intrusion detection system. *IEEE Transactions on Instrumentation and Measurement*, 37–02, 2007.

[18] Humble, T. S., R. S. Bennink, W. P. Grice, I. J. Owens. Sensing intruders using entanglement: a photonic quantum fence. In *Quantum Information and Computation VII*, Donkor, E. J., Pirich, A. R., H. E. Brandt, (eds.). Proceeedings of SPIE Vol. 7342, 73420H, 2008.

[19] Zhang, C. J., et al. Entanglement detection beyond the cross-norm or realignment criterion. *Physical Review Letters*, 77(060301), 2008.

[20] Gittsovich, O., et al. Covariance matrix criterion for separability. In *Ninth International Conference on QCMC. AIP Conference Proceedings*, 1110, 63–66, 2009.

[21] Garcia-Patron, R., et al. Reverse coherent information. In *Ninth International Conference on QCMC. AIP Conference Proceedings*, 1110, 67–74, 2009.

[22] Lippmann, R. P., et al. Evaluating intrusion detection systems: The 1998 darpa off-line intrusion detection evaluation. In *Proceedings of DARPA Information Survivability Conference Exposition*, 2000.

[23] Elkan, C. Results of the kdd'99 classifier learning. *ACM SIGKDD*, 1, 2000.

[24] Kumar, V. Data mining for network intrusion detection: Experience with kddcup'99 data set. In *Workshop Netw. Intrusion Detection*, 2002.

[25] He, D. and H. Leung. Network intrusion detection using cfar abrupt-change detectors. *IEEE Transactions on Instrumentation and Measurement*, 57(3), 2007.

[26] Abhishek, D., D. Nguyen, and J. Zambreno. An fpga-based network intrusion detection architecture. *IEEE Transactions on Information Forensics and Security*, 3(1):163–197, 2007.

Index

* 9 7 8 1 4 3 9 8 2 5 7 9 2 *
T - #0120 - 101024 - C0 - 234/156/15 [17] - CB - 9781439825792 - Gloss Lamination